1982 Sister M. Clare Edwa

second edition

CHILDREN AND COMMUNICATION:
verbal and nonverbal language development

Barbara S. Wood

*University of Illinois
at Chicago Circle*

PRENTICE-HALL, INC., ENGLEWOOD CLIFFS, INC. 07632

Library of Congress Cataloging in Publication Data

Wood, Barbara S
  Children and communication.

  (Prentice-Hall series in speech communication)
  Includes bibliographies and index.
  1. Language acquisition.   2. Communication.
I. Title.
P118.W6   1981   401′.9   80-22595
ISBN 0-13-131920-5

© *1981, 1976 by Prentice-Hall, Inc., Englewood Cliffs, N.J. 07632*

Printed in the United States of America

10   9   8   7   6   5   4   3   2   1

Editorial/production supervision
  and interior design by Virginia Livsey
Cover design by Carol Zawislak
Manufacturing buyer: Edmund W. Leone

Prentice-Hall International, Inc., *London*
Prentice-Hall of Australia Pty. Limited, *Sydney*
Prentice-Hall of Canada, Ltd., *Toronto*
Prentice-Hall of India Private Limited, *New Delhi*
Prentice-Hall of Japan, Inc., *Tokyo*
Prentice-Hall of Southeast Asia Pte. Ltd., *Singapore*
Whitehall Books Limited, Wellington, *New Zealand*

contents

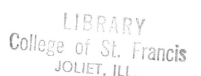

preface

The second edition of *Children and Communication: Verbal and Non-verbal Language Development* places children's language development in a context of communication. Children develop skills that give them communication power, the ability to function autonomously in their environment through communication with others. The text presents a comprehensive view of communication development, considering the development of verbal language, nonverbal language and communication competence. The culmination of learning is the child's acquisition of a broad range of communication strategies for use in everyday communication situations employing selection criteria that help to guarantee communication effectiveness and appropriateness.

The general outline of this edition matches that in the first edition, though much of the text has been dramatically changed. Part I continues to explore the forces that affect children's communication development, with consideration of the intrapersonal forces such as the biological and genetic, as well as the interpersonal forces in this child's environment, especially the family. The first three chapters contain many new sources. Part II on children's development of their verbal language views the emergence of vocabulary, syntax, and semantics in children. Chapters take advantage of recent research and theory in the field of language development. The writings of M. A. K. Halliday, Dan Slobin, Roger Brown, Jerome Bruner and various scholars publishing in the *Journal of Child Language* play a major role in this edition, which is unlike the first edition. As in the first edition, Part III considers children's development of communication through their body language, voice and proxemics. This part has been updated with recent theory and research, but again remains practical for students of children's communication. Part IV presents a view of children's acquisition of communication competence. Children integrate verbal and nonverbal language for use in important everyday situations, and the focus changes to a pragmatic one. This part begins with an examination of the communication situation and then explores children's development of communication in five functional areas: controlling, sharing feelings, informing, ritualizing, and imagining. A systems view of comunication learning is explained, accompanied by instructional guidelines for effective development. This part is a total revision that is practical and specific.

I have tried to share with readers my excitement in studying the development of children's communication. Examples and illustrations are offered which take the child's perspective in their struggle to grow as independent persons in their environment. The text is basic in its treatment, designed for beginning students in education, special education, communication disorders, and communication studies. Designed for those who work with children, the text gives special attention to those going into some phase of work with pre-school and early elementary-aged children.

The first edition of *Children and Communication*, in circulation for about five years, has done well. The response from students and faculty across the country has been very encouraging to me. This edition would not have been possible without such encouragement. Dean Hewes, University of Wisconsin, provided many suggestions which I was able to incorporate into this edition. Doris Seeder, Northwestern University, directed the revision of the chapter on semantics. Colleagues contracted by Prentice-Hall to give feedback on the revisions were helpful in all phases of the second edition. My students have always been my best critics, telling me which ideas made sense and which ones did not. I thank all of these persons for helping to shape this edition. And I would like to give special thanks to my two boys, Jeffrey (10 yrs.) and Gregory (7 yrs.), for understanding why Mommy sat at the typewriter so much. As I read the revision before it went into production, I felt good about what it conveyed. I hope readers share my reactions.

Barbara Wood

PART I

UNDERSTANDING THE CHILD AS A COMMUNICATOR

When we communicate, we share experiences, events, ideas, and feelings with others through verbal and nonverbal channels. We praise a child's drawing by saying, "You did a fine job; your picture of the sun and the apple tree is beautiful." We use words and patterns of words to communicate praise. Our verbal message helps us to share our positive feelings with the child. We also use nonverbal cues to convey our feelings. We move very close to the child to show how much we mean what we say. Our face shows a smile that seems to say, "I like your picture and I like you." And our voice tells the child, "I'm not surprised you have done so well." Because communication involves the sharing of messages through several channels, the study of communication development must include an examination of these channels. Verbal channels include sounds, words, and sentence patterns; nonverbal channels include body motion, the voice, and touch (space).

Children are communicators who must learn to send and understand verbal and nonverbal messages. In this text, we discuss children's development of verbal and nonverbal language in Part II and Part III, respectively. In Part IV we examine how children learn to apply their knowledge of language to important everyday *situations*. In this context, language is viewed as a tool to be used in social relationships. Tools are most effective when they are used appropriately. Children learn to adapt their communication to the listener by taking that person's perspective into account. Part IV presents a communication framework that includes axioms of communication, which say *how* communication works, and five basic communication functions—controlling, sharing feelings, informing/understanding, ritualizing, and imagining. Given this framework, children develop particular communication competencies for use in everyday communication situations.

Before we discuss children's communication on the verbal, nonverbal, and situational levels we must consider the bases of communication development. In Part I we examine the role of communication in children's overall development (Chapter 1) and the forces that affect communication development:

1. *Intrapersonal forces:* factors within the child (Chapter 2).
2. *Interpersonal forces:* models and children's interaction with these models (Chapter 3).

"HELP ME UNDERSTAND"

Children's communication must be viewed as an integral part of their total development as human beings. As they learn to communicate with words and patterns of words and with their voices and their bodies, they also learn about the world they live in. Children have a wish: they want to understand their world, themselves, and others. They struggle to discover a system of beliefs about reality, self, and others. Their most important tool for discovering beliefs is communication.

To function effectively in their families, their peer groups, and their classroom, children must become aware of the power and assistance that communication offers them. To explain an idea, to ask for help, or to disagree with someone, children must have a repertoire of communication options or strategies for that situation. The instructional aim of this text is to help children select appropriate verbal and nonverbal strategies in critical communication situations. In this context, communication allows children to function effectively in their families, their social groups, and their cultures.

FORCES AFFECTING COMMUNICATION DEVELOPMENT

What forces affect children's communication development? The three-part model below will help us visualize the learning process.

1. *Input (Interpersonal forces):* Children learn to communicate in a special communication environment, one that operates according to a "system" in which all members of the group affect one another. The family and its operation affect the child's communication development. Communication models in the family, school, and peer group influence children's communication through the importance of interaction patterns.
2. *Children's equipment (Intrapersonal forces):* Children contribute something to their own development of communication. The maturation of their brain, body, and vocal apparatus

affects the course of their early communication development. Further, children's self-initiated discovery and practice assist them in mastering their language.

3. *Output:* Children's communication is a result of intrapersonal and interpersonal forces. Children communicate in a fashion representative of their level of maturation and their communication environment.

1

"help me understand"

"Children want, more than they want anything else, and even after many years of miseducation, to make sense of the world, themselves, and other human beings."[1] In a matter of years young children must make decisions for themselves, based on their ability to make sense of themselves, others, and the world they live in. They may wonder if they should ask for help on a problem or if they should simply go ahead and try it on their own. They may worry about whether it is more important to talk "like the guys" or talk as their parents suggest. Further, they may question their ability to return something to a store and get their money back. Without the ability to communicate in a variety of situations that are critical to them, children would find the task of making sense an impossible one. To function in their family, their social groups, their classroom, and their community, children need a kind of *communication power*—the ability to perform effectively in communication encounters.

As parents and teachers of children, we must help children build a repertoire of communication strategies with which they can deal with the critical situations they will encounter. We must help them in their struggle to make sense of themselves, the world they live in, and the persons that are important in their lives. Effective communication is the key to making sense, and to be effective communicators children must be aware of the options available to them in each situation they encounter.

[1]From the book, *The Underachieving School* by John Holt. Copyright © 1969 by Pitman Publishing Corp. Reprinted by permission of Pitman Publishing Corp.

Parents and teachers have little doubt that children can be effective communicators. Although children's communication may not be adultlike in terms of pronunciation and sentence structure, the effects of their messages are visible. Consider the powerful effect children have on their mother's purchasing of breakfast cereals. An advertiser sells breakfast cereals to six-year-olds, who in turn convince Mommy to buy Tony the Tiger's Sugar Frosted Flakes or Count Chocula cereal for breakfast the next morning. The television message is simply the necessary stimulus for their sales job. In the case of Count Chocula cereal, a little boy's message may show his excitement about monsters and Dracula-like characters. To sell the cereal to his mother, who is genuinely concerned that he should eat breakfast, is not too difficult for the child to accomplish: his repeated suggestions will probably do the trick. The child may also decide to build his sales case on other arguments. The prize in the cereal box, the chocolate flavor of the cereal, or any other bonus item helps to sell the child and in turn may help the child sell his mother. The child's success may depend on his ability to use a number of communication strategies, such as repetition, statement of advantages, or even a threat ("I won't eat any other cereal!"). Of course, his mother's readiness to listen has some bearing on the outcome.

The sales job of an infant can also be effective, although it will not be as sophisticated as that of the six-year-old child. Picture a five-month-old girl strapped in her highchair. It's time for her baby-food dinner. The menu for the evening sounds exotic: strained beef liver, creamed spinach, and strained beets. Is it any wonder the child wrinkles her nose, turns her head, and grunts every time the spoon approaches her mouth? The child's message is abundantly clear to the mother. (It might interest you to know that spinach, liver, and beets are among Gerber Baby Food's least-popular products.) Apparently, children are capable of influencing their mothers' purchasing of food almost from birth! (Or, maybe the infant is so perceptive that she can read her mother's taste buds.)

The communication strategies employed by our breakfast-cereal salesman were more complex and varied than those used by the dining infant. Yet in both cases it could be argued that the child succeeded in accomplishing the desired communication goal. The two instances differ in the number of communication strategies available to the child. Few options are available to a five-month-old infant, but a six-year-old seems to be a never-ending source of reasons and arguments. As adults, we know that our success in communication, particularly when we are selling an idea or product to someone, depends on our ability to choose just the right approach. A wise selection among alternate strategies is essential for continuing success in communication. The wise selection of communication strategies includes a *repertoire* of strategies from which to choose just the right one and a set of *criteria* to use in the process of selection. Repertoire and selection criteria are two critical components of communication competence that children must acquire in order to be effective communicators.[2] Effective communication strategies are at the core of the research conducted by Burton White of Harvard University.[3] White examined six-year-olds to discover the talents of the competent child, socially and intellectually. The focus in our discussion is on social skills, which are demonstrated in the child's communication behavior.

COMMUNICATION TALENTS OF YOUNG CHILDREN

It is not terribly difficult to decide whether or not a child is together, squared away, or, in psychologists' terms, competent. It is more difficult to isolate the qualities that make the child so. White has engaged in years of research to determine the attributes of children's competence. A discussion of these attributes, which he calls "talents," is essential in this chapter.

gains/maintains attention of adult

The competent child is able to gain and maintain the attention of an adult in a socially acceptable way. The child knows that a call to the adult, a gentle poke in the ribs, or a move toward the adult is an acceptable way to say, "I want to talk to you." Whining, coat pulling, or screaming "Come here!" at the top of the lungs will certainly get an adult's attention, but these methods will undoubtedly be judged socially unacceptable unless the child is quite young. Children acquiring communication power know which strategies are acceptable and which ones are not.

uses adults as resources

The competent child asks an adult for help when a task is too difficult for her to do by herself. A request for assistance, a plea for an explanation of how to do something, and a statement of need are all useful tools in accomplishing a difficult task, whether it is building a house with blocks, riding a new bicycle, or spelling a difficult word in a homework assignment. The child who holds back in asking for assistance may be afraid of being judged as helpless, but the competent child knows that it's okay to ask.

[2]For a presentation of these criteria, see Barbara Wood, ed., *Development of Functional Communication Competencies: Pre-K–Grade Six* (Urbana, Ill.: ERIC Clearinghouse on Reading and Communication Skills, 1977), pp. 1–11.
[3]Burton L. White, "Critical Influences in the Origins of Competence," *Merrill-Palmer Quarterly,* 2 (1975), 243–66.

expresses affection/hostility to children and adults

A competent child knows how to use hugs and kind words to tell his buddy he really likes him a lot for giving him some gum. He also feels comfortable saying "I hate you" or "I don't want to play with you because you ruined my picture." Rather than keeping his emotions inside himself, the competent child communicates them to his peers.

Further, the child is able to communicate such emotions to adults important in his life. While an adult may not really want to hear a little boy's message of hostility directed at her ("I hate you so much!" or "You are so dumb—you don't know anything."), psychologists have learned that the expression of such messages is critical in a child's emotional development. It is a sign of a child's strength when he is able to express both positive and negative feelings to others. While adults can be comfortable in listening to children express positive feelings toward them, many are so threatened by their children's communication of negative emotions such as hostility and anger that they do not allow their expression. The competent child is capable of communicating affection, hostility, and anger to the children and adults important in his life. This talent cannot develop without an understanding, healthy atmosphere in which the child can comfortably express these feelings.

leads/follows peers

If children are engaged in pretend-play with cars and trucks, the competent child can give suggestions about how to play with the toys, saying what the rules of play might be and indicating where the roads and parking places are. If the activity is a simple game of tag, the competent child is able to communicate the rules of the game effectively—of course, saying how you get "times." The competent child is able to lead by communicating effectively with others.

Conversely, the competent child is able to follow the suggestions of others because she knows how to ask questions when things are not clearly presented or how to react if the rules seem unfair. If a friend takes the lead and suggest they play tic-tac-toe, saying "You be O and I'll be X," the follower understands the guidelines or knows how to change them.

competes with peers

Developing children normally exhibit interpersonal competition in many interesting ways. The competent child boasts about how she can ride her bike the fastest, tells others that she finally knows her subtraction tables, or relates to her peers how she was called the best dancer in dancing class that day. According to White's research, a healthy sign of children's social development is that they feel good when they compete with their peers. Competition among children can be physical as well as mental, though we are not talking about competing physically in this section. It is difficult to conceive of children competing in any mental or social way without knowing how to communicate effectively in that critical situation.

shows pride

The talented child is one who is not too modest to say, "Didn't I draw a beautiful picture?" "I really did a great slide into home plate—you should've seen," or "See what a nice outfit I put on?" The competent child shows pride in what he does or what he possesses at any moment in time. He feels good about himself and so communicates this feeling to others in his life.

roleplays adults

If given the chance to play with an exciting toy cash register and play money, preschoolers are delighted in assuming the role of the cashier (the "payer"). They tend to talk like authoritative clerks, demanding money from their peers (the clients) and generally acting like "big stuff." When children role-play, it is natural that they take adult roles, especially as mothers and fathers. They order others around, talk like grownups, phone the doctor for a sick child, and generally show their understanding of what it would be like to be grown up. This type of play expresses a desire to grow up, and psychologists say it's good.

While we could argue that children learn to communicate effectively because they seek to gain our attention, express affection, show pride in their accomplishments, and so on, it seems doubtful that children have such specific intentions in mind as they grow up. A more probable explanation for why children like to communicate in their early years seems to be linked to making sense and then gaining control. The next two sections discuss these objectives.

WHY DO CHILDREN COMMUNICATE?

Children communicate in order to build a set of beliefs about their world, themselves, and others. Their plea, "Help me understand," is a sensitive and penetrating way of explaining why children want to learn their language and why they want to learn it so that it works effectively for them. Once they understand their world, themselves, and others important in their lives, children can develop an independence in that environment.

Then they can develop a degree of control in their world. Communication is really the child's power play, the tool that lets them develop autonomy. The goal is an ability to function on their own, to control their own actions, and to influence the actions and feelings of others. Communication has a verbal code, a nonverbal code, and a set of guidelines for appropriate uses of these codes. To understand why children communicate, we can keep in mind their *goal* of independence and their *tool* of effective communication and explore their particular *method* for beginning to communicate: making sense.

making sense of the world

Children want to know how airplanes stay up in the sky, why leaves fall from trees, and why Daddy goes to work. Parents are quite familiar with the abundance of "how" and "why" questions posed by young children. From the point of view of children, their *questions* constitute an attempt to make sense of the world around them. The following parent-child conversation reflects a boy's concern with understanding the world around him.

Child: Daddy, why is that airplane flying in the sky?
Father: Because it's taking people from one place to another. It's carrying passengers.
Child: But why does it go in the sky?
Father: All airplanes go in the sky; they have jet engines to fly very fast.
Child: Why do they have jet engines?
Father: Because they are the fastest engines for making the airplane go.
Child: Dad—why are they the fastest?

The conversation could go on and on because each answer the father gives his child creates for the child a new question about the reality he is trying to understand.

Children also learn about their world through their *sensory experiences.* A young girl may spend ten long minutes watching a leaf carried down a sidewalk by a gentle breeze. She studies the movement of the leaf with her eyes. She may try to catch it with her hands so that she can examine it through touch. But just as she gets close enough to touch the leaf it may blow away. Now she is more curious than ever.

Touching, licking, and poking are important means of exploring the world and answering questions about it, especially for young children. When the child's senses do not provide the answer, or when the answer seems a bit odd to the child, she may ask for help. Communication takes over in her quest for information. If she is able to formulate just the right question, she may receive an adequate answer about why her world operates as it does. Rarely do adults have to teach the child *how* to use her senses in exploring the world. Rather, they must provide the opportunity or the time for the child to engage in such explorations.

Asking questions about the world is different from explaining it: it's not as easy, for well-framed questions do not come naturally to children. The child's basic tool in making sense of his world is his ability to ask all kinds of important questions about reality. In the home the child's questions are too often viewed as a nuisance and are answered inadequately. Questions such as "Can't it go like this?" and "How come it works like this?" tend to elicit answers that are short and sweet but say very little. In the school little time is spent on how to ask good questions, but plenty of time is devoted to the proper punctuation and grammatical structure of questions. The child's plea to understand the world is aided little by these kinds of responses. What helps is information about the role of questions in understanding what's around us: when questions can be used, how questions can be posed, and why questions are important in discovery. A functional approach to communication instruction, such as that adopted in Part IV of this text, allows questioning to become a critical communication situation for classroom study. From a functional standpoint, then, communication becomes doubly important: it is the *means* of instruction for dealing with communication situations as well as the *end* of instruction.

With the help of sensory experience and an ability to question appropriately, the child is able to formulate a set of beliefs about his world. A young boy knows that "it hurts" his sister when he pulls her hair. He also knows that he is a boy and consequently is different from his sister in several ways. He may even know that putting a box on his head will not make him invisible (if he's old enough!). These are examples of *primitive beliefs* about physical reality, social reality, and the nature of self. The child acquires such beliefs from direct sensory experience, but also from his interaction with others (typically, older children or adults) who are in a "better position" to know about reality. Adults are fairly certain about their primitive beliefs. They feel that they understand physical reality well, and they seldom argue about it. For children, however, the struggle to acquire a set of primitive beliefs is beset with humorous (to adults) examples of incorrect but sensible inferences regarding those beliefs. Eventually, through maturation and learning, children modify their set of primitive beliefs to include complex features and attributes. For example, many young children believe that height is directly related to age: the taller you are, the older you are. Even an extremely short, hunched-over senior citizen is a "funny-looking kid." Soon they learn that while this belief is a pretty good rule of thumb, it doesn't apply to all circumstances. So they add new attributes to the physical dimension of age, and in the future wrinkles and old-looking faces will also play a role when they determine how old a person is.

The following responses were given by two young children in a newspaper survey about what people think they will be doing when they become seventy. Note the interesting beliefs they express about age, activity, and lifestyle:

Interviewer: What will you be doing at age 70?

Child (5 years): Go to work everyday. I'll be a doctor. My grandmother is the oldest person I know. She's 32. For fun she takes naps and goes to the bank. Only kids really have fun. I'll probably live till I'm 10.

Child (4 years): Get my mail. That's what Granny does. For fun she plays cards with me and cooks. She also pulls the string on my doll that laughs and spits in your face. Granny is the oldest person I know. She's 2.[4]

Yes, these children have more to learn in formulating a valid set of beliefs about age. Yet their statements about adult behavior patterns are pretty sound, don't you think?

Our primitive beliefs about reality form the core of our belief system. A visual representation of the human belief system might be helpful at this point. Figure 1.1, a model constructed by Milton Rokeach,[5] organizes our beliefs into five categories. The model visualizes what children must learn as they develop into social beings. The smallest circle in the model—the center of our belief system—contains information on what we know about the world around us. Rokeach calls these primitive beliefs about our world *type-A* beliefs. For adults, these beliefs are not debatable because adults can "see for themselves" or they rely on scientific fact. But for children the set of A beliefs change on a day-by-day basis. Today, a child might believe Mommy makes the sun shine; tomorrow, it could be "Mother Nature"; and some day the child will be amazed at the explanations offered in science class.

In summary, when children are trying to make sense of the world around them, they are trying to formulate the center of their belief system. They ask adults questions because they want to know what things look like, what makes them "tick," and why things work the way they do. To understand children's communication, parents and teachers must understand *why* children talk. One important reason is their wish to discover their world.

making sense of oneself

Getting to know ourselves is quite different from understanding the world around us. Children who want to understand more about themselves are developing their self-beliefs:

[4]"PhotOpinion," *Chicago Sun-Times*, Tuesday, March 27, 1979, p. 34.

[5]Milton Rokeach, "Images of the Consumer's Changing Mind On and Off Madison Avenue" (paper delivered at the Eastern Conference of the American Advertising Agencies, November 6, 1963); a shorter version of this paper is contained in *Etc.: A Review of General Semantics*, 21 (September 1964), 267–73.

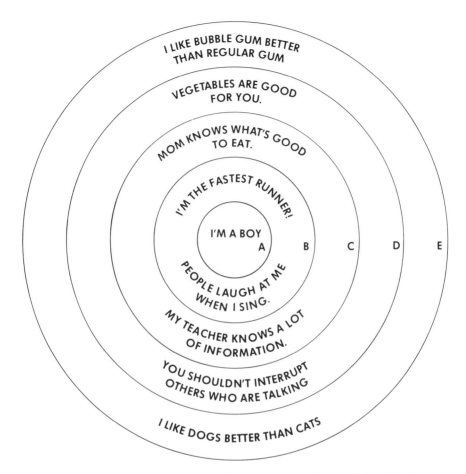

Figure 1.1. *Model of the human belief system. Adapted from Rokeach, "Images of the Consumer's Changing Mind."*

I am a good girl, most of the time.

I am a smart girl because I can count to one hundred.

I am a pretty girl when I get all dressed up.

Beliefs about self, the *type-B* beliefs in the Rokeach model, are basic to each of us. Their content is derived from our interactions with others. When others let us know what they think of us, through their actions and their words, the content of our self-beliefs may be affected. Type-B beliefs are slightly more flexible than type-A beliefs because others can disagree with us about their content. Although you may believe you're not very attractive, your friends may think you're quite attractive.

Our beliefs about ourselves can be positive or negative. Essentially, type-B beliefs are our value judgments about ourselves. Studies have shown that adults' type-B beliefs are highly resistant to change. This conclusion cannot be applied to children, however. Throughout their early years, children are in the process of discovering the content of their type-B beliefs. They do this by learning more and more about themselves, based on their self-images and how others react to them. In this sense, children's self-beliefs "emerge" in their early years. And in contrast with adults' type-B beliefs, those of children are easily affected by the opinions others have of them.

In that type-B beliefs represent value judgments about ourselves, they are based on a *language of morality*. Words such as "good," "bad," "fair," and "just" are key ingredients of self-beliefs. What morality words mean to children constitutes part of their struggle to get to know themselves. For example, a young boy may insist that he has been good because he remembers having done his chores for the day: he did his chores; therefore, he was a good boy. However, his mother might have a different opinion of the matter. She remembers that he was caught cheating in a game at school, that he hit a friend of his, and that he said "I hate you" to her. His excuses—"I didn't like the rules," "My friend took my bike," and "You scolded me, Mommy"—do not alter the mother's judgment.

In this example, the child and his mother hold different meanings of "goodness." To the mother, the chores her child performed were a matter of duty, not goodness. She may not realize, however, that the only concept young children have of morality is one of duty. As children grow older, the morality of duty is replaced by the morality of goodness. Often, the differences of opinion adults and children have regarding the child's self-beliefs are based on the different constructs of morality under which they operate.

Children want to understand themselves. They want to know what is right, good, and helpful about their behavior. They also want to know what is wrong, bad, and unhelpful in what they do and say. The tool they use in finding out about themselves is communication. Through their communication with others important to them, children acquire beliefs about themselves. If others communicate to children that they are clumsy, they will probably believe they are clumsy. We hear so much about the importance of a child's self-concept in education courses and textbooks. Experts in education say that a child needs a positive self-concept to get along with others and to learn. Communication is the child's key to the development of a healthy set of self-beliefs.

Children must be given opportunities to communicate their feelings about their own behavior and about others' reactions to that behavior. Children must be allowed to talk about themselves, to ask questions, and to discuss the *morality* of their behavior—as they see it and as others see it. In short, the second reason why children communicate is to make sense of themselves.

making sense of others

Children depend on others in building the remainder of their belief system—beliefs about authorities, beliefs based on authorities, and other, more inconsequential beliefs. *Type-C, type-D,* and *type-E* beliefs (see the examples in Figure 1.1) are products of children's interaction with important persons in their environment. Children communicate with others in an attempt to determine which authorities are important in their lives:

1. Mother knows a lot about nutrition; she is an expert on what to eat.
2. My coach knows about baseball, and he's my authority on that subject.
3. My friend knows how to dress well, and she's my authority on clothes.
4. Dad knows about tools, and he's the expert on fixing things.
5. My teacher knows about books; she's my information authority.

These are Type C beliefs which illustrate children's authorities. Important persons, religion and the church, schools and teachers, and TV heroes function as models by which children can pattern their behavior, decisions, and communication.

Beliefs derived from authorities are called type-D beliefs. They involve statements about what are appropriate or correct behaviors:

1. "Eating vegetables gives you muscles." (Mother may be this authority.)
2. "You should never throw your bat." (coach)
3. "Jeans should be faded when you wear them." (friend)
4. "Watch your fingers when you're hammering." (Dad)
5. "If you don't know it, look it up." (yes, the teacher)

Type-D beliefs tell us how to act, or, stated more conservatively, suggest appropriate ways of behaving.

Type-E beliefs, the easiest type to change because they are at the edge of the belief system, are the inconsequential beliefs. These are simply preference beliefs about what to do (play with marbles or watch TV), what to eat (Cheerios or Corn Flakes), or which color is prettier (purple or red). People love to talk about their preferences, and children form their preference beliefs in their conversations with others important in their lives. If a child's best friend loves peanut butter on saltine crackers for a snack, the child may change his mind about what he likes best after school and ask for peanut butter on saltines. Persons important in the lives of children assist them in discovering their likes and dislikes, and influence their preferences and tastes.

From the child's standpoint, the discovery of others is often a baffling process. Think for a moment how three-year-olds look at adults. First, young children are constantly looking up. Our voices come down from the tops of legs. In the excitement of play with other children they forget about the "big people" and concentrate on the world close to the floor, which is filled with similarly sized friends. Suddenly, out of nowhere may come a pair of adult legs that obstruct their way, and the result is a collision. Our legs got right in their way. It isn't until children are made to stop, look up, and acknowledge the obstruction as a person that they do so. Children see the intrusion as an invasion of their own activities ("Adults are always in the way"), whereas adults may insist that children apologize for "bumping into them" or invading their territory. Young children live in a "three-foot-tall world" and find it difficult to understand the territorial boundaries adults set for themselves. Apologize for that crashing encounter? Definitely not! You were in my way.[6]

Consider a little girl who cries impatiently, asking to be picked up. She might be saying, "Help me—take me into your world, Mommy." Either her world just wasn't right or she needed the assurance and security of the adult world. The wise adult knows that it is sound advice with young children to squat down to their level—to come into their world—in order to show them understanding. To be an active participant in children's activities in the classroom, a teacher knows that it's best to sit in a little chair, too. But the child must also understand the feelings of adults: adults also have space requirements, or territories, that should be cherished. Just as children have their own little territories, adults have adult territories. Sometimes, adult territories are a bit too large for children to understand.

Children must learn that people reveal themselves through their verbal and nonverbal communication. If children are to understand the persons around them who are very important in their lives, they must know the value of communication with these persons. Our communication with others helps us to get to know them, and in turn to better understand ourselves. To make sense of others, children must learn that communication takes place in several channels:

1. The *words* we use give important information to others.
2. The *pattern of words* we employ gives coherence to the information in our message.
3. Our *voice* communicates how we think, what we feel, and what we hope.
4. Our *body language* conveys important information about what we believe, how we feel, and what we know.
5. Our use of *space* in communication, through distance and touch, is an important part of our message.

[6]The image of the three-foot-tall world was suggested in a paper by an undergraduate student of mine, Jennifer Carter.

Our discussion of the child's three-foot-tall world was concerned primarily with the fifth channel of communication: the use of space. Until recently, space was not even considered an important channel of communication. In fact, in planning instructional units for children in the area of communication the continuing emphasis has been on words (the first channel of communication). However, children should be aware of all channels of communication if they are to function well in their interpersonal relationships.

Children should see how the channels of communication "go together" to produce a message. Only rarely does one channel operate independently—maybe in a letter, for example. In face-to-face encounters all channels of communication operate simultaneously. Normally, messages in all channels must be interpreted at once, and the overall message must be determined. But when channels of communication *interact*—that is, when they operate together to produce something different from the sum of the messages in each separate channel—understanding is difficult, even for adults.

For example, a sarcastic message communicated to a child, even a twelve-year-old child, is nearly impossible for the child to interpret correctly. If the symbols (for instance, "You really did a fine job!") are coupled with a negative voice, a smile of sorts, and a slightly turned head, they are usually misinterpreted by children. Most adults could decode this kind of message, although they might not enjoy the message. Children do not understand sarcasm properly and react to such messages very negatively.[7] The interaction of all channels of communication to produce the "conflict message," as in joking or sarcasm, presents a difficult challenge for even the high school student. To understand others, the child must become a type of communication expert, able to employ and interpret the several channels of communication in various situations. Although words and patterns of words are certainly primary means for getting a point across to someone, they are but one way to communicate. One theory suggests that no more than 30 to 35 percent of the "social meaning" of a conversation is conveyed through words.[8] The nonverbal channels thus carry the load.

On the other hand, children must also develop the ability to put together a message that incorporates all the channels effectively and includes just the right communication strategies. Communication involves more than simply sending and receiving information. When we communicate, we do

[7]Daphne E. Bugenthal et al., "Perception of Contradictory Meanings Conveyed by Verbal and Nonverbal Channels," *Journal of Personality and Social Psychology*, 16 (1970), 647–55.

[8]Ray L. Birdwhistell, *Kinesics and Context: Essays in Body Motion Communication* (Philadelphia: University of Pennsylvania Press, 1970), p. 158.

exchange ideas but we also define our relationships with the person to whom we are talking. In the terminology of some communication experts, we send and receive *reports* (informational messages) and *commands* (relationship messages, such as what I think of you, what you think of me, or what I think you think of me).[9] Children realize early in their lives that words alone are not sufficient to get along well. Other qualities of effective interaction must be mastered. Children learn that they need a rich vocabulary to express themselves, but they also need ways to put their words together sensibly, and some knowledge of good ways of saying things in certain situations. For example, even preschoolers know that it is important to say "please" when asking for something from an adult, but that such polite behavior with their pals may only get them trampled in the rush for toys. Further, they also learn that the way they communicate with their friends affects how their friends treat them. For example, in a playroom of a nursery school a four-year-old boy may say to an aggressive friend, "It's not fair that you're always the winner. You push me too much." Or, in a similar vein, an eight-year-old may tell his mother, "They think I'm a sissy because I don't use bad words." Children struggle with big communication decisions, such as "Should I boss him back?" or "Should I use naughty words?"

What complicates the learning process is that the nonverbal channels play a major but subtle role in establishing relationships, a role that children and adults don't often realize. It has been suggested that about 93 percent of the impact of a message is derived from the facial and vocal channels.[10] This estimate of the importance of nonverbal communication is unusually high, but it indicates that the previously neglected nonverbal channels cannot be neglected anymore.

For children to make sense of the important persons in their lives, they must be given information about the critical communication situations they encounter with others. In short, our third answer to the question of why children communicate is this: to understand others.

To summarize, children communicate in order to formulate their belief system. Children interact with others in order to answer three very important questions: (1) What is the nature of my world? (2) How can I understand myself? and (3) How can I understand the important people in my life? Children rely on communication in answering these questions. Communication is what assists children in their struggle:

"Help me understand!"

[9]Paul Watzlawick, Janet Beavin, and Don Jackson, *The Pragmatics of Human Communication* (New York: Norton, 1967), pp. 51–54.

[10]Albert Mehrabian, "Communicating Without Words," in *Communication: Concepts and Processes*, ed. Joseph DeVito (Englewood Cliffs, N.J.: Prentice-Hall, 1971), pp. 107–13.

COMMUNICATION: THE CHILD'S POWER PLAY

As a result of children's pleas to make sense of their world, themselves, and other human beings, and given the appropriate assistance from adults in their community, children are on their way to becoming functioning members of their social groups. "Experienced" members of their social groups, such as parents, adult friends, and teachers, must equip children with the communication skills that they need if they are to make sense. A philosophy of elementary education that is consistent with our communication approach is the power philosophy. According to this view, we must "free" the child or "move him from a powerless position in society to one of power."[11] This "power" is not physical strength; rather, it involves an internal feeling about oneself in interaction with others. Some theorists call this "personal power," but most people simply refer to the overall talent as self-confidence. If children feel good about themselves, they will feel free to assert themselves or express their feelings. Before we explore children's development of communication from several directions, we must first agree on why the development of effective communication is essential to the well-being of the child. Communication is the child's power play, the tool that will help the child develop a sense of self and a confidence to become independent in a world that is often difficult to understand.

Children are not born with personal powers that they can employ to affect their lives. They gain them in "negotiated interactions with persons who already have such powers."[12] While the mother is usually viewed as the primary model from which children can learn these powers, other persons important in children's lives—the authority figures discussed earlier in this chapter—become important models, as well. The father, doctor, neighbor, friend, and teacher can all serve effectively as power models. Two behaviors are essential to personal power:

1. Children must learn to direct their own activities, take care of their basic needs, and get along well in their daily lives. This does not mean that children cannot rely on others for anything whatsoever. It means that they must be "in charge" of themselves, and this requires that their communication be *clear* and *adapted* to the listener.

2. Children must express their needs, feelings, and ideas in an orderly and acceptable manner. In simpler terms, they must learn to act and talk appropriately and in a socially intelligible manner.[13]

---

[11]Beverly L. Hendricks, "The Move to Power: A Philosophy of Speech Education," *Speech Teacher*, 19 (1970), 151.

[12]John Shotter, "Acquired Powers: The Transformation of Natural into Personal Powers," *Journal of the Theory of Social Behavior*, 3 (1974), 141–56.

[13]*Ibid.*, pp. 154–55.

Children's perceptions of personal powers can be demonstrated most overtly in their playing of social games. Roleplaying, pretend-play, and other forms of social interchange highlight children's awareness of important roles: the child as a child, the child as a grownup, the child as a naughty person, the child as a teacher. Children make sense of themselves, others, and their world by "trying on" various roles in play situations and by participating in a number of different relationships in this play. Recent study in the area of children's play offers new insights into what is important to children. Children's feelings about themselves and their relationships with others stand out as critical when experts analyze children's play.

The key to effective participation in children's pretend-play is communication competence—the ability to select the appropriate communication strategies while performing the task of effectively defining a relationship. If children are pretending to be mothers taking care of their babies, then children playing the role must select the most appropriate communication strategies for enactment of that role. Their pretending becomes a rehearsal for personal powers necessary in future relationships. The purpose of much of children's early play is to give them skills and experience in becoming autonomous and developing the abilities to act independently and to take care of themselves. In order for children to develop a sense of independence, they must acquire a powerful *communication code*. The contents of that code are as follows:

1. an expressive vocabulary capable of communicating a host of meanings and ideas important in their lives
2. a set of sentence structures for communicating ideas, inferences, judgments, attitudes, and opinions
3. an effective nonverbal communication system, including facial expressions and gestures, postures, and prosodic cues, capable of expressing important feelings and relationships

The second set of components essential to children's development of a sense of independence is a powerful set of *communication practices*, which include the following:

1. an adequate range of communication strategies from which to select (for example, different ways of asking for help, such as requesting, stating a need, and bargaining.)
2. a set of criteria for selecting the most effective and appropriate communication strategies to use in a particular situation (for instance, a request is better to use with a parent than an order delivered forcefully.)
3. an understanding of the *content* (ideas and information) and *report* (relationship) in another person's message, so that children are empathic, understanding, and effective in their interpersonal relationships (for example, "I can see that you're unhappy today, Mary. What happened? Tell me about it.")

Communication can be the children's power play if they develop an effective code and an effective set of practices for using that code. Their goal is not simply to master the skills in putting sounds together or to talk with clear voices, but to develop communication talents that will equip them to deal with important issues, relations, and events in their lives. The *communication talents* outlined by White are critical to children's struggle for independence. With the ability to express feelings, ask for help, lead others, and so on, then and only then will children develop into persons capable of taking good care of themselves. Their power will come with the development of skills essential to their independence.

SUMMARY

Children ask for help in understanding their world, themselves, and others. They require a repertoire of communication strategies with which they can deal with critical communication situations they will face in their lives. Children must learn a set of criteria they can use in selecting the most effective and appropriate communication strategies for use in particular situations. The talents of the competent child involve rather specific communication skills essential in their day-to-day functioning: gaining and maintaining the attention of adults in socially acceptable ways, using adults as resources when a task is difficult, expressing affection/hostility to peers/adults, leading and following peers, competing with peers, and showing pride in one's accomplishments. With the development of these talents and others important in getting along with people, children can begin to learn about themselves, others, and the world they live in. Through such knowledge children can learn to be free, have confidence in their communication, and act independently.

The three basic reasons why children communicate are linked to the three types of beliefs they must build. First, children must learn to understand the nature of the world around them. They must therefore build a set of primitive beliefs about reality. Their communication with others, often in the form of questioning, helps them learn why airplanes fly, why leaves fall from trees, and why Daddy goes to work. Second, children must understand themselves and must therefore have a set of beliefs about themselves. Through their conversations with persons important to them, they discover self-beliefs that help them get to know themselves. Finally, children must understand other persons in their lives. By communicating with others and by attending to all the verbal and nonverbal channels of communication, children learn to understand the feelings, beliefs, and ideas of others.

The power philosophy of education is consistent with this text's approach to children's communication. In order to "free" children and to give them a kind of communication power—that is, an ability to communicate effectively in a variety of situations—we need to provide communication instruction that focuses on important communication situations.

SUGGESTED READINGS

HENDRICKS, BEVERLY, "The Move to Power: A Philosophy of Speech Education," *Speech Teacher,* 19 (1970), 151–160.

HOLT, JOHN, *The Underachieving School.* New York: Pitman Publishing Co., 1969.

WHITE, BURTON L., "Critical Influences in the Origins of Competence," *Merrill-Palmer Quarterly,* 2 (1975), 243–66.

WOOD, BARBARA, ed., *Development of Functional Communication Competencies: Pre-K–Grade 6.* Urbana, Ill.: ERIC Clearinghouse on Reading and Communication Skills, 1977.

2

communication development: intrapersonal forces

Children are unique individuals: no two will have quite the same appearance, sense of humor, or tactics for handling frustration. Neonatal specialists firmly believe that children are born with distinctive personalities. They begin life in an active mode, and affect others in ways consistent with their personalities.[1] This chapter focuses on the distinctive role children play in their own development of communication. The intrapersonal factors to be considered are biological maturation, genetic makeup, and creative ability.

A sense of what we mean by intrapersonal forces is illustrated in the following dialogue:

Interviewer: What do you have to have to be a mother, Jimmy?

Jimmy (six years old): Oh, about two childzez.

Interviewer: Two of them? Not just one, right?

Jimmy: Yah, two. If she only gots one, then she . . . well, maybe she could still be a mother.

Interviewer: Does she have to have anything else to be a mother?

Jimmy: Well, she dresses like one. You know, she wears mothers' clothes.

Interviewer: What do mothers' clothes look like, Jimmy?

Jimmy: Like housedresses.

Interviewer: Does she need anything else?

Jimmy: Oh yah, I forgot to mention a purse—she needs one.

[1]See, for example, Malca K. Aleksandrowicz and Dov R. Aleksandrowicz, "The Case History of a Happy Child," *Child Psychiatry and Human Development*, 5 (Spring 1975), 174–81.

Did anyone teach Jimmy to use words like "gots" and "childzez"? And who would have suggested to him that a mother is a woman who has two children (and not one)? Could someone have stressed the importance of housedresses and purses in defining what mothers are? No one but the child is responsible for these intricate bits of learning. Much of children's communication about their world, themselves, and others comes from their ability to figure things out on their own. Their minds work to understand events and issues, and their solutions are often so unique that they could have developed only from within. A set of forces within the child (the mind, body chemistry, and maturation) affect his or her development of communication.

When children acquire certain cognitive processes essential in putting words together, they can use sentences. When children acquire reasoning skills essential in viewing two sides of an issue, they can negotiate. On a conscious level, children ask questions, try out new ideas, and experiment with language and thought; the result is communication learning. On an unconscious level, children grow physically, neurologically, and chemically; the result is communication development. The intrapersonal forces discussed in this chapter are these:

1. *Biological forces:* children's maturation (both physiological and neurological) accounts for their progress in language development.
2. *Self-initiated forces:* children discover their language and practice what they have learned.

BIOLOGICAL FORCES

Why do most children begin to put words together in sentences sometime between eighteen and twenty-four months of age? Could it be that all mothers start some type of language training at that time? Probably not. In fact, language stimulation by parents probably begins much earlier in the child's life. A more recent and persuasive explanation is based on certain biological theories. According to one view that deserves attention, human beings have the innate capacity to acquire language, and much of the language-development process in children is best accounted for by biological factors.[2] This view has been most ably presented by Eric Lenneberg, a biologist who is convinced that language is rooted in biological foundations. His landmark publication *Biological Foundations of Language* received mixed reviews. Many found its hypothesis the most exciting one they had read in years; others doubted that his arguments would be supported with solid evidence. Time has suggested to us that though the validity of his

---

[2]Eric Lenneberg, *Biological Foundations of Language* (New York: John Wiley, 1969), p. 125.

theory has not been completely established, consideration of it is important for anyone who studies the development of communication and language in young children. In this chapter, the basic ideas in Lenneberg's theory are presented.

People learn how to stand up and walk without systematic training, and studies suggest, likewise, that people don't have to be taught to use language. Let's explore the walking/talking analogy for a moment. Most scientists agree that the human being's stance and gait are shaped by evolution: humans are predisposed to stand upright and walk on two feet. If you have cared for infants during the first six months of life, you know how excited they become when they are stood upright. Infants can be fussy, unhappy, and generally irritable, but if you pull them up into a standing position, they smile, breathe faster, and vocalize. Pediatricians believe that if infants show this much eagerness to be stood upright in early months, then there must be an inborn urge to achieve this satisfying position.[3] Their eagerness to be upright is soon followed by their jubilation at being able to walk. Bipedal gait is a characteristic of the human species that has applied to all persons in all cultural groups since the early civilizations. Most important, the emergence of bipedal gait is surprisingly regular among all children.

The development of children's communication proceeds along strikingly similar lines in three crucial areas: (1) emergence of language; (2) readiness for speech; and (3) bodily readiness for communication. Let's now discuss the first area, and with it the evidence supporting a biological foundation for communication.

the emergence of language in children

Parents pay a great deal of attention to charts that tell how a child's coordination will develop. They become concerned if their little Jennifer isn't sitting alone by six to nine months—after all, the charts say this is the "normal" time for the child to reach this motor milestone—and they conclude that something must be wrong with Jennifer. Language milestones are viewed by parents in a similar manner. By four months of age, for example, a child is usually cooing and chuckling in response to someone or something in her environment. Parents have read that their child "should be" cooing or chuckling at this time. An important point to consider, and one that many parents lose sight of in following their child's development, is that milestones are based on averages; they are not criteria for normalcy. In fact, many children develop normally in every respect but do not reach motor milestones and language milestones at the prescribed time.

[3]T. Berry Brazelton, *Infants and Mothers: Differences in Development* (New York: Delacorte Press, 1969), p. 149.

Milestones.   Keeping in mind that milestones are only averages, let's explore the emergence of language and coordination in children. Figure 2.1 is a chart, accompanied by sketches, of children's early progress in mastering walking and talking. The chart indicates that children progress step by step in developing coordination and language. Mastery in the motor area, such as in being able to sit alone, is often accompanied by mastery in the language area, such as in babbling. Everything seems to happen at once from the parents' point of view. It's hard to keep up with a growing infant.

The Delecato School.   Why is there such a striking correspondence between language development and motor development? Is it possible that the latter affects the former? While most experts agree that no such cause-effect relationship can be proven, it is worthwhile to discuss briefly a developmental program based on that premise.

Carl Delecato developed a program to assist children with reading deficiencies and overall language-development delay.[4] He hypothesized that the child with reading problems did not properly master the motor skills that are critical in the establishment of the brain patterns essential for reading. The motor skill of particular concern to him was cross-patterned crawling, the crawling pattern propelled by the coordinate forward movement of left arm with right leg and right arm with left leg. His program focused on the development, at almost any age, of the requisite motor skills for language development, such as cross-patterned crawling. He assumed that children must develop correct motor patterns before they can correct any reading disabilities. His 1963 text *The Diagnosis and Treatment of Speech and Reading Problems* (published also by Charles C. Thomas) put the blame for these problems on *neurological disorganization*—disorders in sleep patterns, creeping, walking, and cerebral dominance (a determinant of handedness, eyedness, footedness). While Eric Lenneberg would agree that Delecato was concentrating on two skills that are somehow related in their development, he would not agree that the Delecato School was correct in supporting a cause-effect relationship between motor-skill learning and reading development. We discuss the school briefly here, however, because it continues to attract many clients.

Delecato exercises stress the sensorimotor development the pre-two-year-old typically goes through before learning to talk. Experts reviewing the Delecato approach are often amazed at the progress his students make, but they are reluctant to attribute progress to the motor remediation. Instead, the special attention and the reading work that follow are more likely to account for this development. Many experts have remarked about the prob-

[4]Carl H. Delecato, *Neurological Organization and Reading* (Springfield, Ill.: Charles C. Thomas, 1966).

4 months

Johnny can hold his head up by himself.

Johnny coos and chuckles when people play with him.

6 to 9 months

Johnny can sit alone and can pull himself up into a standing position.

Johnny babbles continually, sounding like this: "gagagag, yayayaya; dadadada."

12 to 18 months

Johnny first stands alone, then he walks along furniture, and finally he walks by himself.

Johnny uses a few words, follows simple commands, and knows what "no" means.

Figure 2.1. *Johnny's development of coordination and language. Adapted from Eric Lenneberg, "The Natural History of Language," in* The Genesis of Language, *ed. Frank Smith and George A. Miller (Cambridge, Mass.: M.I.T. Press, 1968), p. 222.*

18 to 21 months   Johnny's walking looks stiff   Johnny understands simple
                   and jerky but he does well.   questions and begins to put
                   He can sit in a chair (his   two or three words together
                   aim is only "fair"), he can   in sentences.
                   crawl down stairs, and he
                   can throw a ball (clumsily).

24 to 27 months   Johnny runs well, but falls   Johnny uses short
                   when making a quick turn.   sentences composed of
                   He can also walk up and   words from a
                   down stairs.   300-to-400-word
                                                    vocabulary.

Figure 2.1. *Continued.*

30 to 33 months	Johnny has good hand and finger coordination; he can manipulate objects well.	Johnny's vocabulary increases in size, and three- and four-word sentences are prevalent. His language begins to sound adult-like.

36 to 39 months	Johnny runs smoothly and negotiates sharp turns. He walks stairs by alternating feet. He can ride a tricycle, stand on one foot (briefly), and jump twelve inches in the air.	Johnny talks in well-formed sentences, following rather complex grammatical rules. Others can generally understand what he is talking about.

Figure 2.1. *Continued.*

lem facing older readers who must creep and crawl: either they consider the motor exercises irrelevant or they feel humiliated trying them. A student of mine told us in class that his younger brother went through a Delecato program and advanced dramatically in his reading scores as a result of his crawling machine. We asked him to describe this machine. It was like a treadmill, and on it his brother could crawl while not darting around the house like an animal. Every day, he explained, his brother would work out on his crawling machine. Everyone in the family worked hard with him to develop the motor skills that Delecato thought were related to language skills.

Most experts today agree that when we pay special attention to anyone, including children, we show them that we care about their well-being. Often, this attention is in itself sufficient to promote some kind of change in behavior. Related examples can be drawn from the business world, where studies of employee productiveness show that changes or alterations in the work environment produce increases in productivity. Rather than the new paint or the increased lighting, it is probably the mere changing of work conditions by management that boosts morale and employee output. We know that many methods such as the Delecato method of child development focus on providing increased attention to the children in the program. It seems likely that this attention is perceived as care, concern, and confirmation by the children. Consequently, they may try harder in anything they do. Does it work? In a way, yes it does, though we still don't have a cause-effect relationship.

Probably closer to the truth is the alternate idea that motor-skill development and language development are part of a total maturation process in which, as Lenneberg suggests, the growth of the brain prompts development in all areas of human endeavor. The key to understanding much of human development is being sought by neurologists specializing in the growth of the human brain. Such studies may shed light on the synchronism of language skills and motor skills.

Brain maturation. The brain undergoes a very rapid weight increase during the postnatal period: at the end of the first two years of life the brain is roughly 350 percent heavier than at birth. In contrast, the increase at the end of the next ten years is only 35 percent. By about age fourteen, the brain has achieved its adult weight and no further increases are registered. According to scientific research, neurons in the cerebral cortex grow in volume as one grows older. A significant spurt in the growth of the cerebral cortex occurs at about the age of two. This growth spurt appears to happen at about the same time children join words together in a sentence. The possible relationship is tempting and reasonable. In charting the brain's structural growth, biochemical changes, and neurophysiological changes one notices this trend: a *sharp rise at two years*, a slight leveling off in the remaining preschool years, and a general leveling off at puberty. These biological curves parallel the curve representing language acquisition and development. Apparently, maturation of the human brain and language development are related.

For years scientists have tried to explain language development in terms of physiological and neurological phenomena. Marcus Jacobson presents data that suggest language growth can be correlated with an increase in connections in the cerebral cortex, especially in the growth of particular cells he calls type-II neurons.[5] With some caution he traces the development of the "language neurons" and finds that when they are destroyed, the growth of language is also impaired. André Lecours plotted the myelination of brain tissues through teen-age years, and again a striking correspondence can be noted between the growth of tissues and the development of langue.[6] Lecours studied the cycles of *myelination*—the gradual development of myelin in the sheaths of the fiber system in the brain. Using complex instruments he examined this white, fatty substance that forms the sheath around certain nerve fibers in the brain. He took these cycles of growth as indications of brain maturation, and plotted them as they correlated with the emergence and development of locomotion, manipulation of instruments, articulated speech, and language. Lecours offers an explanation for why a child does not usually learn to read until after five years of age: the myelogenetic cycles of the tissues associated with skills involved in reading have not matured yet.

Many such arguments could be presented, but their language and reasoning are beyond the scope of this text. The point here is that studies of brain maturation show a striking correspondence between chemical and neurological changes and language changes. The evidence from medical studies is persuasive in arguing that brain development is a key force in the development of children's language.

If brain maturation is *slowed*, developmental horizons are reached later; the spacing between milestones is prolonged, but the sequence of milestones remains constant. For example, twelve to fourteen months usually elapse between sitting and putting words together, and in general language is fully established within another twenty months. But in the retarded child the lapse between sitting and putting words together may be as much as twenty-four months, and language may not be fully established for another sixty months. The retarded child's early milestones are delayed by a few

[5]Marcus Jacobson, "Brain Development in Relation to Language," in *Foundations of Language Development: A Multidisciplinary Approach*, ed. Eric H. Lenneberg and Elizabeth Lenneberg (New York: Academic Press, 1975), pp. 105–19.

[6]André R. Lecours, "Myelogenetic Correlates of the Development of Speech and Language," in *Foundations of Language Development*, ed. Lenneberg and Lenneberg, pp. 121–35.

months, and the delay increases significantly with age. This lag behind norms becomes progressively greater even if the child's condition does not change.

The Critical-Period Hypothesis.   Lenneberg believes that brain maturation has a starting point and an end point that are critical to the entire process of language learning. In fact, there is a "critical period" during which a person should learn language; after this period it is virtually impossible to learn a first language. Zoologists use the critical-period notion to explain why certain songbirds fail to acquire the ability to sing: they did not hear an adult bird sing within the critical period of song learning. Likewise, Lenneberg suggests that a child learning to talk must hear others talk within a certain time period or else will not learn to talk. No direct instruction is necessary but, as with the songbird, the child must be "immersed" in hearing language during this critical period. Lenneberg places the starting point sometime during the second year; the end point he argues for is puberty, which usually occurs around the age of thirteen or fourteen. More recent studies suggest a much earlier end point of 5 years of age.[7]

Regardless of the precise age at which the end point occurs, there are many generalizations about language learning that show the importance of acquiring language at the youngest age possible:

1. Recovery from aphasia, in terms of language skills, decreases markedly with the age of the patient. If aphasics are beyond puberty when they become ill, they can make little progress. (The vast majority of aphasia patients have speech and language disturbances resulting from a disorder commonly known as a stroke: brain tissue is destroyed and brain functions are disrupted, temporarily or permanently, because of an insufficient blood supply caused by a clot or a ruptured blood vessel.)

2. After puberty, retarded children seldom make significant progress in language learning.

3. Bilingual children learn their second language with an appropriate accent, while teens and adults acquiring a second language will usually retain the accent of their native language.

4. Most young immigrants will acquire a properly accented form of English, whereas older immigrants will retain the accent of their native tongue when speaking English.

5. American adults moving to a new geographic location will probably not acquire the dialect of the new locale, while children of these adults will adopt the new dialect.

We can conclude that learning a language, or picking up a second language, seems to be increasingly more difficult with age. Whether it becomes impossible after a certain age has never been thoroughly tested scientifically.

To weaken Lenneberg's theory, writers used to cite the case studies of wild children discovered in the jungles, saying that these children, despite their environment, should have acquired some rudimentary form of lan-

---

[7]Stephen Krashen, "Laterization, Language Learning, and the Critical Period: Some New Evidence," *Language Learning,* 23 (1973), 63–74.

guage if language is *innate* or biologically preprogrammed in human beings. Lenneberg responded with a key point about the biological basis of language, that at least some *exposure to language* is necessary in launching the biologically based process of language learning in children. Those who do not accept the biological basis of language do not suggest that language emerges without adequate stimulation from other human beings. Yet they do question what would be the minimal input necessary for the development of effective language. Recently, the terribly depressing case study was published of Genie, a thirteen-and-a-half-year-old girl who endured social and physical isolation in her own home and received the lowest conceivable level of language input. Since she was chronologically beyond puberty when discovered, language theorists were interested in testing Lenneberg's original hypothesis of the critical period, assessing whether or not they could teach Genie language at this rather late stage in her life.

From the age of twenty months, Genie was confined in a small room under very restraining conditions: she was either harnessed in a potty-chair or confined in a crib covered with wire mesh. She was not allowed to make any sounds or her father would physically punish her. Her mother fed her infant food. When she was discovered by a social worker at the age of thirteen-and-a-half (she appeared to be only seven years of age or so) she could not stand or chew food, she was not toilet-trained, and she did not speak, cry, or make any sounds. She was taken into protective custody by the Los Angeles Police Department and then was admitted into the Children's Hospital of Los Angeles. She made excellent progress in the hospital and eventually was placed in a foster home to develop and grow. The cruel details were reconstructed as much as possible through interviews, but the events in Genie's life between the ages of twenty months and thirteen-and-a-half years are incomplete.

Susan Curtiss, a psycholinguist, wrote a book about the development of Genie's language. In it she presented two possible versions of Lenneberg's critical-period hypothesis: (1) the strong version, which would suggest that a human being cannot acquire language by mere exposure after puberty, and (2) the weak version, that normal language acquisition cannot occur beyond the critical period. Since Genie did acquire English in her foster home, no support could be given to the strong version of Lenneberg's hypothesis. Though her progress was far below levels we would expect for children even close to her age, she was able to pick up language simply by being with people.

Curtiss did not dismiss the weaker version of the hypothesis, however, since she was able to present evidence in five key areas that related Genie's language problems to typical language disorders:

1. Genie understood much more language than she could produce, a feature of a language disorder. While most children and adults understand more than they are able to talk about,

the production/comprehension discrepancy is more extreme in cases of language disorders; this discrepancy was extreme for Genie.

2. Genie did not use language rules with great regularity. In fact, her use of grammar was unpredictable.

3. Genie used a lot of the stereotypic speech that characterizes language-disordered children.

4. Genie's rate of language development was far slower than that of the normal child, and closer to that of the retarded child.

5. Certain syntactic patterns that Genie did not master cause problems for language-disordered children.[8]

These findings and the results of brain tests on Genie led Curtiss to conclude that her case *does support* a weak version of Lenneberg's critical-period hypothesis: that language cannot effectively be acquired after puberty. In fact, Curtiss is convinced that an earlier age, perhaps 5 years, may be the end of the period in which children learn language. Her data could not test this point, however.

Another important feature of Lenneberg's biological approach is the notion of laterization, the shifting of brain functioning to one or the other side. Handedness and brain dominance are aspects of a person's neurological character that seem to be related to their language development. Evidence from laterization tests on Genie's brain showed that she developed into a right-hemisphere thinker, whereas most language learners develop a left dominance. In fact, experts agreed that her language seemed to resemble that of a right-hemisphere-dominant aphasic. Curtiss calls Genie's language "non-language area language." Genie developed other right-hemisphere talents such as good visual and tactile orientation, effective holistic thinking, and an analytic ability. What might have happened to the left hemisphere in Genie's brain, which in turn might explain the emergence of the right instead of the left hemisphere in her language functioning, was a "kind of functional atrophy . . . brought about by disuse and suppression."[9]

Though there is still more to learn about the operation of a critical period for language development, there is a fairly convincing case that a certain period is most conducive to language learning in children, and that that period is early in the child's lifetime.

Genetic possibilities.   One of the most impressive studies supporting a biological foundation for language examined the language (basically syntax) abilities of seventy-four sets of twins (thirty-seven fraternal, thirty-seven

[8]Susan Curtiss, *Genie: A Psycholinguistic Study of a Modern-Day "Wild Child"* (New York: Academic Press, 1977), pp. 209–11.
[9]Susan Curtiss, Victoria Fromkin, Stephen Krashen, David Rigler, and Marilyn Rigler, "The Linguistic Development of Genie," *Language* 50 (1974), 543.

identical) in the San Diego area.[10] Based on a rationale of genetic alikeness of identical twins, as compared with fraternal twins, the researchers tested this hypothesis:

> The language abilities of the identical twins should be more alike than the language abilities of either the fraternal twins or pairs of siblings of both types of twins.

Their results strongly supported their prediction: the similarity index for the identical twins (.83) was much higher than those for the fraternal twins (.44) and the siblings (.49).

To assess the possibility that the parents of the identical twins treated them more similarly and thereby contributed to their becoming more alike, the researchers did a validity check of parental awareness of the nature of their twins. Did the parents always know which type of twins they had? They did not. In fact, the alikeness scores of those identical twins whose parents thought they were "only fraternal" were still high (.72). On the other hand, the alikeness scores of the fraternal twins whose parents thought they were identical were not high at all (.47). The researchers concluded that heredity must account for a healthy percentage of children's language-structure abilities. In fact, the researchers suggested that as much as 80 percent of children's language variability can be traced to heredity and the remainder to environment. Few theorists are willing to accept these rather extreme figures for intrapersonal versus interpersonal forces affecting language, even if they apply only to syntax. But even though these results are limited to certain methods of testing language comprehension and syntax screening, they are still very impressive support for the biological foundation of language.

Another type of genetically-based evidence illustrating the intrapersonal forces on language development comes from the study of child psychiatry and human development. The study of inborn personality characteristics and behavioral tendencies in children are of great interest to psychologists and psychitrists. Malca and Dov Aleksandrowicz argued in a case study that a child's inborn personality and communicative behaviors were instrumental in shaping her parent's behaviors.[11] A girl named Debbie was selected for study because she was such a happy child. She was very cuddly, and stimulated her usually passive mother into touching her. When she was two years old, Debbie became active, seductive, and aggressive in coping with her mother's reserved style. Her parents' tolerance and flexibility contributed to Debbie's active approach. The doctors concluded that parents

[10]Harry Musinger and Arthur Douglass II, "The Syntactic Abilities of Identical Twins, Fraternal Twins, and their Siblings," *Child Development*, 47 (1976), 40–50.

[11]Aleksandrowicz and Aleksandrowicz, "The Case History of a Happy Child."

obviously affect children's behavior, but that children also affect their parents' behavior. A "happy child" is one who has a biological fit with her parents: the strengths and weaknesses of both child and parents are worked out in effective and easy ways. A poor biological fit is one where a relatively passive child meets a passive parent: neither excites the other in interaction. Another poor biological fit occurs when both are overactive, aggressive, and excitable: frustration prevails, and the two seem not to enjoy each other.

These two studies illustrate that heredity (inborn characteristics) plays a role in shaping aspects of language, and that the child's inborn characteristics are strong enough to have an influence on his parents. Heredity not only plays a role in the language children acquire, it also helps determine how they behave and how others respond to them.

readiness to acquire speech

Recent evidence suggests that the onset of infants' vocalizations can also be explained biologically.[12] Newborn infants, or *neonates*, are to some extent physically equipped to hear and produce speech. Although neonates are able to hear rather well, they do not demonstrate an ability to produce speech sounds. Their inability apparently results from initial limitations of the neonatal vocal apparatus. The vocal folds are positioned relatively high in the neonate, and consequently the oral cavity located above the vocal folds is smaller and of a different shape than the adult cavity. Medical experts have suggested that, while mechanisms directly related to speech production are present from birth, the lowering of the vocal folds mechanism, essential to proper sound production, develops within a short period of time after birth. In addition, it is nearly impossible for infants to modify their breath stream with their tongues, which, because they virtually fill their oral cavity, are much too cumbersome for such activity. Apparently, neonates fail to reproduce the range of speech sounds not because they have not learned to produce them but because the structure of their vocal mechanism at birth prevents this. The configuration and size of the vocal mechanism changes during early physical maturation: by one or two months of age the child can produce vowel-like sounds.

In contrast, the child's ability to hear adult speech sounds seems to exist from birth. Apparently, no changes occur in the peripheral auditory mechanisms during early maturation. In fact, the infant can discriminate among acoustic signals during this early period. For example, neonates respond differently to different pitch levels, intensities, and durations of speech. Interestingly, infants respond to frequencies in the speech-

[12]See Paula Menyuk, *The Development of Speech* (New York: Bobbs-Merrill, 1972), pp. 11–13.

frequency band in a quiet and attentive fashion, but they respond to frequencies above or below this band with alerting and startling responses.

The results of studies of neonates and infants suggest that human children are programmed for speech in these ways:

1. They are able to distinguish speech from other acoustic signals.
2. They are able to produce speech after their vocal mechanism matures to a certain degree.

So far then, the emergence of language has been explained by the process of brain maturation, while early speech can be linked to physiological and auditory readiness.

bodily readiness to communicate

Our messages consist of more than sounds and words, for we communicate with our bodies as well as our voices. Since this text embodies a total view of children's communication development, we must consider a biological basis for nonverbal language. We must view the intrapersonal forces affecting the emergence of body and vocal messages as well as those affecting verbal messages. Just as we have cited support for the biological foundations of verbal language, we can also find support for the biological basis of nonverbal communication.

Studies of the nonverbal behavior of newborns provide the most exciting evidence in favor of an innate bodily readiness to communicate. In fact, two studies present a strong case that babies are already involved in the communication-acquisition process through their body movement. One study viewed newborns' movement in reaction to adult speech, while the other presented fascinating evidence that newborns are capable of "imitating" body movements and gestures.

Newborns' body movement in response to speech. William Condon and Louis Sander at Boston University Medical Center examined newborns' body movements in response to their mothers' speech.[13] A frame-by-frame analysis of the baby on video tape was conducted along with a coordinate analysis of an audio tape containing the mother's voice. The baby's body motion was plotted on a chart to see if it coincided with the adult's articulatory movements during speech. The results were positive. The two doctors noted a flurry of body movement by the newborns—head, shoulders, hips, and feet—when the mother would begin a word. These movements would

[13]William S. Condon, and Louis W. Sander, "Neonate Movement is Synchronized with Adult Speech: Interactional Participation and Language Acquisition," *Science*, 183 (January 11, 1974), 99–101.

subside or change with the articulation of the next word or so. Patterns of body (child) and articulatory (adult) movement were almost perfectly matched. The researchers concluded that newborns' body movements are *synchronized* with adult speech behavior.

Condon and Sander suggest that this movement early in life may serve as the basis of the acquistion of complex linguistic forms that contain rhythm and structure. By the time the child begins to talk, the form and structure of the language has been "practiced" through the baby's nonverbal participation in adult speech. The infant's nonverbal participation in adult communication may lay the groundwork for the child's acquisition of speech rhythm, vocal patterns, syntactic structures, and body-motion rhythm and style.

Newborn's body motions and gestures. Andrew Metzoff and Keith Moore filmed newborns' body motions as they viewed adult gestures and movements.[14] They found that very young babies, only twelve to twenty-one days old, were able to imitate a series of gestures and movements: tongue protrusion, opening of the mouth, lip protrusion, and finger movement. Their report contains pictures of the newborns' reactions to these gestures. The clarity of imitative bodily behavior in these pictures is astounding. The procedure involved showing the babies the gesture, then showing them a passive adult face, and finally filming any reaction. These films were then judged to see whether or not a successful copy had been made.

The researchers concluded that newborns are capable of imitating manual and facial movements. Further, that this ability shows up so clearly and so early in the child's life cannot be explained on the basis of conditioning. The researchers also reject an explanation based on a biological phenomenon called the "innate release mechanism." Instead, they suggest that the human being has the innate ability to reproduce the communicative movements of adults and that further study of this inborn ability will probably help account for how the baby develops language so effectively and efficiently.

Our discussion of children's "bodily readiness" to communicate has focused rather specifically on the ability of newborns to copy adult body movement and the synchrony of newborns' body movement and adults' speech behavior. In other areas of nonverbal communication, such as the child's acquisition of prosody (the intonation and stress patterns in speech), biological factors are often employed to help explain the particular course of development. The point we must consider in our discussion of intrapersonal forces affecting the development of communication is this:

---

[14]Andrew N. Metzoff and M. Keith Moore, "Imitation of Facial and Manual Gestures by Human Neonates," *Science*, 188 (October 7, 1977), 75–77.

Biological factors are extremely helpful in explaining the emergence and development of children's nonverbal messages.

It appears that children's development of communication behaviors, verbal and nonverbal, are partially explained by the maturation of the human brain and the human body. In the future we may be able to outline communication milestones that children achieve in their language development; such milestones may have a strong biological foundation.

SELF–INITIATED FORCES

Child psychologists often suggest that children are excellent investigators of their world. Children behave like little scientists, trying to discover the rules that make things "tick." According to child psychologist Jean Piaget, the child *acts on things to understand them.* The following account vividly describes the scientific capacities of the young child:

Almost from birth, he touches objects, manipulates them, turns them around, looks at them, and in these ways he develops an increasing understanding of their properties. It is through manipulation that he develops schemes relating to objects. When new objects are presented, the child may at first try to apply them to already existing schemes. If not successful, he attempts, again through manipulation, to develop new schemes; that is, new ways of acting on and thereby comprehending the world.[15]

Equipped with a sort of scientific ability to investigate, the child appears to be well qualified to discover the patterns of language. Linguists say that a very powerful intrapersonal force explaining children's communication development is their *creativity* in learning what the principles of language are. Children demonstrate their creative ability by using the intricate "tools" of the scientist at work in a laboratory. The child's laboratory is the world of language, and he discovers the rules of his language rapidly and in an amazingly scientific manner. The child is a busy little scientist, *practicing* and *discovering* the schemes of language.

practicing language

Many children practice their language—that is, they go through a kind of linguistic drill—before falling asleep at night. Others do the same thing

---

[15]H. Ginsburg and O. Opper, *Piaget's Theory of Intellectual Development: An Introduction* (Englewood Cliffs, N.J.: Prentice-Hall, 1969), p. 221.

upon waking up or when playing by themselves. If parents stand near the bedside of their child who is in the two-word stage of development, they might hear him practicing his new-found language schemes. The first systematic study of this process was reported by Ruth Weir. After analyzing the presleep monologues of her two-and-a-half-year-old son Anthony, she described the fascinating practice procedures that are potentially important in a child's development of language.[16]

Many of Anthony's drills focused on the pronunciation of words: he said a word and then corrected his pronunciation over and over again. Other exercises involved practice with grammatical skills. One exercise was the "build-up": "the block," "the yellow block," "Look at the yellow block." Another was the "breakdown": "another big bottle," "big bottle." Both exercises portray a child working at the intricate operations of his language, able to analyze sentences into component parts. Other drills performed by Anthony showed his ability to substitute nouns in sentence frames: "what color," "what color blanket," "what color map," "what color glass." His practicing covered many realms of linguistic knowledge, such as syntactic negation, verb tense, declarative sentences, and questions.

The accounts of Anthony's practice sessions with language show that he enjoyed his drills. He was playing a game with language. Linguistic form always appeared to be paramount in his drills: the content of his utterances was subordinate to the form. Children's bedtime monologues, or any of their "private" monologues during the day, may constitute an important activity in their development of language. Although the precise role of practice drills in children's development of communication has not been clearly established, the existence of this behavior suggests strongly that it is an important contributor.

discovery: children's creativity with language

Just as a linguist working in a university setting attempts to discover the rules of an exotic African language, so does a child analyze a corpus of speech to discover its underlying rules. The child formulates hypotheses about the way language works, tests them to see how they work, and, if they are confirmed, "obeys" the rules contained in the hypotheses. Upon discovering a hypothesis that doesn't account for the language the child hears, our little scientist will search for a new hypothesis that might work better.

To illustrate the discovery process, one need only survey reports of how children acquire the grammar of their language. We will cite two examples of children's supreme creativity in language learning. One is related to verb tense and the other to adding inflections to words.

---

[16]Ruth Weir, *Language in the Crib* (The Hague: Mouton, 1962).

Picture a child searching for schemes to account for verb tense in the speech of her environment. A two-year-old girl may first refer to a past event by saying something like this:

"Daddy went to office."

This sentence appears to reflect some degree of sophistication in past-tense formulation. However, because the second stage of development typically involves a kind of regression, the child probably did not attach meaning to the linguistic change necessary for the creation of the past-tense form of "go." Instead, she may have been imitating the entire form, "went." The second stage might sound something like this:

"Daddy goed to office."

This stage probably reflects the child's first concern with the rules of her language. She knows that walking, talking, and playing done yesterday are said as "walked," "talked," and "played." It seems reasonable to assume that going done yesterday is said as "goed." The child has discovered a rule of language that accounts for much of the language to which she is exposed— yet that rule doesn't always work. People may tell her that as well. Later in her development, maybe as late as four years of age, the child may search for a new set of rules that account for all verbs, including the past irregular verbs. This attempt may result in:

"Daddy wented to the office."

Makes sense, doesn't it? Yet most parents cringe when a child says something like this; they may not allow such an utterance to go uncorrected. Once the child is able to understand how to apply the rules of past tense to irregular verbs, she is able to perform like this:

"Daddy went to the office."

Now the child is back where she started. She may have said something similar to this at age two, but without any understanding of the rules behind its utterance.

Children in the process of learning verb tense are extremely creative in their use of language schemes. They discover rules according to a kind of scientific procedure. They find rules to account for relationships and they employ these rules to portray such relationships. Even though the rules don't always fit adult language schemes, children's creativity in language cannot be stressed too much.

Another example of children's creativity is their ability to learn a nonsense language composed of made-up words for which they must add appropriate inflectional endings.[17] For example, if children are given the words "wug," "gutch," and "bick," accompanied by imaginary pictures of such phenomena, they can talk creatively about them. If children are shown a picture of a "wug," a birdlike creature, and are then shown two of them, they can pluralize "wug" to "wugz" quite appropriately. Such studies have supported the notion that children approach their language creatively. Children can form plurals, past-tense forms, possessives, and adjective forms for all sorts of nonsense words, illustrating that they work with rules to discover language schemes.

"revised when necessary": a communication rule

Young children can evaluate their success in communicating clearly to others. Even an eighteen-month-old child can revise his strategies when someone does not appear to understand him. A group of young children in early stages of language development, around two years of age, took part in a study simply by playing with toys and books in their homes.[18] Although the mothers were present, they were not asked to interact with their child. During a one-hour taping an experimenter continually interrupted the child to ask "What?", pretending not to understand the child. The question was asked about once every three minutes. The child's response to "What" was then examined.

Rather than simply repeating what they initially said, even the youngest children tried some type of revision. Though the repertoire of revision strategies increased with the child's mastery of language, even the youngest and least advanced children knew they had to change some aspect of their utterance. The researcher, Tanya Gallagher, suggests that the following conversational rule is known by even the least fluent language users:

Revise the form of utterances when you perceive that the listener did not understand.

Revisions can be simple restatements—for example,

Child: I wanna play dolly.
Experimenter: What?
Child: I play dolly now.

---

[17]See, for example, Jean Berko, "The Child's Learning of English Morphology," *Word,* 14 (1958), 150–77.

[18]Tanya M. Gallagher, "Revision Behaviors in the Speech of Normal Children Developing Language," *Journal of Speech and Hearing Research,* 20 (1977), 303–18.

Or they can be more elaborate—for example,

Child: I wanna play dolly.
Experimenter "What?"
Child: Can I play with the dolly?

That children know this rule at such an early point in their development of language and communication indicates a strong intrapersonal force affecting this development.

Intrapersonal forces within children direct their acquistion of communication. Through practice and discovery procedures, children demonstrate creativity in their use of language.

SUMMARY

Children are innately capable of acquiring language. Their predisposition to communicate is shaped by the maturation of their brain, vocal apparatus, and body. Just as children's development of stance and bipedal gait follows a predictable and "natural" course, and just as children's development of coordination can be characterized by their attainment of motor milestones, their language development can be described in terms of biological milestones.

All children develop language, speech, and bodily communication according to a similar development schedule. For example, at about two years of age children are able to join words together in sentences and communicate gender through bodily means. The co-occurrence of these milestones at this particular stage of development can be explained by advocates of the biological-force position.

The evidence gathered in the case study of Genie, the child discovered at thirteen years of age in a locked room, showed that Genie was able to learn a rudimentary form of English. Her progress in language development was thought to have been curtailed by her "critical period" having elapsed, however. Evidence from language analyses of fraternal and identical twins points to a genetic basis for the acquisition of the structure of language. Finally, studies of newborns' bodily behaviors support the idea that they are equipped at birth to copy the body language of others and that they tend to move in synchrony with adult speech. Medical and biological studies of intrapersonal forces affecting children's communication, considered as a whole, present a compelling case for the innateness of children's capabilities to learn their language.

In addition to the biological forces affecting the child's development of communication, it is important to consider a second set of intrapersonal forces affecting development. First, when children are at work discovering the schemes of their language they are like busy little scientists. Once they find the rules or schemes for explaining the speech they hear, they *practice* these schemes in certain situations—for instance, before they go to sleep or when they wake up. The process of discovering rules that account for language schemes shows that children are extremely *creative* in their acquisition of a language. When children perceive that they have not been understood by those listening to them, they know they must revise their utterance. Even one- and two-year-olds are capable of revising their speech when prompted to do so. In short, children learn to communicate partly because of an intrapersonal force that compels them to discover the rules that make language and communication work effectively for them.

SUGGESTED READINGS

CURTISS, SUSAN, *Genie: A Psycholinguistic Study of a Modern-Day "Wild Child."* New York: Academic Press, 1977.

LENNEBERG, ERIC, "The Capacity for Language Acquisition," in *The Structure of Language: Readings in the Philosophy of Language,* ed. J. A. Fodor and J. J. Katz, pp. 579–603. Englewood Cliffs, N.J.: Prentice-Hall, 1964.

MENYUK, PAULA, *The Development of Speech,* pp. 3–23. New York: Bobbs-Merrill, 1972.

3

communication development: interpersonal forces

Having just covered the first set of forces affecting children's development of communication—biological and internal forces—we can now examine the second set: interpersonal forces. These include the child's family, peer group, and school. Thus, to consider interpersonal forces, we must consider the environment in which the child grows up. Some theorists call this complex network of people, events, and relationships "the system."

Consider the family system in the following dialogue. How might you react as a parent to John's request?

John (age five): I know what I want for my birthday. I want that Bionic Woman doll.

Mom: You want what?

Art (age ten): Sick!

John: Can I have one, Mom?

Mom: Well, I don't know. How come you want one of those?

Dad: You don't want one of those dolls, do you?

John: It has bionic powers—it's neat.

Art: Sick.

Mom: How about G.I. Joe? You know that's great for boys.

John: I don't like that one. I want the Bionic Woman.

Dad: Well, I'll have to put my foot down. You can't have one of those dolls. That's sissy stuff. You'll have to think of something else for your birthday.

John: I'm not a sissy!

Interpersonal forces are at work influencing John's communication. All the members of his family are providing him with language and communication choices from which he can select his own strategies in the future. John is very concerned that he act and talk in a way that his father respects, and so his concern over not being a sissy is easy to understand. His mother is also providing John with a model of communication behavior, in the area of relating or negotiating: in this dialogue the mother tries to squelch the controversy. Of course, John's brother Art serves as a model for what older, more experienced children say, though his message is rather brief.

John is also experiencing interaction patterns in his family that will affect his future communication patterns. In this conversation various forces either open up or close down the degree of communication. For example, John's mother's attempt to change the subject to an acceptable and less debatable alternative (G.I. Joe) is actually an attempt to close off controversy. Though John's father eventually objects to the purchase of the female doll, he does open up and present his feelings on the matter: "That's sissy stuff." And brother Art has the opportunity to put in his "two cents"— though one might say that's all his comments are worth.

John lives in a family where interpersonal forces are at work shaping his communication. He will not acquire his communication skills in a vacuum. Rather, he will develop as a product of the family system in which he is growing up. If his parents are supportive of his efforts, John will continue to grow and develop, confident that he is doing well. If John is often criticized or reprimanded for his actions and words, then he will continually have to adjust his behavior to fit the norms or status quo. Most experts agree that the child who is given negative feed back will not flourish as well as the child who is given support. Children learning to communicate learn their skills as they participate in their family, their peer group, their neighborhood, and their classrooms. They learn to communicate in the various systems in which they interact.

This chapter focuses on the interpersonal forces affecting children's development of communication, beginning with a brief explanation of the systems view of communication. The discussion of family systems is drawn primarily from the writing of Watzlawick, Beavin, and Jackson. Their interest in the family system is most apparent when they examine the problem of the schizophrenic: they claim that it is not a single person labeled emotionally ill who is sick, but instead the entire system from which that person comes, usually the family.[1] Their work with people who are typically diagnosed emotionally ill has led them to conclude that sickness or health comes not from within a single person but from within a sick system that includes that person. On a different level, then, children developing their communication skills do so within their family, peer group, and school systems or subsys-

---

[1]See Paul Watzlawick, Janet Beavin, and Donald Jackson, *The Pragmatics of Human Communication* (New York: Norton, 1966), pp. 46–47, 92–94, 129, 134–35.

tems. When these systems and subsystems operate in healthy ways, the children thrive; when they operate in detrimental ways, children's communication is damaged.

The view presented in this chapter does not conflict with the view expressed in Chapter 2, that there are strong intrapersonal forces affecting children's development of communication. Both views can play important roles in children's development of communication, and that is the view adopted here. While we know that the biological foundations of language may likely account for aspects of language structure and nonverbal behavior, among other things, we also know that the interpersonal relationships in which children grow up are very influential in their development of language and communication. And while this chapter could examine many different forces affecting children's development of communication, such as television and pretend-play with peers, it focuses on the family and communication models as being the most important forces.

A SYSTEMS VIEW OF COMMUNICATION DEVELOPMENT

In the simplest terms, an interactional system is two or more persons in the process of relating to one another.[2] Each system operates in an environment that includes anything or anyone that influences or is influenced by the system. For example, a family comprising a mother, a father, and two children is affected by a host of factors, people, and events. If the father changes jobs, that change affects the children and mother as well as the father himself. His job is part of the family environment. Similarly, if the two children in the family continually fight with each other, their fighting affects both parents. Events in the lives of each family member affect the persons involved in those events, but also every other member in the family. In this view of family systems, children are certainly influenced by their parents, but the children affect their parents in very important ways as well.

Most systems are open to some type of exchange with their environment of what Watzlawick, Beavin, and Jackson call "materials, energies, or information." A system that is closed to outside influences, as is the case in an airtight, insulated container, is called a closed system. Few families are truly "airtight" in this sense. The degree to which families are open to outside influences from their environment is thought to influence in turn the healthy development of their children.

A family system is also defined by the quality of communication within that system. Just as an open family deals with its outside environment, such

[2] *Ibid.*, p. 121.

as the neighborhood and the school, it has internal communication patterns that are open. Consider these three characteristics of communciation in the open family:

1. The family operates as a *whole unit*, not simply as a collection of individuals. The actions of each member affect the actions of the others. A problem for one family member is a problem for another.

2. Decisions and discussions are the *joint effort* of the members of the family. Even if each member does not participate in every decision or discussion, family members are encouraged to take part in the activities and discussion in the home.

3. The primary quality of feedback in the open family is *positiveness:* encouragement, praise, and confirmation are characteristic of messages from one to another. Positive messages are related to healthy changes in children and their parents.

Now consider three qualities that characterize closed communication in a family:

1. The family operates more as *individuals,* each member with a prescribed status and role. Usually, the parents are authorities and decision makers on all matters. Children are expected to behave according to certain rules. The actions of one member are treated as though they are separate from all others' actions.

2. Decisions in the closed family are made on the basis of predetermined *rules and guidelines* set by the parents or authority figures. Children are often told the results of such decisions. Discussion about what to do, what plans to follow, or who should do something are made on the basis of status criteria—for example, on the basis of who is in charge, who is the oldest, or who is the smartest.

3. The primary quality of feedback in the closed family system is *negativeness:* criticism, suggestions, and rejection are characteristic of messages from one to another, usually from parent to child. These messages help to keep the family unit together in the sense of maintaining the status quo. Growth and development of relationships are difficult when negative feedback is the predominant mode of response.

Let's refer again to the example of a family whose father just changed jobs. If the family was composed of members who didn't care about each other, didn't live together, or didn't know about the lives of each other, then there would be no wholeness to the family unit and his job change would affect only him. But we know that a dramatic change in a parent's life is likely to affect all others in the family, even if they have the rule, "You can't discuss father's work at home." An open family system encourages its members to become involved in the triumphs and troubles of its members. In a closed family system topics involving parental activities may be taboo for children to bring up. The manner in which parents handle interaction in the home helps determine the type of growth and independence the children will experience.

This chapter explores studies on the interpersonal forces affecting children's development of language and communication. Three areas of research are included in the discussion:

1. *Communication models:* How are children affected by the language and communication of models in their family, school, and peer groups?
2. *Interaction patterns:* What are the effects of various types of interaction patterns on children's development of language and communication?
3. *Family communications:* What are the effects of open and closed family styles on children's development of communication?

COMMUNICATION MODELS

Studies of child language development conducted in the United States have assumed that the mother is the major source of input (that is, the primary model) for the child's acquisition of his native tongue, English. For many American middle-class households this assumption is probably valid. But cross-cultural studies that have tested the generality of the mother-as-primary-model assumption contain evidence that this assumption might not be true in certain countries, cultures, and social groups. Many studies have simply assumed that the mother was the primary model even though in many of the cases studied this was not true. In some instances the mother appeared to be most important, but in other cases the mother was rarely with the child and could not have been the primary model. In a ghetto community in California, for example, a child's siblings are key models for the child's development of language. In certain Chinese cultures, the grandmother may be the key figure in caring for the child and the primary model in the child's language development.

Whether the source of input is the mother, the sister, or another family member, the role of the communication model is about the same. The important factor is that children are exposed to "live" communication, which they can analyze and reproduce in some way. When children copy examples provided by adults or other children, we say they are imitating. Imitation may involve copying single words or phrases. For example, a two-year-old may copy (complete with intonation and bodily movements) adult swearing expressions—"Oh nuts" and worse. Children are adept at imitating body movement in communication; at eighteen months a child will likely imitate a pointing gesture used by his parent. The parent viewing the gesture may be pleasantly surprised as she watches or rather shocked at how like her the child is behaving.

Scientists who study imitation of models as a factor in children's development of communication do not agree about the exact role of the imitation process. It is not unusual to observe children using patterns and expressions that are carbon copies of those employed by adults. However, many of their attempts at imitation fail. Let's examine children's imitation of communication models from four perspectives: (1) the nature of imitation; (2) the role of practice and new language forms; (3) the role of practice and solidification of old language forms; and (4) imitation as rehearsal and "plagiarism."

the imitation process

Sometimes children's attempts to imitate result in a lengthy exchange that appears to lead them nowhere. Consider the following dialogue between a mother and her child.

Child: Nobody don't like me.
Mother: No, say, "Nobody likes me."
Child: Nobody don't like me. (eight repetitions of this dialogue)
Mother: No, now listen carefully; say, "nobody likes me."
Child: Oh! Nobody don't likes me.[3]

As a tool for language instruction, imitation hasn't worked well in this case. Adults often admit that attempts to prompt imitations from children end in failure. Although copying seems to be a favorite game with children, their imitations often miss the mark. Why does this happen? It makes sense to suggest this: Although the child's imitation may not be an exact copy of what the adult says or does, it may approximate *what the child sees and hears.* One linguist concerned with grammar suggests that the child's failure to copy new grammatical forms in adult speech is based on the "relative impenetrability" of the child's grammar to adult models, even under the instruction (given by the mother's "no") to change.[4]

In other words, young children at any stage of grammatical development think in terms of their own grammar and cannot do differently until their grammar changes. Although studies agree that it is important for children to hear grammatical speech, the role of imitation in children's development of grammar is not clear. It is quite possible that from the perspective of children's minds, communication models *change* as children develop. That is, as children develop verbal and nonverbal language the input from models may assume a different form to their eyes and ears.

The same phenomenon that we just observed in children's verbal

---

[3]David McNeill, "Developmental Psycholinguistics," in *The Genesis of Language*, ed. Frank Smith and George Miller (Cambridge, Mass.: M.I.T. Press, 1966), p. 69.
[4]*Ibid.*

communication can be observed in their nonverbal communication. Young children often fail to employ the rules of communication distance (proxemic rules) important in adult communication. Young children seem to follow different rules for communicating "in space." For example, an adult usually conducts a social conversation at a distance of about four feet from another person. A young girl attempting to conduct social conversations like Mommy may stand inches from you if you happen to be her lucky listener. Her attempts to copy the communication patterns of adults may fall short of doing exactly that. It is important to consider, however, that young children follow their own proxemic rules in communication. As they become incorporated more and more into the adult system, their patterns and rules approximate more closely those followed by adults in their family, community, and culture.

It is important to note that children's imitations are very much affected by their perceptions of the communication patterns to be imitated. In other words, children's imitations are a product of their particular stage of development in verbal and nonverbal language. It makes little sense to view the imitating child from an adult's eyes and ears. Instead, we have to "get inside" the child's eyes and ears to see and hear as he does.

Some children seem to be imitators and others not. Two researchers tried to find out why there is such variability in children's use of imitations, hoping that an answer to this question could uncover a greater understanding of the role of imitation in language development.[5] Two of their findings shed some light on this issue:

1. Parents whose speech is highly directive (consisting of requests for action, such as "Get the silverware.") and subjective (statements, such as "You really should use your fork.") may prompt fewer *imitations* by their children. Instead, their children respond with *action.*

2. Parents who imitate their children in some way (for example, an imitative expansion of a child's utterance—child: "Fork"; parent: "Yes, that's a fork"; child: "Dat's a fork.") may prompt a greater number of imitations by their children. In fact, the correlation between children's imitations and parents' modeling imitations was quite high (.77), suggesting that children's tendency to imitate adult speech may arise from their parents acting as models of imitation for them.

With this perspective on imitation, let's examine three approaches to the role of imitation in children's development of language. One view suggests that practice in imitation leads to the *incorporation of new forms* (advanced verbal and nonverbal patterns); the second approach suggests that the key advantage of practice rests with the *solidification of the old forms* (previously acquired verbal and nonverbal patterns). The evidence obtained

    [5]Joseph P. Folger and Robin S. Chapman, "A Pragmatic Analysis of Spontaneous Imitations," *Journal of Child Language*, 5 (February 1978), 25–38.

in testing in both of these approaches is drawn primarily from the grammatical level of language. A third and more recent approach that we will discuss maintains that imitation is a *rehearsal technique* for children learning to communicate, and in many ways resembles plagiarism. This technique helps children become acquainted with new words, meanings, and structures, but it also gives children practice in effective interaction skills necessary for communication. These three views can some day be woven into a more confident account of the role of imitation in the learning process. Presently, however, the picture must be more tentative.

practice and new forms

When children are imitating the speech of others, what forms are they practicing? Are these forms novel, or are they forms already learned? Novel forms (for instance, new words or new grammatical structure) are forms that are absent from the child's "free" speech—that is, speech that does not appear to be a direct imitation of the speech of others. If imitation is a necessary condition for grammatical development, then children's speech with imitations should be grammatically more progressive or advanced than their free speech. Studies have demonstrated, however, that for most children imitated speech and free speech are almost identical in complexity.[6] If children are not producing the progressive inflection "he is running" in their free speech, chances are they will not imitate it.

A young child's grammar seems to be impervious to change. The "Nobody don't like me" dialogue that we considered a few pages ago demonstrates the failure of a child to employ a novel form. Imitation in practice does not appear to contribute directly to the incorporation of novel (and thus more advanced) forms into children's language. On the other hand, novel forms *do appear* in children's speech. Their language does change, eventually. Children do profit from adult models, but how they profit is not clear.

Probably the most important aspect of imitation in regard to new forms is what psycholinguists have called *expansion* of the child's speech.[7] When adults imitate the child's speech but *expand* it, we have a kind of imitation in reverse. Quite often adults repeat the speech of a young child; in doing so they change or alter the child's utterance into a well-formed adult equivalent. Consider the following example of the expansion process:

Child: Daddy outside.

Adult: Yes, Daddy is working outside.

[6]See Susan Ervin, "Imitation and Structural Change in Children's Language," in *New Directions in the Study of Language*, ed. Eric Lenneberg (Cambridge, Mass.: M.I.T. Press, 1965), pp. 163–89.

[7] See Roger Brown and Ursula Bellugi, "Three Processes in the Child's Acquisition of Syntax," *Harvard Educational Review*, 34 (1964), 131–51.

In this case the adult filled out the sentence with the appropriate verb. Expansions typically include the prepositions, verbs, articles, and auxiliaries that young children may "omit." On the surface these expansions seem to constitute a prime explanation of how a child develops a more complex grammar. After all, the expansions direct attention to the missing components of the child's sentence. There is one basic problem with this approach: many adults do not expand their child's speech per se. Instead, they may simply comment on the truth value of the child's sentence, responding to it only in terms of its truth or falsity and rarely in terms of its grammaticality. Consider the following dialogue:

Child: Daddy play ball Markie?
Mother: No, he's busy!

In this case the mother's response to the child's sentence is based solely on its probability of occurrence. Relating truth-value (or probabilty) responses to a theory of grammatical development, we would have to predict that the child who is subjected to such responses to his speech (rather than to grammatical expansions) will develop language more slowly or will develop an inadequate grammar. Since this does not seem to be the case, we must be cautious in using expansion to explain grammatical development.

Moreover, parents vary in their propensity to expand their children's speech. But when they do provide expansions, children are offered a relevant and slightly advanced linguistic model for their language development.[8] About the only conclusion that we can draw from the study of adult expansion of children's speech is this:

> Although many parents are motivated by instructional purposes to expand the speech of their child, it seems likely that the primary reason that adults expand a child's speech is to check their interpretation of the child's meaning: the expanded sentences are offered by the adult, and the child can either accept or deny these interpretations.

Taking the expansion process one step further—to the point where the child attempts to imitate the adult expansion—may prove to be an important criterion in the rapid development of a rich language in children. Dan Slobin examined children's imitations of adult expansions and found that about half of the imitations he studied were grammatically progressive.[9] Although children's imitations of adult speech do not typically contain new forms, their

[8]See Lee K. Snyder-McLean and James E. McLean, "Verbal Information Gathering Strategies: The Child's Use of Language to Acquire Language," *Journal of Speech and Hearing Disorders*, 43 (August 1978), 306–25.

[9]Dan Slobin, "Imitation and Grammatical Development in Children," in *Contemporary Issues in Developmental Psychology*, ed. N. S. Endler, L. R. Boulter, and H. Osser (New York: Holt, Rinehart and Winston, 1967), pp. 437–43.

imitations of adult-expanded versions are more progressive. Slobin's studies focused on the speech of middle-class children; generalizations beyond this population are impossible.

practice and solidification *(overgeneralization*

Let's examine a second approach to the role of imitation. This view suggests that imitations constitute practice for already acquired forms of language. Once acquired, perhaps through the expansion process, new forms entering the child's language system must be practiced in order to become solidified in the system. The issue is whether or not forms receiving more practice become more stable than forms receiving less practice. Susan Ervin attempted to answer this question by examining the speech of children for the emergence of past-tense inflections.[10]

Initially, children utter verbs with no tense markings for past or future action. For instance, a child saying "Daddy go" may intend a past, future, or present action. The first verbs to be inflected (to have tense markings added) by children are the "strong" verbs, such as "sit," "come," "go," and "run." The inflection of strong verbs necessitates total word changes (for instance, "go"/"went" and "sit"/"sat"), not merely the addition of markings. "Weak" verbs, such as "look," "walk," and "laugh," are inflected in the regular way. Studies reveal that weak verbs follow strong verbs in the child's development of language.

Children usually say "He comed" or "I sitted" at the same stage at which they say "Daddy walked" or "I jumped." Utterances such as "Teddy goed to bed" do not simply drop out of the child's speech in a matter of weeks—or months, for that matter. Many such forms persist in the child's speech even into grade school. Children's earliest utterances involving the strong verbs can appear consistent with adult inflections. Children say "He went," "I ran," or "Man came." The "regularizations"—such as "He comed" or "I sitted"—appear later in children's speech. In short, past tense appears *first* in correctly inflected strong (but irregular) verbs. At first glance, this finding may seem surprising. How can a child begin to acquire the more difficult strong verbs before mastering the regular weak verbs? But the finding is not that surprising if we take into account the high frequency with which strong verbs occur in adult speech. Once a child begins to use verbs such as "came," "went," and "sat," she finds many opportunities to employ these verbs. The opportunities for the use of past-tense strong verbs are greater than the opportunities for their weak-verb counterparts. Consequently, children receive much practice with strong verbs in the past tense. According to a solidification view of practice in child language de-

---

[10]Ervin, "Imitation and Structural Change in Children's Language," pp. 177–79.

Susan Ervin-Tripp

velopment, these strong verbs should remain stable in the child's repertoire. Contrary to expectation, however, the correctly inflected strong verbs are soon replaced by the incorrectly (but regularly) inflected strong verbs. The strong verbs become very unstable, despite the great amount of practice they receive. The use of regular inflections for strong verbs (such as "He comed") has been called *overgeneralization:* that is, the child inappropriately extends regular endings to irregular verbs, thereby creating a kind of generalization beyond the rules.

Perhaps overgeneralization of strong verbs should be emphasized as a positive shift from strictly imitative behaviors in children to the more productive discovery behaviors that lead to the formation of *rules.* The discovery of language rules, an important aspect of the child's communication equipment (see Chapter 2), becomes a dominant strategy for learning the structure of a language. Further, although weak verbs are individually less frequent in parental speech, surely the consistency of the past-tense markings on the many different weak verbs must impress the child greatly.

Whatever our explanation for the role of imitation in children's development of language, we know that children imitate the communication patterns of others constantly. Communication models, such as parents, siblings, friends, and teachers, are extremely important in children's development of communication. Only indirectly (through *expansion*) may imitations account for the appearance of new forms in the child's communication. Imitations do not appear to help in the solidification of such forms. But we know that imitation plays some role in the child's development of communication. It may be a crucial learning strategy in the child's acquisition of sounds and words. It may also be valuable in the child's acquisition of nonverbal communication. For example, the body motions accompanying adult speech are often attempted by young children. The results can often be amusing, particularly if the movement or gesture is a prominent one. To understand fully the role of imitation in communication development, we must conduct in-depth studies on children's development of nonverbal as well as verbal language.

function of imitation :

imitation as rehearsal and "plagiarism" *[lack of comprehension*

One of the more interesting yet well-documented cases in favor of imitation as a tool in language development has been advanced by Ruth Clark.[11] She suggests that children's imitations are probably best explained as overt rehearsals that children engage in before they are able to rehearse silently. One of the most interesting imitation tactics of children is to "pad"

[11]Ruth Clark, "What's the Use of Imitation?" *Journal of Child Language,* 4 (October 1977), 341–58.

an utterance with "undigested" portions of the previous adult utterance, a tactic Clark fondly calls "plagiarism." It is a very useful device for keeping the conversation going if the child fails to understand portions of the adult's message; she simply imitates part of it to put it "on the table." For example, I observed a two-and-a-half-year-old in the following exchange with a baby-sitter looking in a picture book:

Baby-sitter: Oh-oh, the doggie's hurt.
Child: Doggie hurt.
Baby-sitter: He's cryin' too.
Child: Cryin' too.
Baby-sitter: Oh-oh, I wonder what's happening here?
Child: Happening here.

It appeared to me that the child did not always understand what she was saying, though she was very interested in having the conversation continue. Note that the child loves to plagiarize the final portions of the baby-sitter's speech. In Clark's words, imitation plays a positive role in children's acquisition of language by "making adult forms available to the child, thus helping him to notice these forms more readily when adults use them, and enabling him to assimilate their function gradually through use."[12]

Compatible with Clark's rehearsal view of imitation is Andrea Ramer's emphasis on the important communicative function of the imitation process. Ramer examined the functions of imitations in children's conversations.[13] She noted variation in the children's use of imitation, as have other researchers. The only function of imitation that seemed to be used by all of the children in her study was a communicative one. She calls this function *lack of comprehension*, and suggests simply that children imitate when they don't understand. Ramer found that even her generally non-imitative children imitated at least one word they had never heard before. The structure of adult utterances may be too complex for children to understand, but the children *keep the conversation going*, though they may respond somewhat inappropriately. They may imitate part of an adult's utterance instead of responding with the action it calls for. For example, a child may hear "Bring me the creamer," and instead of responding to the request by bringing the adult the cream pitcher, the child may simply say, "Oh, the creamer," and stand perfectly still. The imitation serves a communicative function of signaling lack of comprehension.

In summary, children imitate the models in their environment. The

---

[12]*Ibid.*, p. 351.
[13]Andrea L. H. Ramer, "The Function of Imitation in Child Language," *Journal of Speech and Hearing Research*, 19 (1976), 700–17.

function the imitation process serves for all children is not totally understood. Adult expansion of a child's imitations may help incorporate new forms into that child's language. A newer view suggests that imitations are a type of plagiarism of adult communication: children simply copy portions of adults' messages or sometimes even signal a lack of comprehension of those portions that are plagiarized. Under either of these views, the models for children's imitations are not simply static persons in the family, neighborhood, or school. Rather, these models interact with children. Our next discussion centers on the process of interaction as examined in communication-development research.

INTERACTION AND DEVELOPMENT

A second interpersonal force affecting children's development of communication is the interaction of children with their communication models. *Interaction* in this sense is the flow of conversation between a child and others, such as parents, siblings, and neighbors. This section examines three processes that take place in chidren's interaction with their communication models:

1. Children are given information regarding the *content* of their language (the extension process).
2. Children learn about the *structure* of their language.
3. Children participate in an important *transactional* relationship: they are influenced by others, but also influence others themselves.

the extension of children's speech: content

Our experience in talking with children reminds us how important it is to comment on what they say. We can help children understand how to use language if we respond to their utterances with comments, new ideas, questions, and evaluations. Courtney Cazden studied this technique of adult interaction with children, believing that such responses positively affect children's development of their language. She found this to be true.

Initially, Cazden called the technique "modeling." She reasoned that adults provide a type of full-fledged language in response to the child's more immature form of language. Later, she renamed the technique "extension." The extension of children's speech provides children with semantic information that "extends the meaning" of their utterances.[14] The parent, friend, or teacher who is extending the speech of children is doing something like this:

[14]Courtney Cazden, *Child Language and Education* (New York: Holt, Rinehart and Winston, 1972), pp. 124–27.

Child: Doggie bark. (when a dog is barking)
Other: Yes, but he probably won't bite. (or) Maybe he is mad at the kitty. (or) Barking is his way of saying how he feels.

Comments and ideas expressed in the adult's extension give children semantic information that is important to them in their development of language.

In her studies of the effectiveness of extension, Cazden reasoned that children who received daily extensions of their speech should progress more, grammatically, than children whose speech was simply expanded (expansion was discussed on pp. 52–4). Remember that expansion simply involves a grammatical filling out of the child's utterance, as in this example:

Child: Doggie bark.
Adult: Yes, the dog is barking.

The thought behind the Cazden study discussed above was that extension information in child-adult interactions is far more valuable than expansion information. The results of Cazden's study indicate that *extension is an effective treatment in assisting young children (twenty-eight to thirty-eight months) in their development of grammar.* The expansion process, on the other hand, did not seem to produce grammatical progressions—that is, sentences that were more complex grammatically than those the child may have used before the treatment.

Even though Cazden's extension study involved only a small sample of children, her results illustrate the importance of adult-child interaction in a child's language devlopment. The key point is that the nature of adult-child interaction may have a strong bearing on development. The interaction should emphasize meaning—that is, semantic considerations of what the child is talking about. Many parents expand and extend their children's speech, but the important factor affecting the speed and ease with which children learn their language may rest in the richness of the extensions provided by parents and others. In other words, the more that adults truly interact with children, the more quickly and efficiently children may learn to use more complex forms of language. Adults must realize that children believe they have something important to say and that they seek adults' reactions to their speech.

mother-child interaction: structure

A second type of interaction assistance that children receive is found in the form of adult language, as opposed to its content. In recent years several studies have investigated mother-child interaction in order to examine the mother's speech in terms of the assistance it gives her child in structuring sentences. A study by Patricia Broen, which serves as the focus of the present discussion, closely evaluated the speech of mothers to their children.[15] Broen predicted that a mother's language was somehow geared to the age of the child. Thus, the language the mother used with her young child should have been far simpler than the language she used with an older child. The study assumed, and probably rightly so, that the mothers examined *did* play a major role in their children's acquisition of language. The families were of middle-class backgrounds and the parents had professional occupations.

Rarely have studies examined directly the nature of the language parents direct to children. We have assumed, because of the obvious omission of the subject from most discussions, that parental speech directed to children remains relatively constant over the years. The language of the mother has been assumed to be a rather stable factor; the unstable and changing factor is supposed to be the child's language. Broen's study revealed that in mother-child interactions over time, the language a mother uses to her child may change almost as drastically as the child's language changes. Broen found that the language style of mothers with their younger children (eighteen to twenty-five months) was quite different from their style of language with their older children (forty-five to ninety-four months), which indicates that a mother adapts her language to her perception of what her child's language should be sounding like. (Actually, Broen compared mothers' speech to three age groups: younger children, older children, and adults. Using three age groups resulted in more information about mothers' speech to both groups of children.)

Broen found the following generalizations to be true, regardless of children's age:

1. Mothers talk more slowly to their children than they do to adults.

2. Pauses in mothers' speech to children are usually located at the ends of sentences, whereas pauses in their speech to adults are located almost anywhere within sentences, as well as at the ends of sentences.

3. With a child the mother gears her vocabulary to that of the child, but with adults her vocabulary size is far greater.

4. The sentence structures mothers use with children are of two basic types; sentence structure in mother-adult interactions is more varied.

Mothers acting as communication models adapt their language to children. This finding should not startle us, for when we observe adult-child interactions it is quite apparent that they differ in many respects from adult-adult interactions.

The most interesting comparison is between mother–younger child

[15]Patricia Broen, *The Verbal Environment of the Language-Learning Child*, American Speech and Hearing Association. Monograph No. 17 (Washington, D.C.: American Speech and Hearing Association, 1972).

interaction and mother–older child interaction. With younger children (about two years of age) mothers tend to talk in brief sentences:

Child: See?
Mother: That's my purse.
Child: Mommy purse.
Mother: Put it here.

Dialogues of this nature are abundant in mother–younger child interactions. Rarely do mothers speak in complex sentence forms to their younger children. Rather, their sentences represent two basic patterns: (1) imperative sentences, (commands and request) and (2) "be" sentences with "this," "that," "it," "there," or "here" as a major constituent. In the dialogue immediately above, the mother used an imperative sentence, "Put it here," and a "be" sentence, "That's my purse." Imperative sentences addressed to children usually start with one of the verbs "look," "put," and "see." "Be" sentences (questions and statements) directed to young children look like this:

"What's in there?"
"It's a nice dolly."
"There is the box."

When talking to their older children (four to eight years of age) mothers usually employ the same two sentence patterns, but their sentences are more complex. The difference is in the extent of modification in the noun phrases. Consider the following sentences, which are typical of mothers' speech to older children:

Imperatives:

"Please put the purse on the big table."
"See the pretty little dolly."

"Be" sentences:

"What's in that big box over there?"
"That table is really big, isn't it?"
"There is a special treat in my purse."

Mothers adopt common sentence patterns in talking with their children. They expand these patterns into bigger sentences with greater modification when they talk to their older children. Mothers' speech to adults is far more complex, structurally.

In summary, mothers, and possibly all models, tend to provide a simple form of language for their children. The language used by mothers with their children reveals a process of development similar to that of children's language, although the speech of mothers is obviously more advanced. The adapted form of parental speech may or may not assist the child in acquiring language structures. The simpler forms of adult language may help the child in defining major linguistic units, such as the sentence, the end of which is usually defined by a pause. Simpler sentences are undoubtedly easier for children to understand. Since the vocabulary of mothers is geared to their children's understanding, misunderstandings based on word meaning are not likely to occur.

Sentence structure can thus be the focus for interaction assistance. On the other side of the coin, however, the simpler forms of language may only slow children in their grammatical progression. If parents used more adultlike language with their children, would their children progress faster or better than children whose parents used the simpler forms of speech? Further research must be conducted to answer this question.

Interaction opportunities are important in children's development of language. Evidence suggests that the structure of models' language to children is geared to the structure of children's language. Those who talk with children often show in their language a kind of sensitivity to children's language. The child's progress in acquiring language is affected by the content and structure of the model's speech. When others extend the meaning of children's utterances, children seem to progress more rapidly in developing language structure. The structure of the model's speech in the interaction process may or may not play the key role in grammatical progression. A tempting conclusion about the role of interaction in children's development of language is this:

> The semantic richness of a communication model's language in adult-child interaction helps advance children's language and its structure. Syntactic richness may or may not help advance language, but models usually gear their language structure to that employed by children.

a transactional view of interaction

Jerome Bruner, probably the most noted theorist in child development, believes that many of the underlying principles of language, such as those of syntax, semantics, and pragmatics (language principles based on the primary functions of language), are formed before the child uses speech to communicate.[16] One of the key precursors of the prespeech stage of the

---

[16]See Jerome S. Bruner, "From Communication to Language—A Psychological Perspective," *Cognition*, 3 (1975), 255–87.

child's development consists of the interpersonal forces between child and mother. Bruner is quick to point out that this interaction is not simply the mother affecting the child; the child influences the mother's behavior, too. The process is something like this:

1. The infant makes a movement or vocalization; the mother is paying attention.
2. Correctly or incorrectly, but based on a set of cues, the mother interprets the movement or vocalization as having an intention.
3. The mother responds to the child's behavior, starting a communicative exchange in which she continues to support almost any form of the child's involvement.
4. The child continues to make movements and sounds that will elicit supportive behavior from the mother. If the mother is quite consistent with her support, the child is likely to continue to participate in any way that elicits a response.

This pattern describes the *joint behavior* of the child and mother in a *transactional* situation.

Probably the strongest interpersonal force in this transactional pattern is working in step 2, where the mother makes a decision regarding the infant's intent. Bruner does not seem concerned about whether or not the child actually had such an intent. Figuring out intent is not easy anyway, and according to Bruner, it is not a profitable way to spend our time. Instead, Bruner suggests that if the mother *attributed intent* to the child's behavior, then the pattern of interaction has been set in motion and the two are communicating. But how does the mother judge whether or not the infant wants to communicate? First, she probably hears the intonation contour of the child's vocalization and is able to interpret an overall meaning, feeling, or purpose. The babbling may sound like a happy release, a questioning probe, or an angry statement. The tone of voice strikes the mother in a certain way, and she concludes that the infant is purposefully behaving that way. Another cue includes what one writer calls "accompaniments"—pointing, playing with an object, searching, pouting, squealing. These behaviors tend to shed light on the utterance. Finally, the context plays a major role: is the child hungry? just waking up? stuck in her playpen? Any of these situations will help explain why an infant might want to communicate. In support of the transactional view of interaction are several interesting studies on preverbal communication training of infants, training in which games and social exchanges assist children in acquiring the rules of their language concerning turn-taking and role learning.

Preverbal "game training."   When mothers and fathers play games with their babies and young children, they know that the games delight the children. The little games would continue for quite a long time if the children had their way. Parents may not realize, however, that the playing of these games may assist young children in acquiring their language, especially the rules and patterns which relate to turn-taking and role differentiation.

Nancy Ratner and Jerome Bruner video-taped two children from infancy to about two years of age in a game-playing situation with their mothers.[17] They used a toy clown that can be made to disappear into a cone base. They found that the mothers provided a very clear format in which the children could participate in a "clown game." For the very young, the game had several junctures during which the child could participate. Here is a typical "dialogue" (mother talking):

> Jonathan, look what I've got here. Who's this? (clown appears)
>
> Shall Mommy hide him? Jonathan do it.
>
> He's going. He's going to go-o-o.
>
> Gone! He's gone! (clown disappears)
>
> Where's he gone?
>
> Here he comes. He's coming to see you.
>
> Boo. Hello Jonathan. (clown reappears)
>
> There he is.
>
> Babababoo. (moves clown to child's belly)
>
> You mustn't eat him.[18]

Ratner and Bruner analyzed the flow of the game from its start to its completion. With the very young child, the mother tended to do most of the work; the older child participated in a very active manner. Instead of just giggling, smiling, or touching the clown in a particular situation (for example, the reappearance of the clown), the older child sometimes anticipated the situation and smiled or giggled beforehand. Eventually, the child may want to play the active role of making the clown disappear, and so might reverse the roles. Ratner and Bruner conclude that children learn the back-and-forth flow of communication in a game that resembles a conversation. The researchers credit early games like this one with establishing role relationships between speaker and hearer for the child. In addition to turn-taking, the game provides a context in which children can play an active role in varying the flow of the game. The child can learn to take over the game if he has learned the rules, just as children learn to initiate and direct conversations when they have developed verbal language.

Conversational training of babies. Take a look at the following conversation and see if you can tell what is so unique about it:

[17]See Nancy Ratner and Jerome Bruner, "Games, Social Exchange and the Acquisition of Language," *Journal of Child Language*, 5 (October 1978), 391–401.
[18]*Ibid.*, p. 394.

Ann (3 months): (smiles)
Mother: Oh what a nice little smile! Yes, isn't that nice? There. There's a nice little smile.
Ann: (burps)
Mother: What a nice wind as well! Yes, that's better isn't it? Yes. Yes.
Ann: (vocalizes)
Mother: Yes!! There's a nice noise![19]

It appears as if the mother passes the conversational turn to the baby, yet I think all of us would more likely conclude that the mother is just waiting for the baby to do anything that could serve as a turn. Catherine Snow studied mother-baby interactions and found that mothers try hard to pass the turn to their babies, using tag questions ("isn't it?") and other post-completers (such as "hmm?"). When the baby doesn't respond, the mother "repairs" the conversational procedure by stepping in to take the baby's turn or by repeating herself. Mothers talk to their babies as if the infants are quite capable of responding. When Ann (the three-month-old in the "dialogue" just cited) was one-and-a-half-years old she participated in a more verbal way. But notice that her mother was still very active in using anything Ann said to keep a conversation going:

Ann: (blowing noises)
Mother: That's a bit rude.
Ann: Mouth.
Mother: Mouth, that's right.
Ann: Face.
Mother: Face, yes, mouth is in your face. What else have you got in your face?
Ann: Face. (closing eyes)
Mother: You're making a face, aren't you?[20]

How can young children help but acquire the pattern of conversational turn taking when their mothers or caretakers are such patient teachers?

Conversational competence. When persons engage in a conversation, they follow rules about taking turns talking. We advise children not to interrupt someone, yet all of us do this to some extent. In a recent study of conversational turn taking of one- and two-year-olds with their mothers, even little children followed the rules to the letter.[21] Both age groups engaged in

---

[19]Catherine Snow, "The Development of Conversation Between Mothers and Babies," *Journal of Child Language,* 4 (February 1977), 12.
[20]*Ibid.,* p. 18.
[21]H. R. Schaffer, Glyn M. Collis, and G. Parsons, "Vocal Interchange and Visual Regard in Verbal and Preverbal Children," in *Studies in Mother-Infant Interaction,* ed. H. R. Schaffer (New York: Academic Press, 1977), pp. 291–324.

smooth conversational exchanges with their mothers in a play session with toys. Rarely did overlaps in talking occur, and the ones that did seemed to function as promotional devices—to make the conversation more lively, for example. The vocal exchanges occurred in "bouts" (back-and-forth exchanges), more of which were initiated by the children than by the adults. The mother's watchfulness was thought to be instrumental in keeping the conversation going.

How could the flow of conversation be so smooth with children so young? The researchers offer three explanations:

1. Both persons, the child and the adult, *know the rules* for turn-taking, and so the interaction is smooth. While they may be following the rule almost unconsciously, its frequent mention by the adult may account for the synchrony. But does a one-year-old know the rule on any level? Maybe the preverbal games discussed earlier set the stage for learning the conversational rules of turn-taking. A fairly plausible explanation is that even the one-year-olds knew enough about the communication principle to behave appropriately.

2. On the other hand, the mother was pictured as orchestrating the conversation so that the child led while she merely filled in the pauses. While researchers doubt that the child plays such a minuscule role, they do not question their observation that the mother is very watchful as she communicates with her baby.

3. It is possible that some primitive mechanism within the human being explains the smoothness of early turn-taking. This mechanism might be one that does not allow the simultaneous occurrence of vocalization and listening. If this is the case, smooth conversations are biologically based. In fact, when young children vocalize and then hear something their vocalizations decrease. The researchers suggest that the inability of one to speak and listen at the same time may be more a basic truth than simply a difficult thing to do.

It is difficult, and may be unwise, to isolate a single underlying mechanism to account for effective communication behavior at such an early age. It is tempting to link the Ratner-Bruner study, Snow's study, and this one to advance a "watchful-mother" hypothesis:

(1) the structure of communication is introduced to the infant through games and play by a watchful mother;

(2) the mother lets the child lead, gives the child credit for communicative intent in every grunt and move, and so gives even the youngest child "a turn";

(3) thus, by the time the child engages in verbal conversations, she plays by the rules and takes turns effectively.

FAMILY COMMUNICATION

Pragmatic theorists who view growth and development in the family ask us to think about the family as a "space" to take care of.[22] Just as our

---

[22]Watzlawick, Beavin, and Jackson, *The Pragmatics of Human Communication*, pp. 118–48.

home has a thermostat that activates the heat or air conditioning when the temperature of a room slips below or above a certain point, the family unit also has its thermostatic settings. Certain behaviors are "tolerable" within the thermostat's setting and other behaviors fall outside that setting. When children misbehave, their punishment might well be the result of keeping the system functioning by using the rules set by the thermostat. Theorists say that in the healthy home parents and their children grow together. While many believe it's just the children who grow and change, pragmatic experts are quick to point out that parents change and grow too. When their little babies become teen-agers who gain their independence, parents almost have to change (reset their own thermostats) to accommodate their children's changes. How often we find parents of teen-agers express with disappointment, "I can't keep track of her anymore—she's off on her own." At least this parent realizes that the child must develop independence. Some parents do not, and consequently try to take care of their children even when they too have children of their own.

Change and growth come about in children (and parents) when positive feedback occurs. A typical form of positive feedback that fosters change and growth is *confirmation*, a message that says, "Your opinion is important even when it's different from mine." A confirmation message says, "I like you," "I like what you say," or "I like what you do." Confirmation tends to keep the relationships in a system developing and growing. Praise for children helps them realize they can learn more. In their communication development, as in all aspects of children's development, positive feedback—in this case, for appropriate and sensitive communication efforts—is the most effective technique.

Stability, or no change, is also important within the family unit. Negative feedback helps insure maintenance of the status quo. Children are scolded and punished when they do things or say things outside the limits of the thermostat. Negative feedback brings them back within the limits. While the family or its members do not grow as a result of criticism and scolding, the system stays in balance. Negative feedback is not terribly successful in changing children, however. Many parents say with dismay, "I've told her again and again not to act that way—you'd think she would've grown up by now." This kind of statement is based on the underlying assumption many of us have about our role in children's growing up: they'll grow up fine if we keep them in line. While there may be some truth in this statement, most evidence concerning growth and change within any system would support positive feedback rather than negative feedback as the most effective agent of change.

To maintain a required degree of stability within the family unit, parents and others can rely on negative feedback in the face of problems. But to assist children in growth and development, we should consider the importance of positive feedback. When children receive confirmation for their effective communication attempts, they will make more of the same attempts because they believe they will again be rewarded. We can support children in their struggle to learn, grow stronger, and understand their world. Our support can depend on the way we allow communication to take place. Will conversation remain open, where children can participate in decisions? Or will the family unit have a closed communication system, where all rules are spelled out and children are encouraged simply to be quiet and be good?

closed communication in families

Any closed system is best explained by the rules governing it. Thus, closed family communication is best defined by the rules and status relations within the family. When families have rules and strict guidelines based on status relationships within the family, there is the potential for a closed system. Any rule or guideline that "settles issues" and helps in making decisions can close up a system. Here are some examples of rules in a closed system:

1. In matters of money, your father always decides.
2. Never speak angrily with your mother.
3. Male children deserve more (money or possessions) than female children.
4. The female children must take care of the younger ones.
5. Never argue with your father.
6. You must always do as your mother says.

It is important to understand that within a unit such as a family or a group of friends there are always rules on how persons should behave. There is nothing wrong with rules as such, but *too many rules* or rules that are too rigid seem to harm children's development of thought and communication. If children rarely get opportunities to participate in decision making or express their opinions or feelings, their development of communication choices in these areas will suffer. In closed systems, spontaneous communication among members is in many instances not allowed. Instead, the family resorts to rules that settle the issue. For example, in a very closed family unit a decision about how to resolve a conflict over what to watch on TV may not be difficult at all. After all, father's Monday night football is on and he worked hard today. So, others watch Monday night football, watch nothing, or watch the other, probably less attractive TV set in the home (the average number of TV sets in the American home is over two).

Closed situations within the family are those in which the power in the family does not allow a topic, problem, or issue to be presented for consideration by members. In most families there is a set of situations in which bargaining or discussion are not often encouraged. For example, the bedtime hour may not be an issue in a home: the mother sets the rules and the children follow religiously—except when the mother lifts those rules. On other occasions that same home may be quite open. The children and parents may jointly decide what to watch on TV or what to do on a Saturday, for instance.

open communication in families

Resolving disputes in an open communication setting is done by persons talking about what they believe. A sharing of ideas can be the mode, but an argument can also develop. Just because members of a family are arguing does not mean that they are engaged in closed communication. That members can argue shows a degree of openness in the system. Persons can express themselves, even if they are raising their voices and acting somewhat angrily.

The open approach is used to make decisions after some interaction has taken place. That interaction focuses on preferences, opinions, and facts. Issues are settled on the basis of criteria presented by a member or group of members. An argument over what to watch on Monday night TV will have more than a single dimension, the father's desire to watch football. The children and mother are allowed to present their preferences, and while open communication does not mean a child will win, the child may be convincing enough to get to watch her special program. On the other hand, following open communication about the TV situation the group may decide, reluctantly or agreeably, that Dad can watch his game. Outcomes are not as predictable as in the closed families. In the open family alternate outcomes can occur because the rule structure is not so tight.

Why should we discuss disputes about what to watch on TV? First, such disputes are frequent in most families, and are excellent mirrors of a family's communication style. Second, TV disputes tend to become so personal that those involved don't realize how they are behaving. Adults have been known to behave more like children and children like adults. Third, these disputes are excellent opportunities for children to practice communication skills.

Now consider these two situations:

1. The members of the family all wish to view different programs. Since each person stated a desire in strong terms, the mother says, "I'm going to turn off this stupid TV set, and we will all read something instead." Is this open communication?

2. Everyone seems to want to watch a different program, and the father makes the following suggestion: "OK, you can watch your program in the living room, I'll go to my room, and your mother can watch the TV in the family room." Is this open communication?

These examples portray typical methods of eliminating conflict. Each will probably result in circumventing the dispute. But both methods are very closed. The "turn it off" method and the "each one to his own set" approach both avoid the controversy by hiding from it. Both halt interaction about the controversy by changing the conditions, one by not allowing TV and the other by utilizing three sets instead of one. Argument or controversy is usually viewed as a negative process. Everything should run smoothly, and so tactics of communication that stop controversy are viewed positively. When methods of closing discussion or controversy are introduced, communication about the problem is halted. Many who use or experience these "smoothing" tactics find an initial relief, because the tension of argument seems to disappear. However, the problem that all tried initially to resolve together is never really solved.

keeping a balance

This discussion does not suggest that all issues in the family or all issues in the classroom, on the playground, or in the neighborhood should be resolved by the open participation of all members. The purpose of introducing the systems approach to behavior is to highlight the *processes* that we all engage in to keep a group together and growing. The togetherness of a group and our tendency to want to keep things stable result from structure, rules, and certain closed patterns of communication. Rules are necessary if members of a group are to feel balance and peace. On the other hand, if we are concerned about the growth of members within a group—and in this text we are concerned with the growth of children's communication—then we have to realize that such growth occurs in a context of change. For change to occur in children's communication, family, classroom, and peer-group systems, a system must temporarily open up, communication must occur, and the child must play a role in the process of communication.

Probably the strongest force affecting children's development of communication is the family unit. Here the child learns how to express feelings, share ideas, and settle disputes, among other things. While children are affected by what goes on in the family context, their behavior affects others in the family, as well. Take the example of the extremely compliant child who obeys, wants very much to please, and rarely breaks the rules. These behaviors play an important role in how the parents feel about parenting and their own well-being. Just let the obedient child rebel once and you will see how dependent the parent may be upon the compliant behavior of the child. Conversely, rebellious children are viewed in just that way by their parents, so that every time a controversial subject arises a parent may expect griping or arguing by the rebellious one. The influence is not one-directional, parents to children. Rather, children also affect their parents, even in closed family structures. In more open families the interaction is complex and multidirectional.

SUMMARY

Children grow up in an environment where they are influenced by persons and events around them. In addition, they affect their environment, creating a continuous process of change. We discussed three forces affecting children's development of language and communication as they operate in the family system: models, interaction, and family communication.

Models, such as parents, siblings, friends, and teachers, provide examples of language that the child examines and copies. While direct imitation of these models does not seem to account for much of children's communication development, adult expansions of children's imitations do seem related to language development. Recent studies suggest that imitation may serve a more general function for children, either as a rehearsal of new material (a type of "plagiarism" of another's speech) or as a message showing a lack of comprehension of some portion of the adult's utterance. These views of imitation reflect more of a communication orientation than do earlier views of imitation.

Probably more important in children's language development is the nature of communication exchanges (interaction) with models. When others comment on children's utterances—presenting ideas, asking questions, and making suggestions—they are extending the meaning of children's language. This technique is called extension and has been found effective in helping children acquire more complex grammatical structures. The language that mothers direct to their children appears to be structured like the child's language; studies have supported this tendency of mothers (and perhaps other models as well). The transactional view of interaction maintains that while others obviously affect the language and communication of children when interacting with them, children influence the behaviors of these others as well. This view has conversational competence as the goal of mother-infant interaction, and suggests that infants and their capabilities affect how mothers will interact with them. A "watchful-mother" hypothesis helps explain the successful emergence of conversational turn-taking and role differentiation in the conversations of young children.

Maybe the most important interpersonal force affecting children's development of effective communication behaviors is the family communication style. If communication in the family is open—if family members are allowed to participate in decisions, discussions, and exchanges—then children have plenty of opportunities to practice communication strategies essential in their relationships with others. If closed communication patterns are predominant, however, children will not have opportunities to try various communication strategies because the rules of the family unit may settle all disputes or disagreements. Children need plenty of confirmation in their struggle to develop communication competence.

SUGGESTED READINGS

BRUNER, JEROME S., "From Communication to Language—A Psychological Perspective," *Cognition*, 3 (1975), 255–87.

SLOBIN, DAN, *Psycholinguistics*, Chap. 5. Glenview, Ill.: Scott, Foresman, 1971.

WATZLAWICK, PAUL, JANET BEAVIN, AND DON JACKSON, *The Pragmatics of Human Communication*, Chaps. 1–4. New York: Norton, 1967.

WHITE, BURTON, "Critical Influences in the Origins of Competence," *Merrill-Palmer Quarterly*, 21 (1975), 243–66.

PART II

THE CHILD'S COMMUNICATION SYSTEM: VERBAL DEVELOPMENT

Children acquire a communication system that allows them to function effectively in many important situations. A preschooler can convince his mother to invite his friends to their house for the day. A six-year-old can explain how a butterfly grows, using very precise language. A ten-year-old is able to quiet her whining three-year-old brother with a host of reasons why his whining is in vain. Children's ability to communicate effectively is based to a great extent on their mastery of verbal language skills.

Communication can be defined as the sharing of meanings. When we talk with someone, we share descriptions of people, events, ideas, and feelings that we have encountered. We share opinions, arguments, and pleas. The communication of meaning can be traced to three basic levels of verbal language: words (morphology), structure (syntax), and semantics.

In Part II each level of verbal language is discussed in two ways: the level is defined, and then a stage-by-stage account of how children learn that level is presented. Children's verbal-language development is viewed as a process that can best be explained in terms of the development of meaning, whether through words, syntax, or semantics. The best view of children's development of meaning is yielded by a stage-by-stage analysis, each stage offering an explanation of the meanings children communicate to others. Some of the stages of development that we cite are based on a multitude of studies; others are cited with the qualification that further confirmatory studies are necessary. Our purpose in each chapter is to present *what we know* about how children acquire a particular level of language. Studies conducted in the past decade or two have revolutionized our understanding of children's acquisition of language. The new information should be invaluable in helping parents and teachers understand their children.

Chapter 4 is an introduction to the three chapters that follow it. Children's development of language entails the acquisition of linguistic intuitions about how the language should sound. Chapter 4 examines children's linguistic intuitions and explains, with the help of examples, five methods typically employed in studies of these intuitions.

Chapters 5–7 deal with three basic verbal levels. Each chapter outlines one of these levels according to the typical stages of its development. The following sections stress the importance of each of these levels in the communication of meaning.

WORDS AND MEANING

Children's performance in school settings as well as their behavior in social groups is based on their ability to communicate meanings to others. Words can be used to make fine distinctions among objects, events, feelings, and actions. Thus, children who are able to use words to express fine distinctions in meaning will more successfully communciate their ideas, feelings, and attitudes to others. Vocabulary instruction has long been an important component of language-arts instruction in elementary school. It should continue, but in a more meaningful way that is in accord with language-development principles. Children's word meanings do not always match the meanings understood by adults. Research indicates that, as children grow older, words in their vocabulary take on more advanced meanings, so that the expression of more refined meanings is possible with older children.

STRUCTURE AND MEANING

As children acquire complex sentence structures, they acquire a potential for communicating specific and subtle meanings. A sentence containing a high degree of modification and subordination of ideas is quite effective in communicating an idea vividly and accurately. Chapter 6 emphasizes the fact that children learn the syntax of their language in a stage-by-stage fashion. With little help from those around him, a child will eventually utter sentences that reflect the syntax of adult sentences. The most important assistance an adult can give young children acquiring syntactic rules is to employ language that uses these rules. Research has indicated that although it might help toddlers to use a form of "baby language" that is easier for them to copy, the use of any form of baby language for language-learning children may only hinder their development.

Chapter 6 is organized according to six stages in children's development of language structure. These stages were drawn primarily from the work of Roger Brown and from a host of studies on the emergence of structure in children's speech. Since the communication of meaning is accomplished by the use of various syntactic structures, teachers must be given a comprehensive view of syntactic development that covers all the language-learning years. Chapter 6 presents syntactic development in a comprehensive manner, beginning with early forms of toddler language and extending to the complex structures acquired in later elementary-school years.

SEMANTICS AND MEANING

Our approach to semantic development is drawn from the work of M.A.K. Halliday in his book, *Learning How to Mean*. Semantic development is an active process in which children gradually learn how to mean in the context of their environment. Children do not acquire a set of meanings per se. Instead, meaning is an active process of development focusing on function. Lev Vygotsky maintains that the thought-language relationship is the basis of semantic development: he explains children's growth in terms of their development toward self-regulation through language. In the first phase of learning how to mean, children learn a set of basic meaning functions, such as the regulatory and the imaginary. In the second phase, they combine functions into more complex, interpersonal messages. Finally, in the third phase, children make choices about what they mean from among a broad range of functions; their messages are based on scripts and schema for the communication event.

4

children's language: methods of discovery

"I maked dis picture but da guy gots no ears."

Children's sentences such as this one have traditionally been explained as including "mistakes." Current theories of language development, however, regard children as capable speakers of their own rather "curious" language rather than poor speakers of adult language. According to these theories, children *follow their own rules* in forming negative constructions, asking questions, producing past tenses of verbs, and so forth. These rules are not deviations or distortions of adult language rules; they simply differ from the rules adults follow. As children progress through elementary school their language gradually approaches that of an adult. Modern theorists explain language development in children in terms of children's stage-by-stage and rule-by-rule acquisition of adult linguistic competence.

Two general issues facing the person studying children's development of language are these:

1. In general, what do children learn when they learn their language?
2. How can we characterize children's language at any point in its development?

This chapter focuses on a framework that explains what children learn and how we can assess their linguistic development.

LANGUAGE KNOWLEDGE: OUR LINGUISTIC INTUITIONS

Those of us who are native speakers of English all have linguistic intuitions about our language, not because we have studied language but because we are native speakers. We are capable of making certain judgments about the child's utterance, "I maked dis picture but da guy gots no ears." While our judgments will be more general and probably far less accurate than those of a linguist, we are able to say what strikes us about the choices the child obviously made and why the child made those choices. First, we might say that the verb "maked" should be "made," knowing that the child put the regular past-tense ending on the irregular verb "make." We may know that the "correct" pronunciation of "this" and "the" includes the voiced /th/ sound, while the child in the example said "dis" and "da." Finally, the verb "gots" is just not right, though the child's use of this word is not easy to explain. "Gots" is one of the most frequent forms in children's speech and a form that is particularly childlike. Not related to the verb "to get," though at first glance that may seem to be the link, many children use this form to communicate the meaning of "to have," but they do this through the idiom "has got." Adults use this idiomatic verb form most often with the contracted auxiliary (for example, "He's got a funny nose."). It seems that children who say "gots" are using a form of this idiom.

Children learn to make judgments about grammaticality: for example, they soon learn that "gots" is really not right. They learn to make judgments about the clarity or ambiguity in utterances. For example, they may be able to see that the example sentence we've been discussing is clear and unambiguous. In addition, they become aware of meaning in language, and so know that whoever might express a sentence like this one is saying they made a mistake in drawing the human anatomy. Or, to put the observation in the language of a child, "Oh-oh, I mistaked." Of course, now you may realize that the child saying this is following regular rules of verb inflections with a noun ("mistake"), something that children will do.

In this text, rather than call forms such as "gots," "maked," and "mistaked" ungrammatical we talk about the rules children probably follow in using such forms. Their consistency in applying rules and inflections is good proof of the rule-governed basis for language development. The key to understanding children's language, then, is not to discover which rules they "break" in trying to use a form of adult language. Instead, our purpose is to view their language and try to characterize the rules they *follow* in creating utterances. The purpose of this chapter, then, is to examine the intuitions children acquire about how their language works[1] and methods of discovering these linguistic intuitions.

intuition 1: "It's grammatical"

If you are a native speaker of English, you can distinguish well-formed sentences from ungrammatical strings of words. Consider the following examples:

---

[1]The linguistic intuitions examined in this chapter are based on the outline presented by Dan Slobin in *Psycholinguistics* (Glenview, Ill.: Scott, Foresman, 1971), pp. 4–6.

1. Rubber the angry duckie threw the boy.
2. The rubber boy threw the angry duckie.
3. The angry boy threw the rubber duckie.

An adult speaker of English would have no trouble determining which example is merely an unstructured string of words (sentence 1), which one follows grammatical word ordering but makes little sense (sentence 2), and which one is a well-formed and meaningful sentence (sentence 3). (By the way, children attach great significance to little rubber duckies. Ernie, who lives on "Sesame Street," is never without his rubber duckie. It means a lot to him.)

In addition, a native speaker knows when certain word sequences are not acceptable sentences. Consider this example:

4. The boy who was angry and that I knew threw the rubber duckie.

Something is wrong there, and we know it!

A native speaker's sense of grammaticality also includes some knowledge of what linguists call "degree of deviation" of sentences from English. For example, most of us would agree that the following sentences are scaled from top to bottom in terms of increasing deviation from English:

5. The dog looks terrifying.
6. The dog looks barking.
7. The dog looks lamb.[2]

A native speaker's ability to make such distinctions is based on his grammatical intuition.

In a study of children's metalinguistic awareness of acceptable and grammatical (but anomalous) sentences, Diane Carr asked children between two and five to respond to sentences that could be "odd" or "right."[3] The results show a rather interesting pattern of development in children's assessments of a battery of sentences. Carr proposes three stages of development in children's mastery of the ability to make these judgments.

Stage 1: Does it match with my experience? The youngest children, usually between two and three years of age, responded to the question on the basis of whether or not they had experienced the action it described. Carr called this the verification strategy. A stage-1 child-judge responds like this:

Can a baby wake up?	C: Yes.
Can a plate wake up?	C: No.

[2]For a discussion of these three sentences, see R. B. Lees, "Review of Syntactic Structures," *Language* 33 (1957), 375–408.

[3]Diane B. Carr, "The Development of Young Children's Capacity to Judge Anomalous Sentences," *Journal of Child Language*, 6 (June 1979), 227–41.

Can a rabbit wake up?	C: No.
Can a bird wake up?	C: No.
Can a man wake up?	C: Yes.
Can a bus wake up?	C: No.
Can a flower wake up?	C: No.

A child at this stage does not include linguistic knowledge in her judgment of whether a sentence sounds right or not. If the sentence matches her experience (if, for example, she has seen babies wake up), then it's "right." If she has not witnessed something (for example, rabbits waking up), then her response is "no." Since she has not seen birds and rabbits wake up, she assumes that they do not do so, and responds "no."

Stage 2: "Gee, anything's possible, isn't it?" In the next stage of development, possibly starting during the second year but usually in the third, children find all kinds of situations possible. In fact, Carr was quite surprised to find that children in this stage judged many of the anomalous sentences to be possible. Children are now beginning to be aware that something may be true even if they have not experienced it. The only problem in this stage is that children admit that almost anything could be true:

Can a baby wake up?	C: Yes.
Can a plate wake up?	C: Hmmm . . . yes.
Can a rabbit wake up?	C: Yes.
Can a bird wake up?	C: Yes.
Can a man wake up?	C: Yes.
Can a bus wake up?	C: Yes.
Can a flower wake up?	C: Yes.

Children seem to view any thing or person as capable of *acting*, and so believe that plates, flowers, and buses can all wake up, be sad, and rejoice. Psychologists relate this behavior to the child's view of reality at this stage of development, a stage where children consider any moving and living things to be capable of rather human responses.

The children in the study could have employed the "undecided" response, but stage-2 children did not make effective use of it. The stage-2 child responds "yes" with the dogmatic certainty of a stage-1 child saying "no" to the question "Can a table eat?" Children under four years of age seem to be able to entertain a number of thoughts without judging them true or false. Quite possibly the child in this stage of development is saying, "OK, I can entertain that possibility—that a table eats something."

Stage 3: "I can judge correctly." In this stage children are capable of responding in an adult-like way to questons of judgment regarding sentences.

They use the "undecided" category and they weigh the factors necessary in making their decisions. Children are able to weigh factors such as experience and knowledge of reality in their epistemological judgments of the likelihood of occurrence of familiar and unfamiliar events. Here is an example of how a four- or five-year-old might respond:

Can a baby wake up?	C: Yes.
Can a plate wake up?	C: No.
Can a rabbit wake up?	C: Sure.
Can a bird wake up?	C: Yes—and fly around.
Can a man wake up?	C: Yes.
Can a bus wake up?	C: No . . . it can start but not wake up.
Can a flower wake up?	C: Well, that's a tough one . . . maybe, I don't know.

It is doubtful that adults would respond in a more enlightened way than this young child has.

intuition 2: "There's a difference in underlying meaning."

Adult speakers can also distinguish between sentences that look alike on the surface but differ in their underlying meaning:

8. Winnie-the-Pooh is easy to see.
9. Winnie-the-Pooh is eager to see.

The difference between sentences 8 and 9 becomes apparent if we analyze the relations between the words within each sentence. The doll is the subject of sentence 9—it is seeing "eagerly." In sentence 8, however, someone else is the actor—the doll is what can be seen. Our ability to assess relationships between nouns and verbs, to determine which noun is subject and which is object, and to identify which words modify other words enables us to distinguish differences in the underlying meaning of sentences.

Incidentally, five-year-olds will have trouble understanding the difference in meaning between sentences 8 and 9, whereas nine-year-olds will have no difficulty at all. A young child, when asked if a blindfolded doll is "easy to see," will say no because "the blindfold is in the way." Obviously, the child has missed the point of the question and the meaning of the sentence. Children of elementary-school age are in the process of acquiring complex structures related to underlying sentence meaning. Children's development of these structures (stage 6 of the child's acquisition of syntax) is explored in Chapter 6.

intuition 3: "They're saying the same thing."

Adult speakers can also distinguish between sentences that look different on the surface but are alike in underlying meaning:

10. The girl carried the gerbil.
11. The gerbil was carried by the girl.

There is no question in your mind that the girl is the subject of both sentences—the gerbil never "does the work." Experience with language tells us that these sentences are saying the same thing even though their form is different. The difference in form is something we might be able to pinpoint if we recall our high-school grammar. Sentence 10 is presented in an active form, whereas sentence 11 is written in a passive form.

Figure 4.1. *Passive sentence understanding: monster and boy.*

Our intuition about the semantic relationship between active and passive sentence forms is based on learning and becomes a part of our linguistic competence. The linguistic competence of a four-year-old child may not include the ability to make such a judgment, however. As we will see in Chapter 7, preschoolers have trouble understanding the "meaning" of certain passive sentences. If young children are shown Figure 4.1 and the sentence "The monster is being chased by the little boy" and are then asked if the sentence matches the picture, they might reply, "Yes, they match OK." Intuitions regarding semantic rules of a language take time to develop.

intuition 4: "It's ambiguous."

Adult speakers can judge whether or not a sentence is ambiguous. Some sentences have more than one intrepretation:

12. Walking toddlers can be a pleasure.

This sentence could mean "Toddlers who walk can be a pleasure," or it could mean "It can be a pleasure to walk toddlers." The ambiguous verb in this sentence could be rewritten in two different ways:

13. Walking toddlers are a pleasure. (*They* look so cute—that is, until they get away from us.)
14. Walking toddlers is a pleasure. (The *activity* can be enjoyable, unless the wee ones have "ideas.")

Sentence 12 can be "read" two different ways by using stress and pause to illustrate differences in meaning. The words in both readings are the same, but the underlying meanings of the readings, as expressed in sentences 13 and 14, are different.

A general but valuable way to characterize the goal of children's language development, then, is to say that children develop four basic linguistic intuitions in a broad range of language situations. They learn to monitor their own language and the language used by others. Their monitoring tells them, for example, that a sentence sounds all right, that it doesn't make sense, or that it has a double meaning. With greater experience in language, and certainly with classroom experience in composition and grammar, children become better able to express their linguistic intuitions. But unless they pursue a course of study in language or linguistics, they will never be able to characterize their intuitions in a very sophisticated manner. The second section of this chapter focuses on methods of discovering the linguistic intuitions of children.

FIVE METHODS OF DISCOVERING CHILDREN'S LINGUISTIC INTUITIONS

It is easy enough to examine an adult's grasp of language principles. All you have to do is secure a valid test of a language principle and then administer it to the person. Assuming that the scoring procedures are valid and reliable, you can determine to what extent the adult has mastered that language principle. With children, especially those who do not yet read, you have to devise other means for assessing what they know about language. The procedures for young children must be oral and visual and the test must be interesting enough to capture their attention. Consequently, the methods will be indirect, assessing a child's knowledge through rather subtle procedures. Researchers have devised a set of methods for uncovering children's intuitions about language. These methods are arranged in order from the least direct to the most direct, and from general observation to specific questioning.

check for regularities in usage

The first method of discovering children's intuitions about language is to analyze their speech for regularities. The regularities or patterns are noted, recorded, and explained in terms of rules. Consider the following sentences typically produced by children.

"Allgone shoe."
"Allgone Mommy."
"Allgone hot."

Each of these three sentences is composed of "allgone" plus the object word. Children regularly select the descriptive word "allgone" to modify "shoe," "Mommy," and "hot." Children could not have been "reducing," or simplifying, adult sentences in these instances; adults would not produce complete sentences with these words, in an order resembling the children's order. Rather, children follow their own rules of sentence production. By observing regularities in children's speech, then, such rules can be uncovered.

test for the extension of regularities to new instances

A more stringent method of demonstrating the existence of a rule is to search for the extension of regularities to new instances. A good example of this method is that employed by Jean Berko in her landmark study of child language, which we discussed briefly in Chapter 2. Persuaded by the regularity of childlike utterances such as "he goed" and "two mouses," Berko created a nonsense language of words such as *wug* and *bing*. Cartooned pictures of a fat little bird (a wug) and a man standing on the ceiling (binging) were used to elicit responses in this way.

This is a wug. (picture of one wug)
Now there is another one. (picture of two wugs)
There are two of them. They are two_____

This is a man who knows how to bing. (picture of man standing on ceiling)
He is binging. He did the same thing yesterday. What did he do yesterday?
Yesterday he_____[4]

Children followed their own rules in forming plurals ("wugs") and past tenses of verbs ("binged"). Since the children had never heard these words before, Berko and other theorists concluded that children are able to produce new forms in a regular fashion, based on a knowledge of grammatical rules.

look for self-corrections

A third method of uncovering linguistic intuitions requires evidence that children are adjusting their utterances to produce language which follows different rules. In some situations, it is apparent that a child can judge whether or not an utterance is correct according to some linguistic standard. A child's sense of grammaticality can be observed in this three-year-old girl's self-corrections.

"She had a bad headache like me had . . . like I . . . like I did."

This child was monitoring her speech in accordance with rules she simply "knew." In this case the standards were adult rules. In other examples the same girl may adjust her speech to follow her own rules rather than adult rules:

"Why . . . Why . . . Why people have not . . . Why people have no tails?"

After realizing that her attempt to follow adult rules was not working out so well, she changed her utterance to conform with her own rules for negative questions.

A study of five- and six-year-olds' self-corrections[5] produced a number of important generalizations. The younger children self-corrected minor aspects of language, as in choice of words, while the older children transformed sentences structurally or changed the thrust of their message. Based on the greater frequency of self-corrections among the older children, it would seem that as children age they become more active listeners to what they say. A large proportion of self-corrections involve the verb—its expansion, agreement, and elaboration. It seems likely that this area of syntax affords the most difficulty for children.

Examples from the article illustrate the changing importance with age of self-correcting for children learning their language:

[4]Jean Berko, "The Child's Learning of English Morphology," *Word*, 14 (1958), 150–77.
[5]Sinclair Rogers, "Self-initiated Corrections in the Speech of Infant-School Children," *Journal of Child Language*, 5 (June 1978), 365–71.

Younger children: "We can't go no more." "We can't go any more." "Me go." "I go." "He grew bigger." "He growed bigger."

Older children: "You put down it." "You put it down." "I know what them are." "I know what they are." "I'm going to leave school soon." (Are you?) "Well, when I'm sixteen anyway." "Our little dog was hurt yesterday . . ." "Well, it's our neighbor's dog really, but . . ."

ask indirect questions

The use of indirect questions is an extremely effective method of tapping children's linguistic intuitions because this method does not rely on complex verbal elaboration to demonstrate the child's underlying knowledge of language. Typically, indirect questions are used to ask the child to demonstrate competence by using either nonverbal behaviors or by using extremely simple verbal responses which do not require elaboration. Examples are helpful:

"See the animals in this picture Bill? Which one is sleeping? Point to the animal that's sleeping." (pointing nonverbal behavior shows the child's answer to this question)

"Here's a truck and here's a car. Can you show me, 'The car was pushed by the truck?'" (nonverbal demonstration reflects competence with passive sentence structure)

"There are three persons on this felt board. Who is the father? Make the one who is the father sit in this chair." (demonstration behavior portrays semantic knowledge).

Notice that in each of these examples, the question element could be omitted and the command to point or show could be used alone. Indirect probe procedures typically require the child to show competence through simple means other than verbal definition. Another indirect method of assessing children's linguistic awareness is through the use of simple questions such as these:

"See the animals in this picture, Bill? Which animal is sleeping? Is it the goat?" (a simple "yes" or "no" response is all that is required to demonstrate competence).

"Watch the car and the truck. (person makes the car push the truck) Is this true: 'The car was pushed by the truck.'?" (again, a true/false or yes/no answer is all that is required).

The indirect question method is most effective in testing children's linguistic intuitions because it requires only simple and straightforward responses from children.

ask direct questions

The most stringent method for discovering children's linguistic intuitions, other than asking them to state the intuitions explicitly, is to ask them direct questions. Linguists depend heavily on this method in studying adult's knowledge of language, but the method is often unproductive with young children. When asked "Which is right, 'Mom told me' or 'Mom told me'?" a preschooler may just look at you as if you spoke a different language and answer "Hunh?" Direct questions must be clearly stated and based on a vocabulary the child knows.

Margaret Stubbs used a special kind of direct question in her examination of children's knowledge of kin terms in English.[6] First, she asked the children, who were from four to ten years of age, an indirect question—to point to or move on a felt board a character that represented a certain family member (for example, the mother). She then gave them one of two basic, direct probes: "How do you know she's the mother?" or "What do you have to have to be a mother?" In addition, she tailored follow-up probes to the answers of the chidren. The children's responses were examined for the features they mentioned in explaining the meaning of kin terms. Take a look at this dialogue from her study:

Interviewer: Point to the one who is the mother.
Bobby (six years): (points to nursery-school teacher surrounded by children)
Interviewer: How do you know she's the mother, Bobby?
Bobby: She gots lotsa childz.
Interviewer: How many childz you have to have to be a mother?
Bobby: Oh, two.

In this case the "real mother" on the felt board had only one child. But to Bobby, a family of children was so tempting in the definition of a mother that he failed to catch the interviewer's comment about the nursery-school teacher: "Mrs. Brown is a teacher. She has no children of her own, but here she is with her students." The children in this study provided fascinating statements about English kin terms—for example, "Brothers are boys who play baseball," "Fathers read the newspaper and drink coffee," "Aunts wear dresses and carry purses," and "Grandmothers have wrinkles and old faces." When you ask young children direct questions that they can understand, you never know exactly what answer you will get—that is, unless you know how they think and how they express themselves.

Armed with these five methods of determining the rules children follow in using language, developmental psycholinguists have begun to characterize the stages of language development in children. Though not specifically defined in terms of children's chronological ages, these stages represent periods of development in the child's pursuit of adult linguistic competence. By uncovering the linguistic intuitions of children, scientists can postulate

---

[6]Margaret Stubbs, "Children's Acquisition of English Kin Terms" (Master's thesis, University of Illinois at Chicago Circle, 1975).

constructs of children's language competence at successive stages of development. Generally, all children pass through such stages, regardless of their income level, home environment, or cultural background, and they all do so at about the same time in their life.

Most of the information presented in Chapters 5–7 is based on one or more of these five methods. These methods have allowed theorists to account for the development of verbal language in children, thus paving the way for psychologists and neurologists to explain *why* children's language develops as it does.

SUMMARY

The study of children's verbal language is based on the examination of their rule behavior. Linguisitic competence is our underlying knowledge of the rules of a language, knowledge that we speak of in terms of linguistic intuitions—how a sentence sounds and what it means to us. Our judgments about grammaticality, sentence meaning, and sentence ambiguity constitute our linguistic intuitions:

1. "It's grammatical."
2. "There's a difference in underlying meaning."
3. "They're saying the same thing."
4. "It's ambiguous."

The starting point in child-language research has been the examination of children's linguistic competence at successive stages in their language development. We explored five methods of determining children's linguistic intuitions:

1. checking for regularities in usage
2. testing for the extension of regularities to new instances
3. looking for the child's self-corrections
4. asking indirect questions
5. asking direct questions

These five methods are employed by researchers who study the words, syntax, and semantic development in children's language.

SUGGESTED READINGS

SLOBIN, DAN, *Psycholinguistics*, Chap. 1. Glenview, Ill.: Scott, Foresman, 1971.

WOOD, BARBARA, "Competence and Performance in Language Development," *Today's Speech*, 21, no. 1 (1973), 23–30.

5
words in children's communication

A one-year-old child may use only five or ten words to communicate with others. By two years of age, the child may be able to use over two hundred different words. The vocabulary of a typical five year old child is not significantly smaller than the everyday vocabulary of a typical adult. This suggests that a child's vocabulary is almost adult-like by kindergarten, yet this is simply not true. While a child's vocabulary grows rapidly in preschool years, there are some very special qualities in the young child's word choices. These qualities are the focus of this chapter.

Two important principles of children's vocabulary growth appear again and again in studies of children's meanings for words:

1. Children's word meanings may not match adult word meanings.
2. As children age their word meanings may change, reflecting a new viewpoint.

A story illustrates these principles.

Michael was a normally developing ten-year-old; his mother is a secretary in our department. We videotaped him in an experiment on how children understand kin terms such as "mother," "son," and "uncle." The first question he was asked involved the kin term "mother" and followed the presentation of three alternatives: (1) a teacher with three babies in her nursery-school class, but no children of her own; (2) a woman with her husband and a dog; and (3) a woman with her husband and a child of her own. We asked Michael to point to the person whom he knew was the mother. Of course, we expected him to select the third woman because he was at an age where he should have mastered the easier kin terms such as "mother." But instead he pointed to the woman with the husband and no child. We were used to younger children selecting the nursery-school teacher because they tend to be quite impressed by the brood of children surrounding her. But we did not expect the selection of the childless person. Michael told us that she "just looks like a mother, you know, a mother's dress and all that." Using a standard probe we asked, "Do you have to have anything special to be a mother?" Michael responded, "No, but sometimes they wear big hats."

As you can imagine, Michael's mother was shocked when she saw the videotape. When she heard her son's "housedress" definition of a mother she wanted to hide in a corner. We assured her that his definition of a mother was just as unique as those given by other children: some say mothers mop kitchen floors, other say they are ladies who carry purses, and some even agree with Michael that they wear mothers' dresses. Michael's mother said that she always worked and that she rarely wore "mothers' clothes." We comforted her, saying that Michael was probably brainwashed by the pictures of women he saw in magazines and on television.

Not until children reach their early teens do they understand the meanings of kin terms according to a set of semantic features most adults use. Their meanings for kin terms, a typical set of words in their vocabulary, change as they develop, reflecting the features most important in their world. So it is not surprising that a child may at one time say that grandmothers are ladies who walk with canes, next that they are old ladies with grey hair, and later that they have wrinkles and old-looking faces.

A child who defines mothers as ladies who wear housedresses is thinking of the concept of mother according to physical features rather than the adult features of sex and offspring. Is the "housedress" approach wrong? Should the child be criticized for having such meanings? Theorists today would rather examine children's meanings, studying them as they reflect the working of their minds. Rather than suggest that children progressively "correct" meanings, theorists would simply agree that word meanings change as children develop cognitively. To follow children's vocabulary development, it is not enough to simply examine which words the child uses and understands, counting and listing all possibilities. Instead, it is more appropriate to study children's behavior with words. How do children act with different words? How does their behavior with words change as they grow up? This chapter reviews key studies in three phases of vocabulary development:

1. the single-word stage of expression
2. the refinement of word meanings
3. the development of definition making

The discussion centers on principles that explain the changing aspects of children's vocabulary.

ONE-WORD UTTERANCES

Children in the single-word stage of language development have a vocabulary sufficiently large and varied to make sentences, but they do not do this. They know enough words to talk about many objects and events using subjects and predicates, but for some reason they do not use multiple-word sentences. According to Lois Bloom, children under about two years of age do not know the linguistic code for putting words together into sentences.[1] While children of this age realize that people can perform actions, that objects can exist and then disappear, and that events can happen again and again, their speech is simple—"one word at a time."

types of single words

While children in this stage of language development understand sentences more complex than one word, they produce only single-word utterances of two basic types, according to Bloom. The first type, *substantive words*, refer to classes of objects, such as cookies and pants, or classes of persons, such as "Mama" and "baby." The second type, *function forms*, comprise a relatively small number of words in the young child's vocabulary, yet their individual frequency of occurrence in children's speech is far greater than words in the substantive class. The most frequent function forms are "there," "up," "more," "down," "no," and "gone." Bloom stresses that young children do not learn adult parts of speech, such as nouns and prepositions. Instead, they develop conceptual representations of regularly recurring experiences in their lives and use words that "code" these experiences to communicate their needs to others. So, because children regularly want to be carried they may continually say "Up," hoping to be lifted up by a parent. A tasty dessert may predictably be followed by a cry of "More."

Other researchers who have examined this stage of language development classify single words in much the same way as Bloom. The focus of their schemes may not be like the one we just examined, but the relation of the scheme to the needs of the child is usually stressed. A classic consideration of early words was made by Werner Leopold, who examined the early language development of his own child.[2] To illustrate the breadth of the substantive-

[1] Lois Bloom, *One Word At A Time* (The Hague: Mouton, 1973), p. 55.
[2] Werner F. Leopold, "Speech Development of a Bilingual Child," in *Readings in Language Development*, ed. Lois Bloom (New York: John Wiley, 1978), pp. 4–30.

word class, Leopold organized early words into several semantic groups, claiming that children may begin to sort words in this way early in their lives. These groups included words for food, toys and games, animals, persons, parts of the body, clothing and undressing, home routines, and outdoor life. Other categories that seem more related to function forms included words for emotions, social relations (for example, "Hi"), and what Leopold called "abstracts" ("there," "away," and "why," for instance).

Names for person are probably the most frequently used of the substantive words. A study was conducted to see whether or not young children know the difference between common and proper names.[3] Children not quite two years of age were shown dolls and blocks and asked to do certain things with them. They were first given nonsense words for one of a pair of blocks or dolls and then shown "the other one." The researchers wondered if the children would behave differently with potential proper names than with common names. Here is a reconstruction of the common-name task they employed with the children:

Tester: Look what I've brought, Jimmy. This is a zav. (In subsequent conversations the block was referred to five times as "the zav.") (referring to a similar block) Yeah, here's the other one. Oh Jimmy, bring the zav to Mommy, OK?

Because "zav" is being used as a common name for the blocks, the child could have brought either block to his mother, right? But how about the proper-name situation:

Tester: "Look what I've brought, Jenny. This is Zav." (In subsequent conversations the doll was referred to as "Zav" five times.) (referring to a similar doll) Oh yes, Jenny, here's the other one. Oh Jenny, give Zav a bath, will you?

Now if Jenny knows that "Zav" is a proper name and that only the "real Zav" can be bathed, not "the other one," then she will score well, reflecting her understanding of proper names. But if she bathes the wrong doll, then we can suspect that she is using "zav" to refer to a class of objects (zavs) rather than as a name of one doll, "Zav."

The girls in the study were able to discriminate among common and proper names and behave appropriately with the blocks and dolls. While they knew they could select either block in the common-name condition, they knew that they could play with only one doll in the proper-name condition. But the boys didn't do as well. The authors suggest that boys' inexperience in playing with dolls and of course their lack of knowledge that

---

[3]Nancy Katz, Erica Baker, and John MacNamara, "What's in a Name? A Study of How Children Learn Common and Proper Names," *Child Development*, 45 (1974), 469–73.

all dolls have names and are treated individually may have accounted for their poorer performance in the proper-name condition.

Paul Guillaume's studies utilized a classification scheme very similar to Bloom's, in that it included names for persons and words for objects. A third category was related to Bloom's function forms, but Guillaume labeled it in a way parents will find quite appropriate: "the language of wanting."[4] Guillaume was very impressed with the sense of need satisfaction and urgency communicated by young children with the words in this category. In some cases it seemed as if a child wanted everything, and so would use words like "More" and "Up." In other cases a child would say "No more" or "No" when given undesirable food, indicating that she wanted that action to stop immediately. Guillaume stressed that viewing single-word utterances from an adult perspective, such as by classifying these words in a way similar to that used by Leopold, is totally incorrect from the child's perspective. Children under two years of age do not "think" in terms of semantic groups, he argued. Instead, they think in terms of what they want and what they don't want.

circumstances of single-word speech

Researchers have studied children's single-word utterances in context to discover typical circumstances under which they are produced. One such study reports that about two thirds of all single-word utterances are produced while children are performing some action.[5] As they bounce a ball they say "ball," or as they drink their milk they may say "milk." Children say single words *when touching an object*, not before or after contact. Further, their single words do not usually initiate interaction with an adult, but *follow adult speech*.

The particular nature of adult-child interaction at the one-word-utterance stage is a major question for many researchers, however. Different parents talk to their children differently. It is thought that *how parents talk to children*—what style of communication they use or which words they reinforce in their interactions—may account for the types of words their children use in this stage of their verbal development. Some children may use performatives (sounds or words that are appropriate to actions being imitated) in their play, such as engine sounds ("rrr") when playing with a car, or counting words ("two," "three") when playing with blocks. Others name things they see, hardly missing an object in their environment. And some

---

[4]See Paul Guillaume, "First Stages of Sentence Formation in Children's Speech," in *Readings in Language Development*, ed. Bloom, pp. 131–48.

[5]Maris M. Rodgon, Wayne Jankowski, and Lucias Alenskas, "A Multi-Functional Approach to Single-Word Usage," *Journal of Child Language*, 4 (February 1977), 23–43.

will only say words for objects that are part of some distinctive action they have observed: for example, a child who sees a spoon fall from the table to the floor may say "spoon." There may be parental factors that determine, to some extent, these and other focuses of children's first words.

building a repertoire of words

Many of the experts who are trying to explain how young children build a vocabulary from a rather modest set of early words draw from Lev Vygotsky.[6] According to Vygotsky, there are two processes in the development of the young child's meanings. The first, which is called a *chain complex*, involves a series of associations between referent situations and a word. A chain complex develops when a child uses a particular word in situation A, sees a likeness between situation A and situation B, and then "chains" the word and uses it in the new situation. Situation B could then be viewed as similar to situation C, and the same word used in that new situation. In the chaining process each situation relates to the one next to it (for instance, situation A to situation B), but not necessarily to all other situations. For example, a young child who knows "wawa" for the water she splashes in her bathtub may see water coming from the garden hose, splash in it, and say "wawa." Quite possibly, the water or the splashing may relate the two referent situations. But if she then goes with her father to the gas station she might say "wawa" when she sees the hose used to fill up the car with gas. She will learn that this new referent situation does not fit the meaning for "wawa." Nevertheless, the trip to the gas station has probably opened up opportunities for the child to learn a new word.

A second process in children's development of meaning is called the *associative complex* by Vygotsky. In this process children relate a feature or number of features in an original referent situation with a similar feature or features in a new situation. These associations may not coincide with adult thinking, but the associations seem to be clear from a child's perspective. Melissa Bowerman provided an excellent example of the associative complex in describing how her fourteen-month-old daughter used the word "gi" ("giddiup") while bouncing on her spring horse.[7] The child subsequently used the "giddiup" word in other situations: picking up a small plastic horse and trying to ride it, mounting a toy tractor, getting on her trike, viewing horses on TV, climbing into a tiny chair, bouncing in the tub, looking at a hobby-horse, and bouncing on her mother's knee.

Together, the chain complex and the associative complex explain how

---

[6]See, for example, Lev Vygotsky, *Thought and Language* (Cambridge, Mass.: M.I.T. Press, 1962).

[7]See the discussion of this example in Lois Bloom and Margaret Lahey, *Language Development and Language Disorders* (New York: John Wiley, 1978), pp. 120–23.

children extend their words to more and more referent situations. Though children have not really acquired new words by using their old ones in new situations, the interaction that follows such chaining often prompts the use and acquisition of new words. The child who produced "wawa" for gas hose will likely learn a word related to gas, hose, or some other object in the gas station. The child who used "gi" might try new words such as "horsie," "tractor," or "trike." Vygotsky claims that the child develops a repertoire of words for use by expanding words already in use—from one situation to another. In the process children build a repertoire of messages and eventually a rich vocabulary.

overextension of first words

Calling a gas hose "wawa" is an example of an inappropriate word usage typically called *overextension*. A child may call any round object "a ball," or any furry, four-legged creature "a doggie." This is called overextension because children are presumably relating qualities of one object to another and on that basis calling both objects by the same name. The question of interest to child-language theorists is not whether children overextend. The question is *why* they do it. If we agree with Vygotsky that children acquire meaning by chaining situations with words, then such associations explain their overextensions. But alternative explanations must be considered as well.

One alternate explanation suggests simply that children note similarities between two or more situations and use the same word for each situation. This explanation is compatible with Vygotsky's though much more general in scope. Another explanation is that children sometimes have "retrieval" problems: they can't find just the right word with which to say something, so they pick the one "like it." Still another reason is that children with a limited vocabulary simply pick the best word they have for saying something.

Jean Thomson and Robin Chapman examined children's understanding of basic words in both production (using) and comprehension (understanding only) situations.[8] The researchers discovered that overextensions were not consistent in both situations. That is, even if in actual use a child overextended the name he used for "Daddy," he did not necessarily overextend that name in the comprehension situation. Thus, the limited-vocabulary explanation did not fit all instances in this study. The retrieval explanation seemed far more appropriate for these instances, since if the word was given by an examiner the child responded appropriately.

[8]Jean Thomson and Robin S. Chapman, "Who is 'Daddy' Revisited: The Status of Two-Year-Olds' Overextended Words in Use and Comprehension," *Journal of Child Language*, 4 ((October 1977), 359–75.

Any account of typical overextensions in young children's speech probably requires a set of explanations that include difficulties in retrieval, limited vocabulary, and the processes children probably use in referring to all new objects, persons, and events they encounter. Again, parental behavior may play a major role in children's use of words. If children are encouraged to name and talk about everything around them, their overextensions may be plentiful, especially when they are not given specific guidance or heavy coaching.

Eve Clark sums up this stage in children's development of meaning by stressing that children's early word-behavior is best explained from a communication perspective.[9] At the early stages of language development children have only a small vocabulary at their disposal. Although they supplement these few words with gestures, they are still limited in what they can talk about. According to Clark, children often want to talk about things for which they have no words. They "stretch their resources" and use *deictic words* (words that pick out objects), they point a lot, and they rely on a few verbs for describing actions. They do the best they can with the resources they have, because their purpose is to *communicate*. Overextensions occur because they would rather communicate something about what they mean than say nothing because they don't have the right words.

first words: children's choices

Patricia Greenfield and Joshua Smith viewed two children's development of first words from about eight moths until just before two years of age, when the children began to use multiple-word sentences.[10] They found that a description of these early words was best given in terms of their semantic functions—the functions that the use of the words served for the child. By the time the children had acquired a full set of semantic functions for their early one-word utterances, the researchers found that they could predict which words would be encoded verbally and which ones would be nonverbally communicated.

For example, consider one of the first semantic functions that children acquire: positive and negative volition, or demand. The most common form is either "Mama" (used to request something) or "No" (used to reject something being presented). If a child desires an object, let's say, the child could simply reach for it rather than name it, though one could say that the nonverbal "naming" was the reaching gesture. According to the researchers, volitions contain two parts: the volition or demand and the object being

[9]Eve Clark, "Strategies for Communicating," *Child Development*, 19 (1978), 953–59.
[10]Patricia M. Greenfield and Joshua H. Smith, *The Structure of Communication in Early Language Development* (New York: Academic Press, 1976).

demanded. Since one-word utterances can name only one of the components, the other must be coded nonverbally. Greenfield and Smith sought to predict, based on key factors of the situation, which of the two components would be verbally encoded by the child. They found that the Informativeness Principle was effective in predicting which of the two components would be placed into the word.[11] According to this principle, when uncertainty exists, as when a child could encode either the volition or the object, the child selects the component for encoding that reduces uncertainty. So, in the positive situation of demanding, children produce the object word because that is the unknown element in the communication. However, in the negative or rejection situation, children produce the volition word because, again, that element is likely the unknown one.

Adults communicating with young children probably understand children's use of the Informativeness Principle and realize that the uncertainty being resolved is viewed from the child's point of view rather than their own. Conversations often focus on others checking out their interpretation of the child's selection. Taking one final example, let's say that a young girl points to a drinking cup on a table and says "Cup!" She is showing the volition by pointing and the object of that volition by saying "Cup." Her mother might ask, "Do you want the cup?" checking to see if her child wants the cup or something else on the table.

As children begin to use multiple-word sentences, they continue to expand the size of their vocabulary. The number of words available for their use continues to grow as their experiences grow. But their meanings for words do not remain constant. Instead, they are subjected to a process of refinement.

THE REFINEMENT OF WORD MEANINGS

Children's early words often embrace rather broad and undifferentiated meanings. As children acquire more words and more ways of putting these words together (a process discussed in the next chapter), they are also able to differentiate the meanings of these words. This section focuses on the process of meaning refinement by exploring five special characteristics of children's speech: the pronoun "it," modifiers such as "sort of" and "very," comparative adjectives such as "older" and "younger," deictic terms such as "here" and "there," and the terms "same" and "same kind." These words were chosen because they characterize children's development of word meanings in the early stages of vocabulary growth.

---

[11]*Ibid.*, pp. 184–85.

how the pronoun "it" works

How do you think preschoolers would respond to the following questions?[12]

A. There is clay on the table.
   (1) Give me some.   /or/
   (2) Give it to me.
B. There are marbles on the table.
   (1) Give me some.   /or/
   (2) Give them to me.

Would you give the same amount of clay for the request A1 as for the request A2? Or would you take off a chunk in response to A1 but give the person the entire mass for A2? Would you give the person just a few marbles in answer to request B1 but the whole box for B2? Rules of language defining the pronoun "it" suggest that we mean "all of it" when we ask for "it"; we do not mean just a slice, a piece, or a couple. On the other hand, when we want "some" of something we do not expect "all of it," but if we received "all of it" in asking for "some" we would not think the person weird or linguistically foolish.

Children from three to five years of age responded most appropriately to requests for marbles and clay when definite noun phrases were used (for instance, "Give me *the* marbles" or "Give me *the* clay"). The use of definite pronouns (such as "it" and "them") did not seem to produce as accurate results, however. The marble condition (which required "them" and not "it") was more difficult than the clay condition (which required "it"), suggesting that the trouble was not really with the pronoun "it" but with the pronoun "them." By the time children are five or six they acquire refined meanings for "it" and "them," meanings that insist that "all of it (them)" be given, eaten, picked up, and so forth.

Children's use of the word "some" was even more interesting. While we know that some is "more than one but not necessarily all," many children erred by giving only one marble. This behavior may have stemmed from the children's reluctance to give up a desired object (we don't know this from the design of the study). This error pattern was greater for the older children (say, five-year-olds) than for the younger ones, a result that baffled the researchers. They did suggest, though, that the older children's focus on learning the meaning for "some" as being "not all, but only part" may account for their interpreting "some" in such a modest way, selecting only one

[12]For a more extensive discussion of "it," see Christine Tanz, "Learning How 'It' Works," *Journal of Child Language*, 4 (June 1970), 224–35.

flower, one marble, and so on. For continuous quantities such as clay, the problem did not present itself, since a small or large chunk would satisfy the request.

"sort of"; "very"

Linguists who study a class of words called modifiers often speak of vague versus intensive modifiers. We can use intensive modifiers to stress an attribute, such as tall, short, big, or little; the result is "very tall," "very little," and so forth. We can use the vague modifier "sort of" to play down these same attributes, as in "sort of tall" or "sort of little." When does a child develop an appreciation of vagueness in language? How do children's meanings for these modifiers change as they develop?

As a child's vocabulary grows and words are added for objects and events within certain classes of objects, a child compares and contrasts phenomena according to attributes. People, houses, cars, and dogs are compared for their size and speed, for example. Then single members of any word class can be modified by either vague or intensive words:

That man is sort of short.

That house is very big.

That car is very fast.

That doggie runs sort of fast.

Though boundaries between these major meanings for entity attributes are often fuzzy for children, the language to express this fuzziness develops by first grade.

The intensifier "very" is usually acquired before the vague modifier "sort of." The reason for this might be the clarity of the implied comparison: "very" refers to the "best example" of the attribute in an array, and thus offers a rather clear-cut label for the child to use in selecting an object or person in an array. All of the four- and five-year-olds in a study conducted by Rita Berndt and Alfonzo Caramazza[13] were able to select from an array the "very tall," "very short," "very big," or "very little" objects or persons, though the tall/short distinction was more difficult for the children than the big/little one. Their performance with the vague modifier "sort of" was much more varied. While they avoided the selection of extremes, as they should have, the children seemed to use several different strategies in interpreting these vague modifiers. The older children used many more responses to

[13]Rita S. Berndt and Alfonzo Caramazza, "The Development of Vague Modifiers in the Language of Pre-School Children," *Journal of Child Language*, 5 (June 1978), 279–94.

"sort of," indicating their greater appreciation of its vagueness. On the other hand, younger children seemed to use more specific strategies, though their responses varied according to the attributes.

"He's older 'cuz he's taller. silly!"

Ask young children to guess your age, and you may be in for quite a surprise. If you're short, as I am, you will be pleasantly surprised to hear that children say you're young. But if you're tall, and especially if you're nearly six feet tall, better be ready to get the blow: you might be judged thirty or fifty! This is because children begin their meanings for "young" and "old" with a very simple approach related to height. Is it any wonder? They know that the taller they get, the older they get. So why isn't this a principle upon which persons' ages can be compared?

Adults know that while the "height principle" is fairly effective in determining age, it cannot account for such comparisons by itself. We must examine other features of persons in order to judge their age. A young child observing a very elderly four-foot ten-inch woman walking with a hunched back may say, "What a funny-lookin' kid!" They may find it hard to accept the "facts." Children are amazed that women, who are often shorter than men, are sometimes older than men, "Are you sure you're older than Dad, Mom?" a child might ask. When you assure them of that, they don't seem satisfied. One day I was told, "Mom, I bet you didn't eat your vegetables." Not understanding the context from which this remark came, I asked what my child was referring to. When he told me, I had a hard time controlling my laughter. I became short because I didn't eat well, and this explained why I was pretty old but only five feet three inches.

In an experiment assessing children's understanding of the relation between height and age, researchers found that only for the older child does chronological age play a role in determining age.[14] For the younger child this finding does not hold; only height is significant. When presented with two dolls of varied heights, children in the first stage of word-meaning refinement always select the taller one as the older one. If the dolls match in size, close scrutiny precedes the children's guess, but the chronological ages of the dolls, which are announced to the children by the experimenter does not enter into their decision. The strategy in this first stage is that *tall and old are directly related.*

In the next stage children use the chronological ages given by the interviewer only if the dolls are the same height. Otherwise, the children

---

[14]Stan A. Kuczaj and Amy Lederberg, "Height, Age and Function: Differing Influences on Children's Comprehension of 'Younger' and 'Older,'" *Journal of Child Language* 4 (October 1977), 395–416.

use the strategy of relation between tallness and oldness. The two-part strategy used by children in this stage seems to be this: *height is related to age; if the heights are equal, listen for the ages.*

In the final stage height plays a complementary role with all other relevant factors. An eight-year-old child may have all these factors in proper perspective.

the difference between "here" and "there"

Have you ever tried to give someone definitions of "here" and "there"? "Well," you might say, "here is right here and there is over there." You could point out the two places as you talked, but your definition wouldn't pass a careful inspection for clarity, would it? Children don't have to learn how to define these terms either, but they do have to learn their meanings in order to use and understand them. One researcher suggested that since young children are very egocentric in their thinking, their early definitions might relate only to themselves: their understanding of "here" and "there" would relate to places and/or distances in their *own* physical space. Such a possible first stage was not supported by evidence from a study by Rosalind Charney,[15] however. She discovered that even three-and-a-half-year-old children knew that a speaker-perspective was essential in understanding the two pronouns. Children younger than three years did not consistently adopt any particular strategy for understanding "here" and "there," except in one particular condition: when "there" was quite a distance from either the child or the experimenter the child successfully used "there."

is "same" like "same kind"?

Another word that undergoes progressive meaning changes from three to six years of age is "same." It might be difficult to imagine that such a simple word could undergo any changes in the child's repertoire; it would seem that "same" just means "the same." But how about when two toys are alike and the child is asked to do something with "the same" toy? Will children select the toy they've been talking about and playing with? Or will they select one just like it, placed near the focus toy?

Three-year-olds select either the toy being played with or any other just like it when asked to do something with "the same" toy.[16] This response

---

[15]Rosalind Charney, "The Comprehension of 'Here' and 'There,'" *Journal of Child Language*, 6 (February 1979), 69–80.

[16]Annette Karmiloff-Smith, "More About the Same: Children's Understanding of Post-Articles," *Journal of Child Language*, 4 (October 1977), 277–94.

pattern shows that they interpret "same" as "same kind," so that if attributes are alike, entities are "the same." Four-year-olds are in a transition period, according to the researcher. While they are able to consistently identify "the other one" as the non-same toy (three-year-olds did not), they still interpret "same" as "same kind" in certain situations. When there is a *conflict* of attributes (for example, a brown cow standing up versus a white cow lying down) they do fairly well in selecting the correct "same" cow. But if the cows are both brown or both standing, four-year-olds select "the other" cow as "the same" one about as often as they select the correct one. Their responses in the latter situation are accompanied by a lot of hesitation. Apparently, the decision is a difficult one. By age five, children can deal with color differences in selecting the proper toy when told to select "the same." The competent six-year-old performs the same task without a bit of hesitation.

One thing that affected the children's responses, however, was the linguistic specificity of the prompt question: "Is this the same cow?" versus "Is this the same?" Without the use of the noun "cow," children used the word "same" in a fashion similar to any other adjective, such as "big," "brown," or "white." This led the the researcher to suggest that for young chidren, "same" is in a general modifier class rather than a post-article class.

MAKING DEFINITIONS FOR WORDS

Probably the highest level of development in acquiring word meaning is the ability to define words. When we ask children to define words, we are asking them to use a type of metalanguage, a language to talk about their language. This task is a difficult one because it requires a level of thinking that is abstract and complex. The framework for children's development of definitions is outlined in the stages of thought development presented by Jean Piaget, the noted Swiss psychologist. Three levels of definition making in children are then discussed.

development of children's thought

Let's begin by considering a classic experiment in intellectual development suggested by child psychologist Jean Piaget.[17] This experiment illustrates the very important intellectual capacity (or lack of it) in five- and six-year-olds. The concept being tested is the conservation of continuous quantity. (I have substituted orange pop for water, which Piaget uses, be-

[17]The following experiment is adapted from Herbert Ginsburg and Sylvia Opper, *Piaget's Theory of Intellectual Development: An Introduction* (Englewood Cliffs, N.J.: Prentice-Hall, Inc., © 1969), pp. 161–66.

cause I have found that children are far more attentive and perform at their best when the liquid under consideration is attractive.) With the appropriate materials for the experiment (glasses of different shapes and the liquid) we are ready to go:

Tester: Here are two glasses of orange pop. Do they have the same amount of pop or are they different? (The tester and the child made sure they were the same prior to the experiment.)

Child: They're the same.

Tester: OK. Now, I'm going to pour the orange pop from this glass into this glass—all of it. (The tester pours pop from the regular glass into the short, squat glass.) And now, I'll pour the orange pop from this glass into this one. (Tester pours contents of second regular glass into the tall, slim glass.) Now, I poured this pop into this glass, and that pop into that glass. Now, look at the glasses of orange pop. Do they have the same amount of orange pop or are they different?

Child: Different.

Tester: Oh! Which one has more orange pop?

Child: This one. (Child points to the tall, slim glass.)

Tester: Does this glass have more orange pop than this one? (pointing to the tall, slim glass and then to the short, squat glass)

Child: Yes, it does.

Tester: OK. Now, I'm going to pour this pop back into this glass, and that pop back into that glass. (Tester pours orange pop into original containers.) Now, which one has more orange pop?

Child: They're the same.

Try this simple experiment with a five-year-old child; the child will consistently claim that the quantity of the orange pop in the glass is a function of the shape of the container.

In intellectual terms young children equate a one-dimensional scheme, the height of the pop, with a multidimensional concept, quantity. Their understanding of the terms "more," "less," and "same" is constrained by their intellectual capacity. Children's behavior in this test situation fits beautifully with what Piaget considers to be the second stage of intellectual development: *preoperational intuitive thinking* (two to seven years). Table 5.1 outlines Piaget's four stages of intellectual development in children. Notice that the third stage of development entails children's understanding of complex relationships, such as the conservation of volume and weight. This third stage, *concrete operational thought*, occurs sometime after seven years of age, so we couldn't expect a five- or six-year-old child to answer the foregoing test questions appropriately.

Children's development of language to express and understand the meaning of complex relationships can happen only as quickly (or slowly) as their minds develop. Children do not possess the capabilities for formal

TABLE 5.1. *Stages in children's development of thinking.*

STAGE	AGE	CHARACTERISTICS
1. Acquisition of Perceptual Invariants	to 2 years	Children are able to identify the main features of their environment. They understand that words relate to objects and their properties. Things in children's environments are "invariant," despite the various forms in which they appear—for instance, water is still water even though it's sometimes in a glass, a pan, or coming from a faucet. Meanings are related to sensory qualities—for example, how things look, feel, touch, and taste.
2. Preoperational Intuitive Thinking	2 to 7 years	Children understand the relationships among perceptual invariants. Elementary concepts of time, space, and causality are considered. Children make intuitive judgments about relationships. Their judgments of conservation of volume, weight, and quantity, for example, are based on their attention to only one property of experience at a time. They are unable to see how two properties—for instance, height and width—interact with each other.
3. Concrete Operational Thinking	7 to 11 years	Children have acquired an understanding of complex relationships, such as the conservation of weight, volume, and quantity. Children have attained "reversible thinking"—that is, they can trace a physical operation back to its starting point and account for the transformations in its appearance. Children can classify objects according to a wide range of criteria—size, shape, function, and so forth. Children have trouble in dealing with abstractions and with events that are not visible to them.
4. Formal Propositional Thinking	11 years and older	Children can think in terms of purely logical propositions that can be stated and tested against their experiences. Children are capable of understanding syllogistic reasoning and are quite adept in causal reasoning. Children can derive hypotheses about relationships and draw inferences from appropriate data.

propositional thinking until they are upward of eleven years. Children's development of word meanings parallels their intellectual development. The four stages of intellectual development presented in Table 5.1 can be summarized in this way:

1. *Acquisition of perceptual invariants:* Children are able to identify the main features of their environment. (to two years)

2. *Preoperational intuitive thinking:* Children begin to understand the relationships among the features in their environment. (two to seven years)

3. *Concrete operational thinking:* Children acquire an understanding of complex relationships. (seven to eleven years)
4. *Formal propositional thinking:* Children are able to think logically. (eleven years and
   older)

Remember these four stages of intellectual development as we now examine
the child's development of definition making.

the development of definition making

It is often revealing to ask children what words mean. While we must
realize that we are asking them an unfair question—for "words don't mean"
but rather people have meanings—the question does allow us to enter the
minds of the children. Once children are able to communicate with
multiple-word sentences, one can begin to discuss with them the notion of
word meaning as expressed in definitions.

The first types of definitions children are able to present verbally are
based on *concrete action* (stage 2 in Table 5.1). Things, events, and ideas are
defined in terms of visible actions related to them. For example, a bird is
"something that flies in the sky," and a bowl is "where you eat your cereal
in." Let's call this level 1 of children's definition making. According to one
study, 82 percent of a six-year-old's definitions are phrased in terms of
concrete action.[18]

At about eight years of age a dramatic change takes place: children no
longer define words solely in terms of actions. In this stage of intellectual
development (stage 3 in Table 5.1), words are defined in terms of the sentence contexts in which they are used by the child. This is level 2 of children's
definition making. If a girl usually talks about birds in terms of how they perch
on the branches of a tree in front of her house, chances are her definition of
"bird" will include that fact: "Birds perch on branches on the tree in front of my
house." Another eight-year-old girl (in stage 3) might define a bird in this
way: "it's like an airplane except it's little and chirps." This child's association
of a bird with an airplane reveals the use of semantic features in word
meanings. "Bird" and "airplane" share certain semantic features—they fly,
they have wings, and they are found in the sky. That the child understands
the similarity between the two shows that she had begun to incorporate
semantic features into her word meanings.

When children reach twelve years of age, they may be able to define
birds as "warm-blooded animals that use their wings to fly." This is an
example of level 3 definition making. In this definition children associate

[18]Werner Heinz and Bernard Kaplan, *Symbol Formation* (New York: John Wiley, 1964),
p. 184.

several semantic properties in their meaning of "bird." This definition sounds almost like one you might read in a dictionary, and reflects stage 4 in Table 5.1.

To better acquaint yourself with the three levels in the child's definition making, read the following examples of definitions given by children of various ages:

child	definition level	definition type	definition	
Jim (4 years)	1	action	bottle:	"Where you pour something out of."
			mother:	"She feeds me and gives me a bath."
Ann (8 years)	2	sentence context	bottle:	"It's like a can only you can see through it."
			mother:	"She has babies and takes care of them."
Ben (12 years)	3	dictionary	bottle:	"A hollow glass container that holds liquids."
			mother:	"A lady who is a parent of children."

These definitions differ in their mention of semantic features of the word being defined. Jim mentions only what he does with a bottle—the action of pouring something from it. Ann compares a bottle to a can: they are both containers (a semantic feature) but differ in the perceptual quality of transparency. Ben, the oldest child, is able to formulate an adult-like definition of "bottle," which includes several semantic features of the object.

Jim explains "mother" in terms of the actions his mother performs for him—feeding and bathing. Ann sees mothers as having babies and taking care of them, a sentence-context definition. Ben provides a definition of mother that takes into account two semantic features: female and parent.

Studies that explore changes in word meanings are called word-association studies. Children and adults are told to say the first word that comes to their mind when the tester gives them a particular word. Such studies have been helpful in explaining the basic difference between level 1 and level 2 of definition making. Results have indicated that older children (eight years and over) typically respond with a word that is of the same syntactic class as the prompt word. Opposites are often given. Here are some examples:

prompt word	response word
square	round
fast	slow
run	walk
up	down
cottage	house

In each case the response word is of the same syntactic class as the prompt word and could be "plugged into" a similar sentence context. Younger children (ages two to seven) typically give response words that are not in the same syntactic class as the prompt word but that might follow the prompt word in a sentence. Examine these examples:

prompt word	*response word*
square	box
fast	car
run	fast
up	there
cottage	cheese

The responses of younger children are not syntactically related to the prompt words: the only relationship is that the words "go together" in a sentence. Roger Brown and Jean Berko have called the responses given by older children and adults *homogeneous* because of their linguistic likeness to the prompt word.[19] The responses of the younger children have been called *heterogeneous* because of their linguistic difference from the prompt word. The shift from heterogeneous word associations to homogeneous ones characterizes children's shift from action definitions (level 1) to sentence-context definitions (level 2).

Let's consider one of the words used as an example in the foregoing discussion: "square." Paula Menyuk states that this word elicits "box" most frequently from first graders and "round" most frequently from fourth graders.[20] She argues that "square box" is probably not a dictionary entry for the first graders. Instead, "square" and "box" share the semantic feature or property of, say, having corners. First graders have a limited set of semantic features for any lexical item. From another perspective, younger children have a set of semantic properties that link words of different syntactic classes on the basis of sentence usage. Fourth graders undoubtedly understand the semantic property of shape that is associated with their meaning of "square." Because they respond with another shape—"round"—we can be fairly certain that the semantic property of shape exists in a fourth grader's dictionary.

A POWERFUL VOCABULARY

Communication competence is enhanced by a powerful and effective vocabulary. Children first need an adequate repertoire of words with which to communicate meanings, but they must also acquire an accu-

[19]Roger Brown and Jean Berko, "Word Associations and the Acquisition of Grammar," *Child Development*, 31 (1960), 1–14.
[20]Paula Menyuk, *The Acquisition and Development of Language* (Englewood Cliffs, N.J.: Prentice-Hall, 1971), p. 179.

rate set of criteria for selecting just the right words in particular situations. Having the first criterion without the second does not lend itself to a powerful communication code. A child with a big vocabulary can sometimes impress people with words, but this does not guarantee effective communication. But a child who has an adequate vocabulary for her age and uses words appropriately with the persons and situations she meets will likely be judged an effective communicator. The vocabulary component of a communication code is important for saying what we mean.

An effective vocabulary seems to be a necessary component of two specific communication talents of the child: expressing emotions (affection or hostility) to peers and adults and taking the lead with peers. If children are to express their feelings to important persons in their lives, they should have a vocabulary capable of communicating these feelings. While nonverbal cues will certainly play an important role in emotional messages, emotions can be vividly and clearly presented with the right words. Likewise, the task of leading others, as in giving instructions, requires a careful choice of words. A powerful vocabulary allows children to accomplish important purposes.

Relating children's vocabulary development to their development of personal powers, the notion of *listener-adaptation* seems critical, as well. In adapting their messages to others, they must select just the words to express exactly what they mean, but they must use words that their listener will understand. In getting along with peers, family members and teachers, children must learn to select the words which best express their ideas, needs, and reactions, but their vocabulary must be appropriate to the factors of the communication situation (participants, topic, task, and setting). Because of listener-adaptation, children are able to relate to others, while at the same time, develop autonomy. In their search to become better able to take care of themselves, they must be able to relate effectively to others through their communication with them.

SUMMARY

In the single-word-sentence stage of language development, children communicate about their regularly recurring experiences using substantive and function forms. The substantive class contains names of persons as well as names of familiar objects. Often these objects or persons are the focus of a demand, and, thus, these single words are better called "wanting words." The same principle applies to function forms, such as "up," "more," and "no": the child again uses a single word to communicate a need.

In building a repertoire of words children expand their verbal horizon by associating features of various referent situations to a word. In a chain complex, children use the same word for successively related situations, while in the associative complex, they relate several situations through their similar features and use the same word for all the situations. Extending the vocabulary through such chaining probably accounts for what others perceive as overextensions in children's use of words.

Word meanings and concepts are refined as the child ages. Relatively simple meanings for words such as "older," "same," "it," and "there" change into more complex meanings. A study of vocabulary growth must also center on changes of word meanings within the vocabulary.

The making of definitions for words requires children to use metalanguage, words that talk about words. Children first define words verbally in terms of their concrete actions. For example, a bowl is "where I eat my cereal from." Next, children define words in terms of the sentence context in which they use them, so that an eight-year-old might define a bowl as "a thing that holds my cereal or soup." Finally, at the dictionary level of definition making (about age twelve), children are capable of defining words in terms of their semantic properties. For example, a bowl is a "container in which food may be placed or eaten."

SUGGESTED READINGS

BROWN, ROGER, *A First Language: The Early Stages*, pp. 168–201. Cambridge: Harvard University Press, 1973.

BLOOM, LOIS, *One Word At A Time*, pp. 1–141. The Hague: Mouton, 1973.

BLOOM, LOIS, ed., *Readings in Language Development*, pp. 1–30, 129–65. New York: John Wiley, 1978.

6

children's syntactic development

The utterances of children have a special quality that tells us children follow unique schemes in putting words together into sentences. The children who produced the following sentences thought they were perfectly all right:

Gregory: What today is, Jeff? Monday?
Wayne: What we're having for dessert?
Corrie: Why he's pushing her like that?

All of these children are using a simple pattern of question making that they acquire early in stage 3 of their syntactic development. The rules of this pattern are something like this: to ask a question, start with the wh-word ("what" or "why") and continue with the statement for which you want an answer (for example, "today is _____"). While we know the rule of inverting the subject and helping verb, young children early in their grammatical development follow a set of rules that do not require that inversion.

Now consider these two sentences, which also include features that are unique in a child's grammar:

Jeffrey: My friend Jimmy comed over this afternoon.
Susie: I can read the calendar—today's the twenty-twoth.

Both of these children are producing forms that adults would not employ, "comed" and "twenty-twoth." But a common-sense examination of Jeffrey's sentence reveals that he is using a standard procedure for forming the past tense of an irregular verb ("Today I come, yesterday I com*ed*"). In addition, Susie is using a standard procedure in forming an adjective from a counting number: most conversions simply require adding "th," as in fourth, fifth, sixth, and so on. So, twenty-two becomes "twenty-twoth." While we would not use the forms employed by Jeffrey and Susie, they are typical of child-grammar forms in stage 5 of syntactic development.

Children learn the syntax of their language when they learn to understand and produce multiple-word utterances. They learn the basic structures necessary for effective communication, as well as the more complex structures that allow the communication of more complex meanings. While children have acquired most of the basic syntactic structures by the time they enter kindergarten, their syntactic learning does not stop at this time. Instead, children struggle with more complex aspects of syntax as they advance through their elementary-school years.

The importance of syntax in children's development of communication is enormous. Children's ability to combine words properly and effectively into sentences that express what they mean determines how well they function in their families, peer groups, and schools. In the discussion in Chapter 1 of the requirements for personal power we noted two essential behaviors:

1. Children must learn to direct their own activities, take care of their basic needs, and get along in their daily lives. If they are to achieve these goals, their messages must be clearly stated and adapted to others.
2. Children must express their needs, feelings, and ideas in an orderly and acceptable manner. ,

Both of these requirements for the healthy development of children include a belief that our expression must conform to standards. The form of our sentences must be orderly, acceptable, clear, and adaptive. These qualities are certainly considerations in the study of syntax, for word order and arrangement could theoretically take several forms. Our syntactic choices, however, are guided by rules and procedures that are considered standard by the language models in the community.

Before outlining the several stages of the child's development of syntax, let's consider the operating principles that underlie children's learning of their language.

OPERATING PRINCIPLES

Children learn the syntax of their language in a rather predictable way: certain forms are acquired before others, and the general pattern of development is constant. In fact, Dan Slobin examined about forty languages and found that the rate and development of structures to express ideas is comparable among them. The results of his investigation led to the publication of an article in which he outlined a set of operating principles that explain children's learning of their language.[1] Some of these principles are strategies for giving utterances a sensible thrust (semantic coherence), while others deal with more superficial aspects such as word order. These operating principles set the foundation for syntactic development: they outline the general strategies that children the world over use in their struggle to master the form and use of language. Now let's examine six operating principles that Slobin identified in his article.

principle 1: pay attention to the ends of words

One of the first principles operating in children's acquisition of grammar is based on the importance of word endings. Children learn to direct their attention to information contained at the ends of words. They hear the difference between cookie and cookies and between climb and climbed. Information at the ends of words is acquired in a meaningful context: children will equate flea and fleas but not free and freeze.

principle 2: pay attention to the order of words and morphemes

Before children produce utterances similar in specific form to those of adults, their more modest utterances have a word order that resembles that used by adults. While a three-year-old child may not say, "The cowboy just fell off of his trusty horse," she may say, "Cowboy fall down horsie," retaining the order of the basic content words in the more mature-sounding sentence. In addition, children sometimes incorrectly interpret the word order of sentences. Fraser, Bellugi, and Brown suggest, for example, that children interpret passive sentences (such as "The cowboy was pushed by his horse") in an actor-action-receiver strategy, using the order in which words are mentioned to interpret the meaning of the sentence.[2] Thus, preschoolers will certainly say that the cowboy is doing the pushing in this case. Only with more experience will they realize that the passive-verb construction suggests a reverse order of actor and receiver.

Word-order processing in children is also the reason R. F. Cromer offers for why children misinterpret an utterance like "Barbie is easy to see" (they say a blindfolded Barbie is not "easy to see"): they judge the first

---

[1]Dan I. Slobin, "Cognitive Prerequisites for the Development of Grammar," in *Readings in Language Development*, ed. Lois Bloom (New York: John Wiley, 1978), 407–32.

[2]C. Fraser, U. Bellugi, and R. Brown, "Control of Grammar in Imitation, Comprehension, and Production," *Journal of Verbal Behavior*, 2 (1963), 121–35.

content word, "Barbie," as the subject-actor and are strongly influenced by the blindfold.[3] The children don't realize that the real subject is the person looking at the doll. By seven years or so, children have adjusted their strategy for interpreting this type of sentence.

principle 3: avoid interruption or rearrangement of linguistic units

When children first learn to use wh-type questions (questions beginning with what, where, or when), they may simply attach the wh-element to a basic sentence:

Where I can go?
What we are eating for lunch?
Why she has no shoes?

They learn later to invert the subject and auxiliary verb to complete the interrogative function. Children may continue to preserve a basic order of the words that follow the wh-element well into their elementary-school years before they begin to use the more subtle rules by which word order is changed. When these children combine clauses into sentences they retain the order of elements within each:

I don't know/where's the bat.
You know/what color is this?

Older children will understand that they must switch the word order in the embedded question ("Where's the bat?") in order to incorporate its meaning into the new assertion ("I don't know where the bat is.").

principle 4: underlying semantic relations should be marked overtly and clearly

The more clearly we mark our semantic intentions, the easier it will be for others to understand what we mean. Note these instances of overt marking that are typical of children:

1. Use of the full form "I will . . ." rather than the contracted form "I'll . . ." or "will not" instead of "won't."
2. Use of what is called nominal-pronomination reduplication. This seems to be an overt marking technique for the sentence subject:

[3]R. F. Cromer, "'Children Are Nice to Understand': Surface Structure Clues for the Recovery of a Deep Structure," *British Journal of Psychology*, 61 (1970), 397–408.

"My sister, she gots red hair."
"My neighbor across the street, he drives a truck."

Likewise, children have an easier time understanding utterances that are clearly marked for grammar. For example, while children may misinterpret "Promise John to come on time," they may have no trouble understanding the more overtly marked form "Promise John that you will come on time."

principle 5: avoid exceptions

The classic example of this principle is the child's development of past-tense forms. The learning progression is something like this: (1) break (no marking), (2) broke (often appropriate), (3) breaked (an overgeneralized marking that follows child rules), (4) breakted (an overgeneralized and redundant marking that again uses child rules), and (5) broke (adult form). That children produce such forms as "twoth" for second and "goed" and "makt" for "went" and "made" illustrates that they apply rules of grammar in a very *consistent* and *predictable* fashion. Only with greater experience do they realize that exceptions are abundant in English.

principle 6: the use of grammatical markers should make semantic sense

Children's tendency to use markers in a consistent, sensible way leads them to mark plurals even when they don't differ from singulars (for example, "sheeps"), mark all plurals regularly ("childz" for children"), mark an irregular, already marked verb ("woked," as in "I just woked up"), or make sure that a comparative is being signaled ("more funer"). Aspects of grammar such as agreement and inflectional rules offer opportunities for children to follow rules of some type. Selections they make show children's awareness of regularities in language that relate to meanings.

With a basic understanding of these six operating principles, the stages of syntactic development may appear as a rather sensible progression. The framework of syntactic development that most influenced the outline presented below is that offered in a landmark book by Roger Brown.[4] The following stages are explained more fully in this chapter:

Stage 1. *Basic relations:* Eight basic utterance patterns characterize children's first stage of syntactic development: at least two words are combined to produce each of these eight major meanings.

Stage 2. *Modulated relations:* With the addition of fourteen grammatical morphemes, children's utterances grow in length and complexity.

[4]Roger Brown, *A First Language: The Early Stages* (Cambridge: Harvard University Press), 1973, pp. 168–98.

Stage 3. *Simple sentence modalities:* Once children have acquired the basic noun and verb phrases with which to form a simple sentence, they acquire other modalities, such as questions and negatives.

Stage 4. *Advanced sentence modalities:* More advanced structures, such as indirect questions, relative clauses, and coordinated structures, are acquired.

Stage 5. *Categorization:* Children refine their sentences with a more particular choice of words, reflecting a complex system of categorizing word types.

Stage 6. *Complex structures:* Structures involving complex syntactic relationships are mastered last.

Table 6.2 at the end of this chapter provides a series of illustrations of syntactic patterns being developed in each of these six stages of syntactic development.

STAGE 1: BASIC RELATIONS

In principle, one-word utterances are distinct from the multiple-word utterances produced in the first stage of syntactic development. However, children do occasionally produce multiple-word utterances during their one-word period. Some researchers claim that these early multiple-word utterances are better thought of as double "words," because it seems that children have learned the two words as a single unit. For example, while many parents consider "kittycat," "allgone," and "go bye-bye," as two- or even three-word sentences, most experts in children's language agree that these utterances contain only one "word" each.

A research team who visited children every week during the transition period from one- to two-word utterances found that after a child first produced ten different multiple-word utterances during a seventy-five-minute visit, the number of sentences per visit steadily increased.[5] It seems that the child takes off slowly but then develops rapidly once this syntactic production begins.

That children understand multiple-word language before they use even two-word sentences is a generalization no linguist would argue with. However, one might ask how strong the understanding of two-word instructions is by children who produce only one-word utterances. Does the understanding of two-word instructions precede the use of two-word utterances? Two researchers set out to test children's comprehension of certain two-word instructions, many of which were what they called "unusual"—for example, "tickle book," "smell truck," and "kiss ball."[6] Now if children do understand

---

[5]Susan Starr, "The Relation of Single Words to Two-Word Sentences," *Child Development*, 46 (1975), 702.

[6]Jacqueline Sachs and Lynn Truswell, "Comprehension of Two-Word Instructions by Children in the One-Word Stage," *Journal of Child Language*, 5 (February 1978), 17–24.

two-word instructions requiring such unlikely actions, then we have solid evidence for their ability to understand two-word instructions in general. The children in the study carried out some of the unusual instructions correctly, showing that they were able to respond to the structure itself. While we could have expected that they would successfully carry out familiar instructions, such as "throw ball" or "pat teddy," their ability to perform successfully with unusual instructions gives evidence of their ability to decode syntax in the speech of others before they produce such structures themselves.

Roger Brown followed the language development of three children on a week-by-week basis for a period of several years. Sometime around eighteen months of age, children begin to put words together into sentences. At this point, according to Brown, two-morpheme meanings develop. (A morpheme is a minimal unit of meaning.) These "major meanings" are composite meanings and not just the result of two word meanings joined together. A major meaning, then, is a basic-sentence meaning. There are eight major meanings that children around two years of age express:

MAJOR MEANING	EXAMPLES
1. agent and action	"Mommy laugh."
	"Doggie bark."
	"Billy cry."
2. action and object	"Hit car."
	"Push door."
	"Hug baby."
3. agent and object	"Daddy car."
	"Kitty ball."
	"Wendy bike."
4. action and locative (or location)	"Fall down."
	"Eat highchair."
5. entity and locative (or location)	"Daddy home."
	"Mailman here."
6. possessor and possession	"Kari teddy."
	"Mommy dress."
	"Suzy duckie."
7. entity and attribute	"Silly doggie."
	"Pretty Mommy."
8. demonstrative and entity	"That car-car."
	"These cereals."
	"This one."

Let's check for a moment the definitions of the terms in the list above:

1. *agent:* someone or something capable of causing an action or process, such as "Mommy" or "doggie"

2. *object:* usually something receiving the force of an action or a change of state, such as "door"

3. *action:* a perceived movement, as in "hit"

4. *locative:* place or locus of an action, as in "down"

5. *entity:* any thing or person having a distinct existence, such as "mailman" in "mailman here"

6. *possessor:* usually a person who owns something or has prior rights of use for it, as "Kari" in "Kari teddy"

7. *possession:* usually an object thought to belong to someone, as "teddy" in "Kari teddy"

8. *attribute:* a quality of an entity, such as "silly" or "pretty"

9. *demonstrative:* a word pointing to a certain thing or person, as in *"that* car"

Note that children's stage-1 utterances incorporate a word order that an adult would use to convey the basic relationship. This ordering clearly follows operating principle 2: pay attention to the order of words and morphemes. We would say the possessor before saying the possession, for example, and so would the child. Children from many different parts of the world express the basic relations inherent in the major meanings listed above. Brown found these relations to exist in languages such as French, German, Finnish, Samoan, Luo (a language spoken in Kenya), and a Mayan language spoken in Guatemala, as well as English. This rather small set of basic relations accounts for about 70 percent of children's utterances in stage 1, a time at which the average length of an utterance is two words or less. When a category that one researcher calls statives is included in the set, nearly 93 percent of children's two-word utterances are accounted for.[7] Stative verbs do not refer to a perceived movement but describe the effect an entity has on an animate object (in 95 percent of the cases the child is the animate object). Most of Starr's statives consisted of "want" plus an object desired—for example, "Want milk," "Want juice," and "Want cookie."

Why does the child in the first stage of syntactic development talk in these eight or nine basic patterns? An explanation that is used very frequently by language-development theorists draws heavily from the writings of Piaget. Jill and Peter de Villiers, for example, contend that

> Piaget . . . would allow that the eighteen-month-old infant can distinguish agents from objects of action and can recognize recurrence and identity and location. Piaget regards these concepts and distinctions as the culmination of the sensorimotor period of intelligence, which ends at around eighteen months of age. The child in the first year of life is preoccupied with objects, the results of his actions, and the stability of objects over time and place.[8]

In short, objects, actions, and locations seem to be among the major focuses of young children. The differences of opinion regarding stage 1 relate to the

---

[7]Starr, "The Relation of Single Words to Two-Word Sentences," p. 703.

[8]Jill G. de Villiers and Peter de Villiers, *Language Acquisition* (Cambridge: Harvard University Press, 1978), p. 75.

issue of how broad or how narrow the semantic categories should be. For example, for the utterance "Kari hit teddy," Brown's guidelines would suggest a description something like this: agent, action, and object. Why don't we use a set of categories that are defined more specifically, such as human actor, physical action, and receiver of physical action? On the other hand, Brown's categories might be too specific an account of what the child thinks about in the creation of utterances. In any case, many writers conclude that an approach centering on basic relations best describes what young children sound like and why their utterances might be syntactically arranged in these typical basic patterns.

STAGE 2: MODULATED RELATIONS

The next stage of syntactic development assumes that children have acquired the basic relations and can even combine them into slightly more complex and longer strings of words. For example, a child who has acquired the agent-and-action relation as well as the action-and-object one can then produce utterances that combine these two basic patterns:

agent and action + action and object = agent and action and object: Susie play + Play blocks = Susie play blocks.

In this second stage of syntactic development, utterances such as "Susie play blocks" are altered to include the nuances of meaning and expression Brown calls *modulation*. The changes add less in information than in what Brown calls fine tuning. For example, the utterance "Susie play blocks" could represent a broad range of sentence patterns:

1. Susie is playing blocks.
2. Susie played blocks.
3. Susie was playing blocks.
4. Susie has played blocks.
5. Susie wants to play blocks.
6. Susie will play blocks.

These are among the many possible intentions this stage-1 utterance might have. All six of them assume the child is using "blocks" as a special kind of object-game—in this sense "blocks" is similar to "checkers" (as in "Susie is playing checkers"). If this is not the case, we can add several other sentence patterns that might account for Susie's behavior:

7. Susie is playing with the blocks.
8. Susie played with blocks.
9. Susie will play with her blocks.

Our list could go on and on.

Stage 2 in syntax development begins with the notion that children wish to communicate more specific intent in their sentences to disambiguate meanings a bit. The context of their communication can help do this. If we overheard a child refer to Susie playing with blocks, we would know whether the reference was to action past, future action, or some statement about what is happening now. Stage-2 children seem to pay attention to the ends of words (operating principle 1) and thus reproduce word endings frequently in their speech:

"I be go*ing*."
"I want two candies."

In addition, they follow operating principle 4 religiously, marking their semantic relations overtly and clearly. The sole purpose of stage 2 is the acquistion of grammatical morphemes that allow for specification of elements of grammar such as tense, number, and location.

When children begin to adapt their sentences more carefully to the needs of other persons, the length of these sentences grow from two to as many as seven morphemes. The filling out of sentences is done primarily by the incorporation of one or more of the fourteen grammatical morphemes listed below.[9] Though we introduce these morphemes in stage 2, some children do not fully master morphemes at the end of the list until they are in the final stages of syntactic development. The morphemes are presented in the general order in which they are acquired.

GRAMMATICAL MORPHEME	EXAMPLES (RELEVANT PORTIONS ITALICIZED)
1. present-progressive verb ending	"Billy cry*ing*."
	"Mommy eat*ing*."
2. the prepositions "in" and "on"	"Sitting *on* potty."
3.	"Playing *in* sand."
4. plural endings	"Hide eye*s*."
	"Play block*s*."

(continued)

[9]The list is adapted from Brown, *A First Language*, pp. 259–73.

GRAMMATICAL MORPHEME	EXAMPLES (RELEVANT PORTIONS ITALICIZED)
5. past irregular verbs ("came," "fell," "broke," "sat," and "went" are used most frequently)	"Daddy *came* home." "Billy *went* to the potty."
6. possessives	"Mommy*'s* purse." "See Teddy*'s* eyes."
7. uncontractible copula	"What *is* this?" "Mommy *is* silly."
8. articles	"*The* baby is crying." "Teddy has *a* hat."
9. past-regular tense endings	"I lift*ed* the plate." "Billy carri*ed* it."
10. third-person-regular tense ending	"She carri*es* her teddy." "He pat*s* the doggie."
11. third-person-irregular endings	"Mom go*es* shopping." "He sit*s* down."
12. uncontractible auxiliary	"The baby *is* crying." "Mom *is* going away."
13. contractible copula	"What*'s* this?" "Mom*'s* silly."
14. contractible auxiliary	"The baby*'s* crying." "Mom*'s* going away."

Our discussion of children's acquisition of these stage-2 morphemes focuses only on English. Other languages contain methods for expressing the same meanings. However, a discussion of these devices is not possible in the limited space of this chapter.

Notice the greater maturity of the sentences in the list above. Words are incorporated into the rather telegraphic two-word major meanings from Stage 1, and the result is the communication of more precise adapted meanings. Brown calls this process modulation because children are now capable of filling out the core idea with less ambiguous statements.

Before children can use one or more of the grammatical morphemes in their communication with others they must be able to distinguish them in the speech of others. While tense endings, prepositions, and articles are not stressed in adult speech, either in terms of volume or through phrasing, children must sense their presence in speech enough to learn that they have special purposes. The basis for the acquisition of grammatical morphemes is a process called *segmentation*, the dividing of the stream of speech into meaningful segments. Utterances have a continuous flow of sound and do not, as many people believe, contain breaks or brief silences between words. Children must learn to break apart the stream of speech into the appropriate units. In stage 1 of syntactic development, a child may segment an utterance into a few large chunks. For example, the utterance "I watched the program on TV" might be segmented as "I/watch/TV." Stage-2 segmentation is much more complex, particularly if the child is advanced in the acquisition of the grammatical morphemes: "I/watch/-ed past tense/the/program/on/TV." In this case the child hears seven meaning units compared with the three in stage 1.

A discussion of segmentation has to include the possibility of errors, as well. When I was a child I heard a story about the hymn "Gladly the Cross I'd Bear." I remember chuckling about how easy it would be to improperly hear this phrase (actually, segment its word boundaries incorrectly) as "Gladly, the cross-eyed bear." Some typical examples of children's improper segmentation are contained in these utterances:

It'sa hurting the dolly.

Emme see it.

I'ma gonna do it now.

The examples are "it'sa," "I'ma" "gonna," and "emme" (or "lemme"). Why do children produce lumped-together words such as "hafta"? It seems likely that these segmentations are due to lumping (sloppy but accepted articulation) by adults.

Because they can segment speech, children hear past-tense endings such as /-d/, /-t/, and /-id/. Verb endings involve complex morphophonemic rules, and children produce correctly generalized and overgeneralized forms of past-tense verbs. Children may use the /-d/ ending correctly in "played" and "drained," but they may also say "torned" and "knowed." They may use the /-t/ tense ending for "slipped" and "kicked" but then say, "I just fliptid this coin," as if they want to make sure they have added something for past tense.

Why are the grammatical morphemes acquired in the particular order in which they are listed above? Are certain forms, such as the contractible be-copula (as in "he's hot"), more complex than other forms, such as the possessive (as in Mom's coat)? Are the earlier acquired morphemes produced with greater frequency by parents and adults and so learned faster by children? Brown found no evidence that parental frequencies of use of the morphemes influence the order of development. Instead, he offers two other explanations that seem to account for the order of development: semantic complexity and grammatical complexity.[10] Counting the number of grammatical transformations and the number of distinct meanings conveyed by each form, Brown was able to provide statistical evidence that the acquisition order has roots in language complexity. For example, the be-copula form requires more "linguistic work" than the possessive form. Brown cautions the student of language development about the variability of acquisition, however. Some children acquire the grammatical morphemes in a fairly

[10]See Brown, *A First Language*, pp. 368–79.

short time, but others are still learning the later grammatical morphemes in their fifth stage of syntactic development, as late as five or six years of age.

STAGE 3: SIMPLE SENTENCE MODALITIES

One of the results of stage-2 syntax development is the ability to produce sentences of up to seven words in length. These longer sentences are far more explicit in their reference. While the two-year-old child first produces sentences of a single noun and a single verb and then expands these sentences by including the grammatical morphemes, the older child further expands the constituents of the noun phrase and verb phrase. Before children are able to produce more advanced structures, such as sentences employing relative clauses, they must more firmly assimilate the phrase structures of their language, such as noun and verb phrases. Our discussion of stage 3 begins with an explanation of the development of noun and verb phrases as precursors to children's mastery of the operational changes necessary for forming sentences, as for example, word inversion essential in forming questions.

Roger Brown and his colleagues found that young children typically produce four types of noun phrases in two basic sentence types:[11]

animate

· object
inanimate

The girl hugged her teddy bear. *Object noun phrase modified*
1 *transitive* 2

The teddy bear is soft and furry. *predicate Nominative*
Subj. noun phrase *intransitive*
3 4

Noun phrase 1 is the subject of the transitive-verb sentence, while noun phrase 3 is the subject of the intransitive-verb sentence. Noun phrase 2 is an object and noun phrase 4 a predicate nominative. The researchers discovered certain generalizations about the ways in which children use noun phrases. First, the pronoun, such as "that" or "it," can substitute for the subject of the copular ("to be"/"is") sentences but not for their object. Second, type-1 noun phrases (the subject of a transitive sentence) are usually animate ("the girl"), while type-2 noun phrases (the object) are usually inanimate ("teddy bear"). Third, children modify object noun phrases earlier than subject noun phrases.

Expansion of verb phrases takes on a slightly different character. In addition to the use of inflectional endings, such as third-person singular and

[11]Roger Brown, Courtney Cazden, and Ursula Bellugi, "The Child's Grammar From 'I to III,'" in *Minnesota Symposium on Child Psychology,* Vol. 2, ed. J. P. Hill (Minneapolis: University of Minnesota Press, 1969), 28–73.

simple past tense, children must learn to add auxiliaries such as "will" and "can." Forms such as "wanna," "gonna," and "hafta" are abundant in three-year-olds' speech. With experience and practice, children acquire the negative forms with auxiliaries, as in "don't" and "can't." The positive forms, such as "do" or "can" appear later, followed by forms such as "doesn't." In imperative sentences children rarely produce auxiliaries and inflections improperly or out of place: they might say "Please tie my lace," but they would not say "Please tying it" or "Please will tie."

questions

At this stage of syntactic development, questions such as these are altered operationally and adult forms are mastered:

> "Mom, you will go on these?"
> "Do you know what day is it?"
> "What color it is?"

Questions include an implied proposition—"tell me." When we ask a question, then, we combine "tell me" and an assertion, such as "the baby is crying," with some interrogative marking of that assertion. Thus, our question is: (Tell me) "Is the baby crying?" Actually, there are two basic types of questions that children acquire. Here are some examples of each (the underlying assertion is in parentheses):

Yes/no questions

> "Is she making my lunch?" (She is making my lunch.)
> "Did the baby cry?" (The baby cried.)

Wh-questions

> "What can we feed her?" (We can feed her something.)
> "Where did the policeman drive?" (The policeman drove somewhere.)
> "Who took my crayons?" (Someone took my crayons.)

Questions 1a and 1b are yes/no questions because their user expects either a "yes" or a "no" answer. To form question 1, the child must learn to invert the subject and auxiliary verb. Because there is no auxiliary (such as "be," "have," or "can") in question 1b, the child must learn to add some form of "do"—in this case the past form "did." Rising intonation is used at the end of yes/no questions.

Questions 2a–2c are called wh-questions because they begin with an interrogative word such as "who," "what," or "where." Inversion of subject and auxiliary is again necessary when the wh-element is at the end of the underlying assertion ("something" and "somewhere" in 2a and 2b, respectively). When the potential wh-element is at the beginning of the underlying assertion ("someone" in 2c), inversion is not necessary. All wh-questions consist of a wh-word placed in front of a transformed assertion.

Now let's consider three stages in the child's development of questions.[12]

Stage 1: The use of rising pitch and wh-words. Yes/no questions at this early stage consist of an underlying assertion spoken with rising pitch to show the interrogation. For example, "Bobby eat?" and "Go outside?" are questions because the child raises the pitch of his voice in uttering the words. Wh-questions at this stage simply attach a wh-word to an assertion—for instance, "Where Dougie truck?" The most prominent wh-questions at this stage are "where" and "what" questions, which also make up a large percentage of the questions parents ask their children. Operating principle #3—avoid interruption or rearrangement of linguistic units—characterizes this stage of development.

Stage 2: The use of a greater variety of wh-questions. Children at this stage add "why" questions to the repertoire of wh-questions and seem to use "what" questions more frequently and with greater accuracy. Although "why" questions tend to be interpreted as either "what" or "where" questions, the child has expanded the wh-question repertoire significantly. Inversion is still not done for either wh-questions or yes/no questions. As in stage 1, rising pitch is used to signal the yes/no question.

Stage 3. The use of inversion. Children at this stage of development regularly invert the subject and verb of an underlying assertion in order to produce a yes/no question:

"Can I have a cookie?"
"Will you help me?"

Children still have trouble with other elements of grammar, such as tense and number of the auxiliary:

"Did you found the candy?"

Wh-questions seem to lag behind yes/no questions in their acquisition by children. At this stage, the inversion that produces a wh-question develops

[12]Our discussion of interrogatives and negatives is based on Herbert H. Clark and Eve V. Clark, *Psychology and Language: An Introduction to Psycholinguistics* (New York: Harcourt, Brace, Jovanovich, 1977), pp. 347–54.

over a longer period of time than inversion for the easier yes/no questions. Some studies have concluded that inversion in positive wh-questions may be easier for children than inversion in negative wh-questions:

"What can I do next?" (positive wh-question)
"Why I can't do that too?" (negative wh-question)

By this stage, the operating principle most critical to structural usage is the fourth one—underlying semantic relations should be marked overtly and clearly. In addition to wh-words, which clearly mark questions in all three stages, children use word inversion to signal a question. They follow operating principle 3 when they fail to invert the subject and auxiliary, as in this stage-3 question:

"What he can have for dessert?"

Eventually, children add to their interrogative repertoire the tag question, a structure that assumes a number of key operating principles. Here are two sample tag questions:

"She rides fast, doesn't she?"
"He isn't being bad, is he?"

Though children use questions as early as two years of age, it is not until the age of four or later that children are capable of producing tag questions. Why are tag questions so difficult? If you were to trace all of the transformations necessary in changing an assertion into a tag question, you would see that complexity is the main reason.[13] First, inversion is necessary in the tag portion, which is attached to the assertion. The pronouns must always be matched, as they were in the examples above. The "do" auxiliary must be added to the tag, and a correct form employed. The affirmative assertion must be negated ("She rides fast, doesn't she?") and the negative affirmed ("He *isn't* being bad, *is* he?"). Then, the subject and auxiliary must be inverted. No wonder this type of question comes late in the child's development of syntactic structures.

negatives

As with questions, negatives are acquired in about three separate stages. Typical negatives contain "no" or "not," although negatives can be signaled in many other ways by the use of words (such as "off" or "allgone") or gestures (for example, shaking the head). Some theorists suggest that

[13]See de Villiers and de Villiers, *Language Acquisition*, pp. 107–10.

children acquire three semantic forms of negation: nonpresence ("Mitten allgone"), rejection ("No wear mitten"), and denial ("No mitten there").

Stage 1: Attachment of the negative.   A "no" or "not" is usually placed in front of a positive assertion, which is often called the "nucleus":

> "Not him go there."
> "No he fall down."

The operating principle playing a key role in this stage of negation development is again the third one—avoid interrupting the nucleus with the negative word.

Stage 2: Incorporation of the negative.   With greater usage of negatives, children begin to incorporate the negative word into the assertion:

> "Spot no bite you."
> "That not mine."

In addition, children in stage 2 begin to use "can't" and "don't" as negative forms. They do not use them as combinations of the auxiliary and the negative, but seem to incorporate them into assertions as unitary negatives:

> "You can't catch me."
> "I don't want that."

"No," "not," "can't," and "don't" are used similarly, and are typically placed inside the positive assertion at this stage of negation development. Operating principle 4, the clear and overt marking of semantic intentions, seems most obvious here.

Stage 3: The mastering of basic rules of negation.   When children use both positive and negative forms of auxiliaries, the negative system seems to be complete in its basic elements:

> "It's not loud enough."
> "I not hurt him."
> "He won't do it now."
> "You can't have it."

Because children place "not" in *all* sentences they want to say in a negative form, they also produce sentences like these:

"I'm not doing nothing."
"I don't got no money."

Operating principle 6—avoid exceptions—characterizes children's across-the-board placement of negatives inside assertions. The acquisition of negatives, as with the development of questions, seems to span about two years.

STAGE 4: ADVANCED SENTENCE MODALITIES

At this stage of development of their grammar, children use sentence structures that combine propositions in a number of unique ways. Three advanced sentence structures are discussed in this section:

1. *Complementation:* "She drove to visit the dentist."
2. *Relativization:* "The dentist that I know best is my uncle."
3. *Coordination:* "The dentist cleaned my teeth but I wasn't scared."

Each of these structures is discussed briefly in terms of the developmental processes children go through.

complementation

Although there are several types of complement structures in English, we will focus on the simpler forms that children learn in their early years. Consider the following sentences which serve as examples (complements italicized):

"I want *to buy a tootsie pop.*"
"Remember *how we sneaked up on her?*"
"Show me *where you got that.*"

In each of these sentences, the main portion of the sentence is coupled with a clause that in some way modifies the verb. Probably the easiest complement structure for children includes the verb "want":

"I want to go outside."
"I want her to tie my shoe."

The first complement structures children use with the verb "want" tend to have the same subject for the main verb and the complement:

"I want to go home." (rather than "I want her to go home.")

By age three, children use several verbs—want, hope, make, guess, like, show, remember—with complements. The rule for detecting the subject of the complement of many English verbs is this: find the subject closest to the left of the complement verb.[14] Consider these examples:

"I'll show you how to play it." (subject of complement: "you")
"Lookit the kid throwin' the ball." (subject of complement: kid)
"Try to guess how many I'm holding" (subject of complement: "I")

Children mark many of their complement constructions with "to" or "what":

"I want *to* get outa here."
"I remember *what* to do next."

But when the subject of the complement is different from the subject of the main verb, children do not follow the operating principle of marking the complement overtly. Instead, they omit the marker:

"I want you fixin' my shoe."

Consider one complement-structure that causes difficulty for even seven-year-olds: the complement-sentence including a transformed question.

"I wonder what they are." (referring to certain objects in an array of objects)

It would not be uncommon for the child to produce the complement structure with the question-clause attached in a form which is not transformed for use in an assertion:

"I wonder what are they."

With greater experience in dealing with both advanced sentence modalities, such as the complement, as well as the inversion operation necessary for implanting questions into assertions, children begin to sound adultlike in their advanced structures.

relativization

In relativization a proposition is combined with a part of another proposition. Relative clauses can restrict, or qualify, the meaning of a portion of a sentence. For example, by placing the clause "The ducks were wet" into the

---

[14]This rule does not apply to a number of English verbs that are learned in the final stage of syntactic development, such as "ask" and "promise."

proposition "The duck quacked," we create the following sentence, which utilizies a relative clause:

The ducks *that were wet* quacked.

Any of the relative pronouns "who," "which," or "that" can introduce a relative clause in a sentence. However, the relative pronoun does not have to be used:

She caught the butterfly we were chasing.

Note that in the sentence about the ducks the relative clause interrupts the main clause, while in the butterfly sentence the relative clause follows. On the basis of operating principle 3—avoid interrupting the order of words—these differences in ordering should result in different levels of understanding in young children: those relatives marked overtly and without interruption should be easier for children to understand. Research indicates that children's first relative clauses are attached to the end of main clauses:

"I want the one you're holding."
"I like the shoe he's wearing."

Children at this early stage of relativization do not produce utterances like these:

"The one you're holding is better."
"The shoe she's wearing has better grips."

Operating principle 3 may be having such a strong influence at this stage that children are reluctant to break up the word order in any way. In their early relative clauses children use the words "kind," "one," and "thing" frequently:

"See the one I got from there."
"I like the kind you bought yesterday."
"Guess what thing I'm coloring?"

Overt marking of relative clauses is not done at this early stage.

    With time and experience children begin to mark the relative clause with the relative pronoun, "that." However, the other relative pronouns do not appear until six to twelve months later. The children have been following operating principle 3 (no interruptions), and now they begin to mark overtly (operating principle 4). Research in the area of comprehension of relative clauses by four- and five-year-olds indicates that when such clauses are overtly marked, children do much better in understanding the meanings of the sentences.

coordination

Children who are learning to link two propositions with a coordinate conjunction such as "and," "but," "or," or "while" are learning coordination. Consider the following propositions:

I rode my bike.
My friend rode the big wheel.

These two propositions could be coordinated in any of the following ways:

I rode my bike while my friend rode the big wheel.
I rode my bike and my friend rode the big wheel.
I rode my bike but my friend rode the big wheel.

If the subject of both propositions is the same, then we can delete part of one proposition:

I rode my bike and my big wheel.

Some of the evidence from studies of the spontaneous speech of children suggests that they learn reduced coordinations later than complete sentences conjoined by "and."[15] Children who are asked to imitate an adult's coordinated sentence first produce the two components conjoined. For instance, they imitate "The baby cried and hit her head on the crib" as "The baby cried and the baby hit her head on the crib." Here they seem to be following operating principle 4 (marking overtly and clearly one's semantic intentions).

Coordination is a complex process for combining sentences. Children's attempts to coordinate sentences sometimes have results like these:

"We didn't get anything to eat, either something to drink at the party."
"Before we go into our room we first gotta line up real straight."

The first child seems to be trying an either-or construction, but the result has "either" where "or" is usually placed and no coordinator introducing the sentence. In the second example, which involves a before-after sequence, the initial segment is overtly marked with "first," a strategy typical of young children.

---

[15]See de Villiers and de Villiers, *Language Acquisition*, pp. 110–11.

STAGE 5: CATEGORIZATION

The categorization stage begins in the late preschool years and continues through the early elementary years. A five-year-old child uses sentences that show an understanding of noun phrases, verb phrases, and complex adverbial clauses. The kindergarten child produces complete sentences that incorporate more sophisticated use of word classes—for instance, nouns, pronouns, adverbs, and adjectives. As members of each word class multiply, however, the child begins to realize that members of a word class are not alike in all respects. Further *categorization* of the words within word classes is necessary. For example, nouns become either singular ("child") or plural ("children"). Categorization of a word as a singular or plural dictates the proper selection of a determiner and verb to use with the noun:

That *child* is happy. (singular)
Those *children* are happy. (plural)

Using a singular for a plural form, though not extremely common among children, certainly does occur:

"Both child crying, Mom."

Children may also confuse the singular and plural auxiliary forms:

"He haves a dog."

Some nouns are mass nouns ("milk") and others are count nouns ("toy"). Selection of the appropriate determiner depends on how a noun is categorized:

She has some *milk*. (mass noun)
She has some (many) *toys*. (count noun)

Mass/count categorization seems to cause children more difficulties than singular/plural categorization. For example, children may use "money" or "macaroni" as count nouns in a context where a mass noun is appropriate:

"Give me some moneys."
"I want more macaronis."

Verbs are categorized as either transitive (taking a direct object) or intransitive. For instance, "make" is transitive and "go" is intransitive. Categorization of the verb helps determine whether or not an object is used and which modifiers are appropriate:

Help me *make* it. (transitive)
I *am going* there. (intransitive)

A unique quality of children's speech is the use of intransitive verbs in a transitive fashion:

"I'll win you, Greg."
"Who votes the game raise your hand."

Prepositions are categorized according to time and place so that appropriate use can be made of prepositional phrases:

He slept *during* the game. (time)
He went *to* the game. (place)

Often, however, children produce utterances containing time prepositions instead of place prepositions:

"For recess our teacher taked us at the playground."

Many other categories continue to be refined at this stage of development. Pronouns serve as an interesting example of the developmental process. Children continue to use pronouns when the pronoun referent is also included in the sentence:

"My sister, she gots red hair."

When children produce such *noun-pronoun pleonasms*, they are making certain their utterance is understood by the other person. A study of the frequency of noun-pronoun pleonasms in the speech of seven-, eight-, and nine-year-old children found a steady decrease with age in structures such as these:

"My *sister, she* gots red hair."
"We played English games, *me and Patsy.*"
"She kept running to *us, me and my sister.*"
"Tonight we're gonna have *it, the meat,* for supper."
"My *aunt and uncle, their daughter* is coming."
"*The ranger, he* was wrong, *the ranger at El Vado.*"
"My *mom, she* and my uncle drove *it* home, *the car.*"[16]

[16]Eleanor Cotton, "Noun-Pronoun Pleonasms: The Role of Age and Situation," *Journal of Child Language,* 5 (October 1978), 489–99.

While these utterances are typical of the speech of young children, Cotton found that children rarely engage in such nominal-pronominal reduplication with their peers. It's with adults—parents and teachers—that the incidence of these forms is the greatest. The child may wish to be more informative or specific with adults than with peers.

Another aspect of pronouns that children find puzzling is the number, person, and gender agreement that marks pronoun usage. The results of a study indicate the struggle children go through in their acquisition of pronouns.[17] A child was presented with Barbie-Doll and Ken-Doll cutouts by an experimenter and then asked a number of questions:

1. What are *they* wearing? (meaning Barbie and Ken)
2. What are *we* wearing? (meaning the experimenter and the child)
3. What are *you* wearing?

Children should be able to distinguish the referent or referents of each of these pronouns if they have mastered their meanings. The study found, however, that children frequently mixed up "we" with "I" (losing the number distinction but retaining the first person). Other frequent error patterns included mixing up "he" and "she" (Barbie and Ken), responding to "you" with Ken or Barbie, and responding to "they" with only one of the two dolls. The error pattern that intrigues adults the most is the use of "he" for "she" or the other way around. Children are quite capable at this early age of making distinctions between girls and boys and between men and women. (However, costumes may trick children into an incorrect response: a girl with a baseball uniform and bat may be called a boy by young children.) Still, in everyday utterances of children, not counting tricky situations involving gender, one hears pronouns with incorrect gender, especially from preschool-age children.

Children's acquisition of the rules of categorization comprise the four periods listed below.[18] Paula Menyuk's studies indicate that the process of acquisition is fairly consistent among children and that a striking correspondence exists between age and acquisition period.

Period 1. Nursery-school children frequently omit the word class or modifiers. (ages 3–4)

Period 2. Kindergarten children substitute an inappropriate word class. (age 5)

Period 3. First-grade children use the correct word or modifier redundantly to "insure appropriateness." (age 6)

Period 4. Second-grade children (and older children) use word classes correctly. (age 7+)

---

[17]Jonathan Baron and Anne Kaiser, "Semantic Components in Children's Errors with Pronouns," *Journal of Psycholinguistic Research*, 4, no. 4 (1975), 303–17.

[18]These four periods are adapted from Paula Menyuk, *Sentences Children Use* (Cambridge, Mass.: M.I.T. Press, 1969), pp. 32–52.

Table 6.1 portrays these periods of development within stage 5 for four word classes. The examples in Table 6.1 demonstrate children's increased sensitivity to what linguists call the "context-sensitive" rules of a language. For example, the determiner to be joined to a noun or the preposition to be joined to a noun phrase must *agree* with the noun context. Consequently, prepositions must be sensitive to either time or place, just as determiners must be sensitive to either mass nouns or count nouns. The selection of words within a word class must be based on the linguistic context. Children learn the context-sensitive rules of categorization in their early school years.

Two operating principles have special relevance to stage 5 of syntactic development. The first is that underlying relationships in meaning should be *overtly marked* (principle 4). At this stage of syntactic development, children are struggling to mark number, gender, person, and other aspects of meaning. In doing so they may form hypotheses about the grammatical system they are learning that are simple and straightforward. For example, they may treat all sentences as actor/transitive action/receiver. This leads them to produce sentences like "I'll win you!" Another such hypothesis may lead them to form plurals such as "sheeps," "childz," and "moneys." In these cases children are following the operating principle of using semantic markers that make grammatical sense (principle 6). Children use language markers in a sensible way, though the results may not be adult-like.

STAGE 6: COMPLEX STRUCTURES

Many of the structures of our language are difficult and require careful attention when we use them. These complex structures are the focus of syntactic learning for children between five and ten years of age. To assess whether or not children understand the structural differences among the command, request, and promise verbs, direct methods of research are necessary. Children may produce appropriate utterances for each verb, but they may respond to instances of their use by others in inappropriate ways, signaling an incomplete mastery of the structures. Researchers of stage 6 syntax use indirect and direct-question methods to uncover children's linguistic intuitions regarding these complex forms. Let's examine three verbs that take an object and a complement verb:

1. *Command:* "I told Bill to leave."
2. *Request:* "I asked Bill to leave." "I asked Bill (for permission) to leave."
3. *Promise:* "I promised Bill to leave."

When you use the command verb "told," the complement verb "to leave" relates to Bill, not you. The request verb "ask" relates to either you or Bill,

TABLE 6.1. *The child's development of categorization.*

WORD CLASS	PERIOD 1: OMISSION	PERIOD 2: SUBSTITUTION	PERIOD 3: REDUNDANCY	PERIOD 4: MASTERY
count noun	"The people are there."	"Pretty much people are there."	"Pretty many peoples are there."	"Many people are there."
plural noun	"Both child crying."	"Both childzez are crying."	"Both children, they're crying."	"Both children are crying."
transitive verb	"Help me—the bicycle."	"Help me go the bicycle."	"Help me ride it, the bicycle."	"Help me ride the bicycle."
preposition of place	"Daddy took me circus."	"Daddy took me at the circus."	"Daddy took me there to the circus."	"Daddy took me to the circus."

135

depending on whether the verb "ask" involves a request for permission. The English language has several *command* verbs (for instance, tell, order, force, compel, require) two *request* verbs (ask and beg), but only one *promise* verb. The promise verb is very different from the ask and tell verbs. A sentence with "promise" has a complement verb that relates to the subject of the sentence in the main clause—never to the object. You are the one who must "leave" if the promise is used—not Bill. Linguists call the promise verb an exceptional case in the English language.

Carol Chomsky conducted a series of research studies investigating the more complex structures of English, including the verb "promise." She studied children from five to ten years of age and demonstrated that elementary-school-age children are still acquiring the more complex structures of their language. Let's examine three of the complex structures studied by Chomsky:

1. The doll is *easy to see*.
2. Donald *promises* Bozo to lie down.
3. Mickey Mouse *asks* Bozo to go first.

Following the discussion of these structures, we will consider one final hurdle in children's syntactic development: the proper use of factive and nonfactive predicates. Subtle distinctions about what we know to be true distinguish factive predicates ("I know . . ." and "I'm surprised . . .") from nonfactive ones ("I think . . ." and "It's possible . . ."). Children must learn these distinctions.

easy to see

Consider the following experimental situation. A child is given a doll that is wearing a blindfold. The experimenter begins to talk to the child.

Experimenter: Here's Chatty Cathy. Can you tell me whether she's easy to see or hard to see.

Child: Hard.

Experimenter: Could you make her easy to see?

Child: (removes blindfold)

Experimenter: Can you tell me why she was hard to see in the beginning?

Child: 'Cause she had this over her eyes.[19]

Obviously, the child related the action of "seeing" in the initial question to the doll, not to himself. Although the linguistic considerations that distin-

[19]Reprinted from *The Acquisition of Syntax in Children from 5 to 10* by Carol Chomsky by permission of The M.I.T. Press, Cambridge, Massachusetts. © 1969 by The M.I.T. Press.

guish "easy to see" (from, say, "eager to see") are many, it seems clear that a five-year-old child is not able to determine the subject of the sentence or the subject of "see." There is a great deal of variability in *when* children acquire the complex rules necessary for interpreting the "easy-to-see" structure, but most children acquire this structure between five and a half and nine years of age. Children nine years and older know this structure perfectly.

promise

We described the promise verb as a problematic one in our language. Its use is subject to rules beyond those normally required for most verbs. Chomsky calls "promise" a *nonconforming verb.*

At first, the child knows what a promise is but understands the structure of promising only in a very specific context. Consider this interview with Kathy (five and a half years old):

Tester: What do you do when you promise somebody something?

Kathy: When you don't fool.

Tester: OK now, if you were going to promise your teacher that you will listen very carefully, what would you say to your teacher?

Kathy: I'd say, "I will." (adequate response)

Tester: Good. Now, if you were going to promise your friend to come over and play this afternoon, how would you say that? What would you say?

Kathy: I'd say, "Come over and play with me." (not an adequate response)[20]

Children of five and six years of age, such as Kathy, know what a promise involves and have learned some of the syntactic structures related to promising. Nevertheless, they understand the promise verb only in a highly specific sentence. For example, the phrase "that *you* will listen" is more specific than the phrase "to come over" in indicating *who* will promise.

An older child better understands the structure of promising but can occasionally be "tripped up" in performing correctly. Consider this interview with Peter (age eight):

Tester: Can you tell me what you would say to your friend if you promise him to call him this afternoon?

Peter: I would say, "I'll call you up this afternoon."

Tester: OK, now, here is Bozo and here's Donald Duck. (gives Peter the dolls) Donald tells Bozo to hop across the table. Make him do it.

Peter: "Bozo, hop across the table." (makes Bozo hop).

Tester: Good. Now, Bozo promises Donald that he will do a somersault. Can you make him do it?

---

[20]Adapted from Chomsky, *The Acquisition of Syntax,* pp. 32–41.

Peter: "I'll do a somersault, Donald." (makes Bozo do it)
Tester: Very good. Now Donald promises Bozo to hop up and down. Make him do it.
Peter: "I promised you you could do it." (making Bozo hop [wrong one!])
Tester: Would you do that again? Donald promises Bozo to hop up and down.
Peter: "I promise you you can do it." (again, making Bozo hop)[21]

Peter did very well until the tester omitted all the syntactic cues from the fourth instruction. Then Peter made the wrong doll (Bozo) do the hopping. Peter is in one of the final stages of acquiring the promise structure.

The acquisition of the promise structure, as with that of the "easy-to-see" structure, is slow for some elementary-school children. In fact, not until age nine do all children fully understand the "promise" verb, although some children do so as early as age seven.

ask

Chomsky employed three cases containing either an "ask" or a "tell" verb in order to test children's understanding of the more difficult "ask." Whereas "tell" is acquired fairly early, "ask" causes a number of difficulties. Consider the three cases:

Case 1:   Ask (tell) Bill what time it is
Case 2:   Ask (tell) Bill his (your) first name
Case 3:   Ask (tell) Bill what to feed the doll

At first, children confuse the two verbs, interpreting both as "tell." Eric (age six) imposes a "tell" interpretation in all cases:

Tester: Ask Bill what time it is.
Eric: It's two o'clock.
Tester: Tell Bill your first name.
Eric: Eric.
Tester: Ask Bill his last name.
Eric: Smith.
Tester: OK, now, ask Bill what to feed the doll.
Eric: Feed him cake![22]

Another child (age eight) understands "ask" for cases 1 and 2 but has trouble with the case-3 "ask":

---

[21]Adapted from Chomsky, Ibid.
[22]Adapted from Chomsky, Ibid.

Tester: Ask Bill what time it is.

Jill: What time is it?

Tester: Good. Now, ask him his last name.

Jill: What's your last name?

Tester: Fine. Now, tell Bill what to feed the doll.

Jill: Feed the doll liver.

Tester: OK, ask Bill what to feed the doll next.

Jill: Feed the doll ice cream.[23]

Children acquire the "ask" verb in a stage-by-stage fashion, first learning case 1, then case 2, and finally case 3. Some ten-year-olds have difficulty with this verb, showing that its acquisition is sometimes slow.[24]

"know" versus "think"

The proper use of factive and nonfactive predicates is a major hurdle in the child's acquisition of language structures. Before we explore their development in a study of children from age three through age eight,[25] let's examine the two forms. Here are the factive predicates: know, be surprised, be happy, be nice, and be sad. When these predicates are used in sentences, the complement activity is always true:

"I'm happy Sally won." (Sally did win.)

These are the nonfactive predicates: think, be possible, desire, be true, want. Complementary activities in sentences containing nonfactive predicates may or may not be true:

"I think Sally won." (Maybe she didn't, however.)

Can children detect whether or not the complementary activity is true in the presence of various predicates? Further, consider the added element of negation, whose presence should not disturb the truth of the complement in the factive condition:

"I'm not happy Sally won."

[23]Adapted from Chomsky, Ibid.

[24]Frank Kessel found that children acquire the "ask-tell" and "easy-to-see/eager-to-see" distinctions somewhat earlier than Chomsky has indicated. See Frank Kessel, "The Role of Syntax in Children's Comprehension from Ages Six to Twelve," *Monographs of the Society for Research in Child Development*, 35, no. 6 (1970), 48–53.

[25]Marita R. Hopmann and Michael Maratosos, "A Developmental Study of Factivity and Negation in Complex Syntax," *Journal of Child Language*, 5 (June 1978), 295–309.

The researchers thought that children might generalize the negation from the nonfactive predicate to the interpretation of the truth of the complement activity (in other words, say that Sally did not win).

The results were rather interesting. With negative nonfactives, the pattern of denying the complement increased with age:

> "I don't think Sally won."
> Response: Sally *didn't* win. (But she may have.)

In the other conditions, affirming the complement increased with age:

> "I know that Sally won."
> Response: Sally won.
> "I think Sally won."
> Response: Sally won. (But maybe she didn't.)
> "I didn't know that Sally won."
> Response: Sally won.

Children denied the complement for negative factives more than for affirma-forms, something they really shouldn't have done. However, this tendency was much less apparent with the older children. Most important, the difference between the affirmative- and negative-factive responses vanished among the older children, a finding that shows eventual mastery of the two types.

The results of this study show a slow progression in children's understanding of factivity and negation. The researchers claim that reasonable competence with the forms comes in middle childhood (six years to seven years, eleven months). In their acquisition of factive and nonfactive predicates, children must learn the core meaning of the predicate itself. Then they can analyze whether or not the predicate takes complements and whether the complement is true, probable, or false.

Most of the forms of syntax mastered in stage 6 are not marked in any uniform way by special forms, word endings, or word order. Consequently, when children acquire these forms in their elementary-school years, they follow the general principle of avoiding exceptions (operating principle 5) and they interpret sentences on the basis of other fairly straightforward principles:

1. "Ask her the time" may be interpreted as "tell" + the time, rather than the more complex "you" + "tell me" + the time.
2. "I don't think she has the ball" may be interpreted as "She *doesn't* have the ball" rather than being viewed as an uncertain case. The *general rule* that "no" or "not" means that something is not true is employed even when inappropriate.

POWER IN LANGUAGE STRUCTURE

At the heart of English grammar are the many syntactic structures that allow us to express with words an infinite number of ideas, feelings, and relationships. Children master the basic syntactic structures of their language in their early years, but the more complex forms require work well into their school years. With the sophistication of complex syntactic forms, children are capable of making sense on almost any topic, assuming they understand the situation.

Children do not need to have mastered the complex syntactic patterns to communicate their needs and intentions. Even one-, two-, and three-year-olds are quite capable of expressing themselves without these forms. But for the more complicated tasks of leading others, competing in situations, and asking for help in difficult situations, more complex structures are required. Children who have mastered all forms of questions are better equipped to ask for help. Children who have mastered the more complex forms of relativization and coordination are better able to present issues in a group. At the same time, children who have acquired an understanding of the complex syntactic patterns are capable of understanding complex grammar in the speech of others. These children can handle themselves well in situations requiring a sophisticated level of language use. One of the key components in children's development of personal powers is their ability to regulate their own lives, to act and communicate "on their own." The ability to use mature, clearly-stated syntactic structures that allow children opportunities to express themselves effectively is important in developing autonomy. Without the ability to employ syntax effectively, children will be dependent on others.

SUMMARY

An important aspect of children's communication is the syntax of their language—that is, the rules of word order.

Eight basic utterance patterns constitute the first stage of syntactic development, the stage at which the child masters the basic grammatical relations. Children at this stage combine two or more words to form a basic relation, such as an agent and an action or an entity and an attribute.

At the second stage of syntactic development meaning is modulated through the addition of fourteen grammatical markers, sucha s articles, auxiliaries, and copulas. Now the child is better able to express intention in a fashion that will more likely be understood by a variety of persons.

The third stage of syntactic development assumes mastery of basic structures and progresses to the acquisition of simple sentence modalities, such as questions and negatives. These modalities develop in three stages and seem to span two years of development.

Advanced sentence modalities—indirect questions, relative clauses, and coordinated structures—are the target of the fourth stage.

During stage 5 (the categorization stage) children of early-elementary-school age develop an understanding of the subcategories of the major word classes (such as nouns and verbs). For example, they learn that nouns can be categorized as singular or plural and as mass or count. Assignment of a noun to a category dictates the form of other words in a sentence. At this stage children learn to categorize verbs, prepositions, and other word classes as well.

In the sixth stage of syntactic development children learn the complex *structures* of their language. These include the "easy-to-see," "promise," and "ask" structures. Factive and nonfactive predicates are also acquired at this stage. Often, children struggle with complex structures until age ten.

Table 6.2 summarizes the stages of syntactic devopment.

TABLE 6.2.   *The six stages of children's syntactic development.*

STAGE OF DEVELOPMENT	NATURE OF DEVELOPMENT	SAMPLE UTTERANCES
1. Basic relations	Eight basic relations constitute the grammatical forms of children's first sentences: e.g., agent and action entity and attribute action and locative	"Mommy laugh." "Billy cry." "Silly doggie." "Silly Mommy." "Fall down." "Ride there."
2. Modulated Relations	Children implement fourteen grammatical morphemes that add clarity and meaning to their utterances.	"Mommy is laughing." "This doggie is silly." "She fell down." "I'm riding there."
3. Simple Sentence Modalities	The basic subject/predicate structure can be changed into a question or a negative structure.	"You will play with me?" "What time it is?" "Will you play with me?" "What time is it?"
4. Advanced Sentence Modalities	Children are able to combine clauses through complementation, relativization, and coordination.	"Lookit the kid throwin' the ball." "See the one I got from there." "We didn't get any crayons, either any pencils."
5. Categorization	Word classes (nouns, verbs, and prepositions) are subdivided.	"I would like *some* milk." (use of "some" with mass noun) "Take me *to* the store." (use of preposition of place)
6. Complex Structures	Complex structural distinctions are made, as with "ask"/ "tell" and "promise."	"Ask what time it is." "He promised to help her."

SUGGESTED READINGS

CLARK, HERBERT H., and EVE V. CLARK, *Psychology and Language: An Introduction to Psycholinguistics*, Chap. 9. New York: Harcourt, Brace, Jovanovich, 1977.

DE VILLIERS, JILL, and PETER DE VILLIERS, *Language Acquisition*, Chaps. 3–4. Cambridge: Harvard Press, 1978.

SLOBIN, DAN, "Cognitive Prerequisites for the Development of Grammar," in *Readings in Language Development*, ed. Lois Bloom, pp. 407–32. New York: John Wiley, 1978.

———, *Psycholinguistics*, Chap. 3. Glenview, Ill.: Scott, Foresman, 1971.

7

learning how to mean

At the supermarket:

Beth (three years): I want Sugar Pops.
Mother: Let's look for another kind of cereal. OK?
Beth: Buy it for me.
Mother: Sugar Pops has too much sugar in it. Sugar is bad for your teeth and for your body.
Beth: I want it. I like it. Why you not buy Sugar Pops?
Mother: I have an idea. Let's pretend. I am the Sugar Pops and you are the tooth. Ready?
Beth: Ouch . . . ouch . . . no more. . . .

For some parents this conversation may seem typical. Beth wants something, and because she knows how "to mean" it in a public place, the supermarket, she feels free to express her wish strongly. Her mother reacts to her request in several ways. First, she would like to include her child in the choosing of another cereal. Next, she informs Beth about the possible dangers in the product. Finally, she engages her child in an act that, as it turns out, shows her that Beth has understood, that Mom's meaning was clear.

M.A.K. Halliday has offered an exciting perspective on the development of children's meaning. Halliday observed carefully his son's behavior as it seemed to be related to the child's language. Then, in a landmark study on the development of meaning,[1] he described in functional terms the way in which children learn their language. When Beth uses what Halliday terms

---

[1] M.A.K. Halliday, *Learning How to Mean: Explorations in the Development of Language* (New York: Elsevier, 1975). The approach to meaning development in this chapter, as well as the title itself, are based on this major work on meaning.
Consulting Author: Doris Seeder.

the *instrumental* function of language, she is demanding goods and services—the Sugar Pops. The mother's response is *interactional*, because it denotes the need and wish for human contact. "Buy it for me" illustrates the *regulatory* function, since it is saying "Do as I tell you, Mommy." When Beth says "I like it," she is functioning on a *personal* level, for she is expressing her own preferences. The question "Why you not buy Sugar Pops?" clearly identifies her curiosity. This is a version of the "Tell me why . . . ," or *heuristic*, function. Finally, when the mother begins the "Let's pretend" sequence and Beth answers by acting out her mother's scenario, the *imaginative* function comes into play.

The meanings in this conversation are viewed in terms of the interpersonal functions of the mother's and child's words, not in the forms or sounds of their words. The mother and child relate to each other through language, but the particular words they select do not contain meanings per se. Their meanings are derived from the social interaction between the two as they relate through communication. To understand what they mean when they relate to each other, it would be ideal if we could view from inside their minds what they think about themselves, others, and their environment. That is not possible, however. The adult's *perspective* is accessible to us, but the child's is probably often misunderstood. It is important that we try to see interaction from the child's point of view.

Adults seem to go out of their way to try to understand what children mean when they communicate. Often they succeed in their interpretations and the process of interaction continues without a disturbance. But at other times an adult may fail to understand what a child means and the process of communication breaks down. Older siblings often act as interpreters, helping parents decode young children's intentions. However the process of communication occurs, children deal with their environment by relating to those around them.

Long before children are able to say words, they are actively involved in trying to manage their environment. As infants children have a strong bond with their parents, who have an impact on them as individuals and as members of their culture. Once children have mastered the "I want" function satisfactorily, they are able to expand their territory from things very close to them to anything that is within their reach with words. There comes a time in children's lives, usually before their second birthday, when they seem to realize that the "I need," "I want," and "Do it" approaches are not the only ones they can use with persons in their environment. They begin to try other approaches and they combine approaches into more complex schemes. It's no accident, then, that language develops in complexity as the child's perspective of the social system enlarges from child-parent interactions to a broader network of relationships.

The question for us to answer about meaning development is not "How does the child acquire meaning?" Acquiring meaning for children sounds more like the passive process of acquiring a sun tan or getting the measles.

Learning to mean is an active process, as in making new friends and becoming a more cooperative member of a group. Learning to mean requires interplay among the child, the family, events, and the entire network in which that child lives.

This chapter is divided into two sections. The first addresses general questions about the nature of meaning, while the second explores the development of children learning how to mean.

WHAT IS MEANING?

If you were to ask your friends what "meaning" means to them, they would probably look at you as if you were crazy. The question might make some people think about their identity. In a class discussion the question could generate an exploration of the meaning of life, or of meaning as a religious quest, but seldom do people simply chat about a theory of meaning or about a dictionary definition of a word they don't know. Psychologists, linguists, and all the other professionals interested in communication, however, are very much concerned with the concept of meaning in language, and with the related subject of meaning development.

One approach to the study of meaning is structuralism. Ferdinand de Saussure and his followers consider meanings of words in terms of relationships among words.[2] For example, they may examine the meaning of a particular kin term, such as "mother," as it relates to all kin terms in the family structure. Much like dictionary definitions, which define words by using other words, meaning, according to this view, is a linguistic phenomenon. The structuralists allow students of meaning to analyze the words and symbols humans use for their meanings, though they do not encourage examination of events surrounding the use of these signals.

One structural view of meaning is based on the notion that every word can be analyzed in terms of a set of more general components, or *semantic features*. For example, we could say that the molecule-word "mother" contains the following atoms (features) of meaning: female, adult, offspring, human. These features could be contrasted, then, with those that define a "father": male, adult, offspring, human. This componential approach to the study of meaning has led to the rather interesting theory that children acquire meanings in a feature-by-feature progression, as is suggested in the classic study by Susan Haviland and Eve Clark.[3] The validity and universality of the componential approach to semantic development has been seriously questioned, but it remains as probably one of the most attractive theories for study because it provides a clear framework for developmental research.

---

[2]See Ferdinand de Saussure, *A Course in General Linguistics* (New York: Philosophical Library, 1961).

[3]Susan E. Haviland and Eve V. Clark, " 'This Man's Father Is My Father's Son': A Study of the Acquisition of English Kin Terms," *Journal of Child Language*, 1 (May 1974), 23–47.

Eve Clark is one of the primary researchers of this approach to the study of meaning. She argues that children acquire their meanings in a feature-by-feature fashion.[4] At first, words are defined by perceptual features—qualities that are visible, such as size, shape, and texture. For example, children might think of the sun as a "round, bright thing in the sky." Children's later definitions are likely to be more abstract and adultlike: an older child might define the sun as a "round and fiery body in space that heats our air."

A graduate student of mine asked children from age four to age ten various questions relating to hypothetical families represented on a felt board.[5] Her purpose was to examine the features by which they understood kin terms. She discovered that young children define various kin terms on the basis of accessories (for example, purses and hats) and physical features (for example, wrinkles and grey hair), perceptual features tbat are typically noticed by young children. Older children in the study provided different features for distinguishing kin terms: for example, some were capable of saying that a person's dress or accessories could be misleading in defining kin term, but that parent status and sibling relations are relevant.

Clark also suggests that the more general features are acquired before the more specific ones, so that the concept of sex, for example, would be acquired before the more specific notion of *sibling*. This helps to explain why many of the young children in Stubbs's study pointed to *all* the boys in the four families (including two "only children") when they were asked, "Who are the brothers who can go to Cub's Park for the ball game today?"

Children learning kin terms must learn meanings for words such as mother, father, brother, uncle, and niece. These words constitute a semantic field called *kinship*, and they are defined by each other. Research with children suggests that acquisition of the entire field of meanings is not complete until the child reaches the early teens. At that time the semantic field of kin terms includes a configuration of components much like that of the complex adult system. Semantic maps which visually portray the spatial relationships among meanings can be helpful in the study of children's semantic development if they contain features that reflect children's perceptual strategies for sorting out their world. As we have noted, in the Stubbs study on children's acquisition of kin terms children cited "accessories" as a reason why a mother was a mother ("She carries a purse"), a father was a father ("He's holding a newspaper"), and a brother was a brother ("He has a baseball mitt"). Just as *sex* (male or female) and *offspring* (having or not having children) are features that the linguistic expert searches for in the

---

[4]Eve Clark, "What's in a Word? On the Child's Acquisition of Semantics in His First Language," in *Cognitive Development and the Acquisition of Language*, ed. T. E. Moore (New York: Academic Press, 1973), pp. 65–110.

[5]Margaret Stubbs, "Children's Acquisition of English Kin Terms" (Master's thesis, University of Illinois at Chicago Circle, 1975).

study of meaning development, *accessories* must also be plotted as a perceptual strategy important in children's semantic field. In this way, purses, slippers, hats, and baseball mitts take on a meaningful role as overt cues of kin status.

Other studies relying on Clark's semantic-feature approach to semantic development examine children's acquisition of adjective pairs, such as "long" and "short" or "high" and "low." Generally, these studies suggest that children's acquisition of word pairs follows a rather predictable sequence. First, the positive member of the pair is learned—for example, "high" or "long"— and then the negative member. Clark suggests that this is probably because the basic notion of the dimension must be mastered before its "lesser form" (the absence of that dimension) can be understood.

In the most general terms, Clark believes that children learn to more sharply perceive the perceptual qualities of objects and events around them. As they develop sharper tools of language, their semantic features increase in richness. Children view similarity and dissimilarity among objects and events and classify accordingly. As they build their meanings for words, they gradually refine that set of qualities that describe each and every referent situation with words.

The major difficulty with this perspective of meaning is that the list of features that is said to represent the total meaning of a word varies and grows depending on the items with which the word is compared and the sentences in which the word is used. To represent all the ways in which one event differs from another, or all the ways in which two events are similar in terms of possible relations, would require an almost infinite list of features. Semantic-feature theory may be too cumbersome in accounting for how we *mean* in our everyday conversations. Since feature theory is so careful and systematic in its view of meaning, however, many of the studies of meaning and its development published today are based on it.

The overall logic and clarity of the semantic-features approach to the study of meaning has attracted many scholars and researchers. The approach provides a workable method that can be extended to the developmental issue of how children learn to mean. Yet many theorists argue that this approach says little about why children develop meanings as they do. To adequately understand the process of children's semantic development, these theorists stress, we must first have an underlying account of *why changes in meaning* take place. Such an account has been provided by Lev Vygotsky,[6] a Russian psychologist, and it is a viable framework for the functional approach to meaning development discussed in this chapter.

[6]Lev S. Vygotsky, *Thought and Language*, trans. E. Hansmann and C. V. Vakar (Cambridge, Mass.: M.I.T. Press, 1962).

functional changes in children's language:
the shift from other-dependence to self-dependence

Children use language as a tool to guide their development of thought. Vygotsky focuses on the interplay between thought and speech in a social context. He explains why children change in their view of language and their world, not why they go through a specific number of language stages per se. To study children who are talking, thinking, and feeling, one must study them in their biological and social milieu as they interrelate with words. The key phenomenon that separates biological and social development is self-regulation, the controlling or monitoring of one's own behavior. When children are very young, they can only react and act with words; they cannot regulate their own behavior with language. Regulation must come from outside elements, such as parental messages to them. The transference of regulation from social (parental) to individual (self) depends on a gradual and complex process of gaining more and more awareness of one's actions and feelings and the control of actions through words. Let's use an everyday example to explain the developmental process:

Johnny is having bad dreams in the middle of the night and awakes crying, calling for his mother. When she enters the room, Johnny points to a shadow and says, "Dat a boogeyman, Mommy. It's gonna get me." If the mother realizes that he needs comforting and touching more than the assurance that the shadow is really not a boogeyman or an explanation that there is no such thing as a boogeyman, she can probably help the child settle down and go back to sleep soon. The child viewing his world in this way sees everything as coming toward him, doing something to him, or controlling his every move. Accordingly, the child's language reflects this perspective of "other-regulation."

Take this same example with an older child. Again calling in his mother, Johnny might talk like this about what he is experiencing: "I'm so scared, Mom, 'cuz I thought that was a boogeyman or a burglar. I know there's no such thing, and I know I shouldn't be scared, but. . . ." Here Johnny is able to reflect on his own behavior through his use of language. Maybe he is even able to talk himself out of being extremely frightened: "I know better than to think that's a boogeyman!"

In addition to providing a way for children to deal with the unknown, as in dreams, language functions in other self-regulatory ways. For example, children learn that saying something "out loud" may help them accomplish a task. They might also learn that explaining a process to someone may help them better conceptualize the steps. In their growth as human beings, children learn to mean in relation to what is going on in their lives. It is no accident that children of about six years of age show dramatic changes in their language meanings; according to Vygotsky, this is the point in children's lives where school, and in particular instruction, takes on a very important role. As children's social and learning repertoires are enlarged, through classmates and teachers, their horizons expand to accommodate new thoughts and new language.

Children mature by taking greater and greater control over their lives and their language. As we discussed in Chapter 1, the power of children's communication manifests itself when children are able to exercise some degree of control in their environment. During this period of their lives children show some independence in their family and school lives. What we called "personal power" was simply children's ability to function effectively in their environment through appropriate use of communication. What we are suggesting in this chapter is that children gain autonomy in their relationships with others because they are able to use language functionally and meaningfully. This process of maturation or growth is accompanied by a fine-tuning of the language functions necessary for coping with everyday situations.

The next portion of this chapter outlines several functions of language that children acquire in the three stages posed by Halliday. All are presented in a framework that is consistent with Vygotsky's notion that the child grows from an other-dependent to a self-dependent communicator.

a functional approach to meaning

Halliday considers children to be active agents who *create meanings* from their experiences and involvements with people. The social system children grow up in is also a meaning system waiting to be acted upon and learned. Since meaning is a part of the entire system, which includes people, places, and events, different people can participate in the same system yet still mean differently. Why is this? The answer is that meaning does not exist in the world—in objects or events—nor does it really exist within people. It exists in the interaction of the two, so that different people in the same ecological system can have different perceptions and different meanings.

Children learning how to mean are really learning how to function within their system—their peer group, family, neighborhood, and culture. Words are important in the communication of meanings, but there are other ways to express meaning, such as through use of the body, the voice, and our personal space; we must also weigh the factors of the communication situation. The remaining chapters of this text focus on the nonverbal and situational factors important in meaning. While nonverbal factors are often considered minor in the process of meaning, Halliday and this text view nonverbal and situational factors as paramount in this process.

When we study children's meaning from a functional viewpoint, we can understand more about why children act and learn as they do, and also why language has evolved with its heart in functions, acts, and doing. The functions of communication which account for the process of meaning development constitute the major *social uses of language* for children. Children and adults use language to accomplish major social purposes that are important in their day-to-day relationships. Halliday considers several functions to be the driving forces behind children's struggle to learn how to mean.

Phase 1. Even before children reach their first birthday they *do* something with their voices. They form sounds that are interpreted as meaningful. Children have purposes that underly the sounds they use to convey various meanings. They use their voice to demand goods and services; this is the *instrumental* function of communication. Sometimes children primarily want to make contact (e.g., "Hi!") with people; here they use the *interactional* function, in order to feel closer to others. For children in this phase, using sounds and words are actions as much as throwing a ball or running. Four other functions (regulatory, heuristic, personal, and imaginative) are mastered in this phase.

Phase 2. Once children recognize the boundary between themselves and their environment, they seem to want to explore it. It is this wish of children to know about their environment that gives rise to the second phase of meaning development, in which children begin to practice more sophisticated functions of communication. Children use language to demand responses from others or to initiate actions (the *pragmatic* function) and to make statements or inquire about what they know or want to know (the *mathetic* function). Dialogue and grammar are used to mean, to interact with people.

Phase 3. As children depend more on language as a system to express themselves, the third phase of semantic development is born. Children draw from a variety of sources to communicate successfully: they use the *interpersonal* function of communication and express *ideational* meaning. In this phase, "every act is a blend of action and reflection."[7] A characteristic of phase 3 is *text*, a combination of meaning and choice. Children's communication in this stage takes into account the full backdrop of what was said, what was done, what is being said and done, and, more important, what could have been said and done that was not. Options are the key in this phase: communication is formed "out of a continuous process of choice among innumerable interrelated sets of semantic options."[8] Since develop-

[7] Halliday, *Learning How to Mean*, p. 110.
[8] *Ibid.*, p. 124.

ment is continuous, the child has functional choices from all three stages of meaning.

Halliday's basic approach was to note carefully what his son, Nigel, said over a nine-month period. During this time Halliday observed Nigel frequently. Sometimes he took part in the situation he was describing, and other times he hid behind doors and furniture and simply observed. Halliday chose the field method to record everything he observed—intonation, contextual factors such as who was saying what to whom, and even antecedents to some of the utterances. For example, if Nigel said something strikingly new, Halliday asked for information about where he had been that day and what he had done, information that might suggest to him a basis for this utterance.

LEARNING HOW TO MEAN

Persons who care for young children often witness interesting exchanges like this one:

Johnny (pointing to a ball Amy is holding):   Mine, gimme my ball!
Amy (whimpering, dropping her head):   I want my Mommy.

It may seem that Amy is not responding in a functionally appropriate way to Johnny's request. After all, she says nothing about the ball or about whether she should hand it over to Johnny. But if we were to analyze the *meanings* communicated by each child, we would have a rather different picture. Johnny uses the strong instrumental function; he demands the ball immediately. While the form of Amy's response seems also to fit the instrumental function (demanding her Mommy), her whimpering and asking for Mommy is much more strongly an expression of the personal function; Amy is dealing with "forceful Johnny" by showing a part of herself in that situation—her discomfort.

In this way we begin to examine children's communication from a functional, meaningful perspective. This section traces children's development of meaning by focusing on Halliday's three phases of meaning. The process of development extends from the basic functions in phase 1, as expressed through meaning as communicated mainly through sounds to the more complex functions in phase 3, which include three levels (called "tristratal" by Halliday): phonological (sounds), semantic (meaning), and grammatical (structures). Functions learned earlier are, of course, retained and used later.

phase 1: sounds and meaning (nine months to sixteen months)

Table 7-1 presents the three phases of semantic development outlined by Halliday. Phase 1 seems like the most fruitful stage of learning because so many functions are listed. Halliday stresses that these functions do not disappear in the phase to follow, but combine to form more sophisticated and complex functions. Understanding the development of the six basic functions is our first task.

One introductory note is important before we begin, however. Since this phase of development includes many uses of sounds that may not seem meaningful to an observer, we do not include specific sounds and utterances in our discussion. Rather, we use Halliday's "gloss" of the sounds Nigel used, which is simply a paraphrase of the meaning according to his observation. We will put the glosses in quotes.

Halliday identifies beginning meanings as those words and actions that children use consistently to mean only one thing. At ten and a half months,

TABLE 7.1. *Phases of meaning development.*

PHASE 1 (9 TO 16 MONTHS) SOUNDS AND MEANING	PHASE 2 (16 TO 24 MONTHS) GRAMMAR AND DIALOGUE	PHASE 3 (24 MONTHS AND UP) TEXT
a. One meaning at a time. b. Meanings are not understood by everyone.	a. Two or more meanings simultaneously. b. Grammar and dialogue for meanings.	a. Ability to distinguish between *old* and *new* information; choices are made to produce text. b. All utterances are both ideational and interpersonal.
Regulatory "Do X."		
Instrumental "I want."	*Pragmatic* "Catch me, 'kay?" "Help me tie."	*Interpersonal* "Yet's play dolls—I be da Mommy."
Interactional "Let's . . ."		
Heuristic "What's that?"	*Mathetic* "There's a star." "That's my dolly."	*Ideational* "Dat's the sun—it's fire!"
Personal "I'm sleepy."		*Text* (choice + meaning)
Imaginative "Cock-a-doodle-doo."	"Next train is coming." (pretending)	"Can't eat train, can't eat man, can't eat book."

Examples are Nigel's utterances, from Halliday, *Learning How to Mean.*

Nigel was already using four of the six phase-1 functions. He exhibited the *instrumental* function with one utterance that meant something like "I want it," referring to a specific object in his environment. For the *regulatory* function, Nigel expressed a generalized request directed at one individual, again about a very specific object in his environment but in this case directing the person to do something with it. The meaning of this regulatory function was something like "Do this again" or "Do it now." The *interactional* function was represented by a few initiating utterances and one response. To greet someone who entered the house, Nigel directed his attention to the visitor and used sounds to mean something like "Good to see you." He might follow that greeting with a more regulatory meaning: "Read this book for me!" Another form was a response to a greeting, and meant something like "Glad to see you, too." These utterances were made during a stage at which Nigel had twelve distinct meanings. By the end of phase 1 his repertoire had expanded to fifty-two meanings.

The sound patterns used in this phase are not simple imitations of adult language. In fact, Halliday suggests, some meanings come from "self-imitations." The expression Nigel used before going to sleep, /wigwig/, meant withdrawal for him; it was hardly something his parents had used for that situation. Children's phase-meanings do not necessarily correspond to adult meanings, nor do the linguistic distinctions made by children correspond to those made by adults. For example, when Nigel was about twelve months old he said /yiyiyiyi/ with a high tone, meaning "I want that." He also used /yiyiyiyi/ with a high rising and then falling tone. This meant "I want you to do what you have just offered to do ," in response to questions like "Do you want your orange juice now?" or "Shall I put the new record on?" Both of these are examples of the instrumental function, since they are related to the offer of goods or services.

If sounds and meanings produced by children are not simple imitations of adult language, where do they originate? Whatever the origins of children's meanings, we know one thing to be certain: children's messages *are understood.* In fact, it is in the context of always seeming to be understood that some theorists, such as Vygotsky, suggest the real origin of meaning lies. Meanings emerge from the *transactional* quality of games and exchanges between adults and their babies. Chapter 3 stressed the important role parents play in forming the interactional and functional basis of language through games, such as hide-and-seek and "Where did it go?" Jerome Bruner is probably the expert most closely associated with this area of research; a brief review of the section "A Transactional View of Interaction" in Chapter 3 will help promote an understanding of the origins of meaning in phase 1.

In another study Bruner followed the development of a game in children from seven to thirteen months.[9] The game consisted of the children exchanging objects with their mothers in a back-and-forth pattern. For the youngest infants, the mother took over both the manipulation of objects and the verbal task accompanying it. Then, the activity changed from the mother giving to the mother offering and the baby taking. In the eighth and ninth months the children became more possessive of what was given to them, beginning to express approval and disapproval. By the tenth and eleventh months the children were more actively engaged in the game, and were assertive about wanting what was being exchanged. As they passed the year mark they became increasingly confident and participated even more actively in the interaction. The progression described by Bruner is very much in step with the phase-1 progression of meaning development outlined by Halliday. While Bruner approaches the study of language from an interactional perspective, Halliday focuses on the meanings that emerge from such a perspective.

As children move from phase 1 into phase 2, their most important development is to combine functions to produce more complex meanings. A one-year-old child may say "Coke" to mean "I want a Coke," using the instrumental function. By two years of age the child may combine three functions to produce the utterance "Please, pretty please, gimme Coke." This utterance, when given with feeling and yearning, reflects a combination of the instrumental (wanting), regulatory (do-it-for-me), and personal (feelings) functions.

phase 2: grammar and dialogue (sixteen to twenty-four months)

"Please, pretty please, gimme Coke" is an example of the *pragmatic* function of phase 2. This phase opens up new options in the children's functional system of meanings. The children involve others in their actions and language. Further, they acquire more language structures, so that their meanings are no longer identified with just one of the earlier functions, but include two or more. At eighteen months a dialogue like this one might occur; note the variety of functions communicated with the food-words.

Mother: Did you tell Daddy what you had for lunch?

Anne: (to mother excitedly) Ice-n, Ice-n (ice cream, ice cream). Mmmmmmm. Toasie, Toasie (toast; mentioned because of what mother is preparing).

Mother: You didn't have toast for lunch!

Anne: Hotdaw (hotdog) (teasing). (returning to what was asked) Tooona, tooona (tuna)

[9]Jerome Bruner, "The Ontogenesis of Speech Acts," *Journal of Child Language*, 2 (April 1975), 1–19.

Children increase their repertoire of meanings suddenly, from 50 at sixteen months to 150 at eighteen months. This happens because they are expanding their horizons: children typically make friends at this time and engage in dialogue with people other than their parents. As children become involved in broader situations they learn to observe, recall, and predict. Nigel used the following progression when a new word—in this case "stick"—came to his attention. First, he said /stick/, translated as "I see a stick." A few weeks later he used /stick/ in a recall situation: "Sticks, holes, stones, trains, balls, and buses." And later yet, on his way out of the house, Nigel used /stick/ to express the prediction "I shall see sticks when I go out for a walk."

A qualitatively new function of communication emerges in phase 2: the *mathetic* function. It is used for *learning* purposes, though not necessarily for learning language. Halliday suggests that this function is very different from the earlier *pragmatic* function, where children use a rising intonation in their utterances to signal the need of a response. For the mathetic function, children use a falling intonation to refer to aspects of their environment and people close to them.

The mathetic function arises as a combination of the personal and heuristic functions practiced in phase 1. Children learn to organize their environment and apply their observations of it to their own experiences. While their pragmatic utterances invite others to participate in an action with them, their mathetic utterances invite only others' attention. Examples of the mathetic function are as follows:

> "Look, that'sa birdie."
> "I saw Superman!"
> "Da doggie cryin', Mom."

Each of these utterances needs no verbal response from those the children are communicating with. In contrast, the rising tone of voice used in conveying pragmatic meanings requires some kind of response. Consider these pragmatic utterances, which ask for responses:

> "Cathy go night-night?"
> "Help-a me button, 'kay?"

The difference between these phase-2 pragmatic meanings and the phase-1 instrumental or regulatory meanings is that the former may require responses on two levels: action (helping, buttoning) and language ("Yes, it's bedtime" and "Okay, I'll help you").

Children in the second phase make an astonishing discovery: in any use of language, a person can be either an observer or a participant. As observers children use language to register their experiences apart from the communication situation, while as participants they use language as action in a specific context. In the beginning of phase 2, children are either observers or participants:

"Doggie bite him."
"I hit doggie."

But as they develop their phase-2 strategies, they are able to be two things at once:

"I see doggie bite. He not nice."

Grammatical structures are necessary to accomplish the task of being observers and participants at the same time.

In addition to learning the observer-participant distinction, children must also master communication roles: they must learn to engage effectively in dialogue. Dialogue involves using language to express social roles. When adults speak, they adopt rules and assign roles to those they are speaking to. The phase-1 child has no concept of role, and hence no notion of dialogue, but toward the end of phase 2 the child learns that "language itself is a form of interaction."[10]

When children act on their environment, they do so with differing degrees of control. James Wertsch explored the idea that as children develop, their ability to regulate themselves grows accordingly.[11] Since Halliday firmly believes that social interaction gives rise to advances in semantic development, and since a crucial aspect of interaction is self-regulation, Wertsch's study helps explain the progress children make from phase 1 to phase 3. Wertsch was able to view three levels of interaction as mothers and their children participated in a "copy-the-puzzle" task. The purpose of the game was for the children to make their puzzles match the model, using any help from their mothers. At the first level of interaction children's understanding of the situation was so limited that communication was restricted; the mother had to provide a great deal of assistance in order for the task to be accomplished:

Child: (picks up window piece) What goes with it?
Mother: I think (points to other window piece in pieces pile) . . .
Mother: What do you think . . .
Mother: I think that's a window. It doesn't look like a window. No. (child looks away from puzzle task materials and looks at windows in the classroom)

---

[10]Halliday, *Learning How to Mean*, p. 31.
[11]James B. Wertsch, "From Social Interaction to Higher Psychological Processes: A Clarification and Application of Vygotsky's Theory," *Human Development*, 22 (1979), 1–22.

Mother: But it's a window to this truck. (mother points to location in copy where window piece is to be inserted)
Child: (drops window piece in his hand back into the pieces pile)[12]

This is an example of the *heuristic* function, and of a beginning attempt toward dialogue. But certainly in this example the child does not use his mother's assistance efficiently, nor does he engage her in dialogue that will help him accomplish the task.

As children begin to understand the puzzle situation more completely they take advantage of their mother's assistance. Still, though they understand and make use of the dialogue between their mothers and themselves, they are not yet able to engage in the complete forms of dialogue characteristic of phase 3.

Mother: So where do you want to put the black one on this puzzle? (child picks up black cargo square from pieces pile, looks at copy)
Child: Well, where do you put it there? Over there? (inserts black cargo square correctly in copy)
Mother: That looks good.[13]

At the third level of interaction children are able to function successfully and regulate their own behavior, even when the directions from their mother are not explicit. Children are now capable of using the interpersonal and the ideational functions simultaneously. This reflects a mastery of the "text" of the adult semantic system: the child chooses to hear and understand what is meaningful and responds in order to solve the puzzle.

Child: Where's the black one go?
Mother: Where's the black one go on Mom's (child looks at copy and inserts black cargo square correctly).
Child: Down there.
Mother: Um-hm.[14]

In this case the mother did not have to regulate the child's behavior. The child used the interaction to complete the task successfully. The child's meanings and use of language in this final dialogue serve as an excellent transition to the third and final phase of meaning development: text development.

[12]*Ibid.*, p. 9.
[13]*Ibid.*, p. 13.
[14]*Ibid.*, p. 15.

phase 3: text (twenty-four months and up)

What characterized the second phase, among other things, was the polarity between the mathetic and the pragmatic functions. This distinction becomes the driving force for the union of functions in phase 3. The greater the gap between the phase-2 functions, the mathetic and the pragmatic, the more children find they need an alternative. The interpersonal and ideational functions of the third phase satisfy that need. Children are now able to freely express ideas in context.

When people use two functions simultaneously it is difficult to decide which of the functions should be emphasized, or how to properly observe meaning dynamics. For example, if a child says "I want to be a soldier," it may be hard to determine whether he is saying "I want to be a soldier so that I can shoot you," using the interpersonal function, or "I want to be a soldier because soldiers are nice, like policemen," using the ideational function. It is usually helpful to be a part of the communication event in figuring out the meaning dynamics: watching, listening, and seeing what went before may help untangle the meaning puzzle. But in too many cases even our presence will not help us decide what someone really means. We may wish we could "stop the movie," in order to look more carefully at the flow of communication events; even that may or may not help us decide. The task of clear and effective communication is difficult for children in phase 3 and for many adults with a lot more practice.

The third phase of meaning development includes the *ideational* function, arising from the use of language to learn, and the *interpersonal* function, arising from the use of language to act. Among the possible meanings, children choose one(s) that fits the situation for them at that moment. In this phase of children's meaning development, environment and meaning interact. The environment affects their choices of meaning, but communication practices (meaning choices) affect their new view of the environment.

In phase 3, children have the ability to impart both new and old information. A child saying "Doggie bite" is relating that he is seeing a dog bite something (new information), and that he has seen dogs previously and that he knows they sometimes bite (old information). In addition to processing new and old information, children also need to *remember* information while they are in the meaning situation. Here is an example from Nigel at twenty-one months: As father and son were walking, they stopped to note a street clock that was not ticking.

Father: I wonder why the clock's stopped. I've never known it stopped before. Perhaps they are cleaning it, or mending it.

They returned home. Some hours later, Nigel returned to the subject.

Nigel: Why that clock stop?
Father: I don't know. Why do you think?
Nigel: Mend it.[15]

Delayed reactions are the child's way of bringing new meanings into the system, almost as if it takes time to work out the novel meanings. Previously known meanings act as radar to pick up new meaning components close enough to the child's prior meanings. Halliday describes well what children must do to develop novel meanings in phase 3: "For the child the overall context is one of survival, and he develops semiotic strategies such that he can use his meaning potential as he is building it and build it as he is using it."[16] In short, children learn how to mean *by meaning*—in the context of social interaction and in the context of meaning.

Let's look now at some other areas of investigation concerning phase 3 of meaning development. According to Clark and Haviland, we make an agreement with our communication partner called the "given-new contract."[17] We cooperate about the use of given (old) and new information. Let's take a few examples from a conversation between two children:

1. "*I wasn't invited* to Bert's party."
2. "*Bert was the one* who had that party."
3. "*I heard they had movies* at Bert's party."
4. "Bert's party *was last Saturday.*"

Notice that a portion of each sentence is italicized; that portion contains the new information. The portion of the sentence not italicized is the given information that is probably agreed upon by the participants. The factors that help identify which information is given and which is new are many: the structure of the sentence, the context of the discussion, intonation patterns, and of course gestures and facial expressions. A sentence in isolation may be ambiguous about what information is assumed and what information is new, but individuals relating to each other are expected to communicate that information clearly.

Another area of investigation related to the third phase of meaning development focuses on what experts call "scripts."[18] We have to learn various scripts for talking and behaving appropriately in various settings. For

---

[15]Halliday, *Learning How to Mean*, p. 134.
[16]*Ibid.*, pp. 135–36.
[17]Eve Clark and Susan E. Haviland, "Comprehension and the Given-New Contract," in *Discourse Production and Comprehension*, ed. R. O. Freedle (Norwood, N.J.: Adler, 1977), pp. 1–40.
 · [18]See Roger Schank and Robert Abelson, *Scripts, Plans, Goals, and Understanding* (New York: Lawrence Erlbaum, 1977).

example, we learn that there are scripts for acceptable ways to behave in public places, as well as at the dinner table in the home. The more we uncover the scripts that are a part of our expectations for appropriate behavior of our children, the more we will understand what meaning choices children are asked to make.

Scripts are determined by many factors, important ones being the nature of communication in the family and cultural rules. The dinner hour (five-to-ten minute rush) may be orchestrated according to this script: First, at a certain hour family members and friends await the announcement for dinner. When dinner is announced, persons seat themselves in their respective places and begin to make some pleasant conversation about the nice dinner, the events of their day, or the enjoyable company; they are expected to carry on some kind of conversation rather than remain totally silent while they eat. After completing dinner, depending on the rules of the home or culture, persons "excuse themselves" in some proper way. Children learn meanings in the context of the dinner hour, and the dinner script helps them decide what choices to make. In this situation the following utterances might be judged as *inappropriate* by persons at the table, and children would be urged to create more appropriate meanings:

1. (just after sitting down at the table) "Yuch, this looks sick!" or "Oh darn, not this again" or "What is this funny-looking stuff?"
2. (during dinner) "You shoulda seen Billy's dog go poop." (Since many conversational topics are acceptable dinner-time chatter, we were hard-pressed to come up with a variety of examples here.)
3. (after finishing dinner) "Well, I gotta go—bye." (abruptly leaves table)

As children grow up, they learn hundreds of scripts that help them make meaning choices in particular situations.

Schemas are mental frameworks for our social, cultural, and personal experiences. These frameworks organize the information we have already gathered and new facts and perceptions as we experience them. Schemas are acquired in everyday life. A child who frequently experiences someone telling him bedtime stories will begin to notice that each story begins with a phrase such as "Once upon a time" and ends with a phrase such as "And they lived happily ever after." As they hear more and more stories they also learn that something exciting or bad often happens to the good guy, but that the good guy triumphs while the bad guy loses. They learn that stories have a sequence and structure, and that actions are often predictable. This framework is probably one schema for the bedtime story. Another schema could be a social one, as in how characters in the story typically talk to each other. In much the same way that children acquire schemas for bedtime stories, they learn schemas for vacations, parties, the dinner hour, and many other social events.

Relating this concept to our main concern in this chapter, we could argue that children really learn schemas for language functions. People must have some knowledge of how language is used in various social contexts. For example, they must know how individuals relate to each other through the regulatory or interpersonal functions of communication. As children grow up, their functional schemas mature; they grow in complexity, as for example into the pragmatic and then interpersonal functions.

Let's explore an example in greater detail. A young child has a schema for the pragmatic function. She knows that to get someone to do something for her she must approach the event in a particular way that is determined by the applicable social and cultural guidelines. The following might be a list of steps in her pragmatic schema: capture the person's attention, be polite if necessary, say what you want in clear terms, repeat yourself if necessary, and use appeals. A three-year-old children may not be aware of these steps explicitly, but she acts as if she know them perfectly well.

PERSONAL POWERS AND MEANING

Probably more than any one chapter in this text, this chapter outlines the underpinnings of language as the development of self-regulation. The key component of human development, according to Lev Vygotsky, the theorist used to lay the foundations for meaning development in this chapter, is the change from other-regulation to self-regulation. According to Halliday, the pathway to self-regulation is through the process of learning to mean in the context of one's life, one's family, the neighborhood, all society.

Using the foundation presented in this chapter, then, the pathway to self-regulation is the effective development of learning how to mean. Children begin the process of meaning using singular functions of communication, such as the regulatory or the heuristic. In this phase of their development, they do not have the personal powers to regulate their own lives. Even in the second phase of development in learning how to mean, they are not properly equipped to deal with regulating their own lives, though in this phase they do have capabilities to initiate actions and responses from others, (pragmatic function) and learn about their environment (mathetic function).

In phase three of meaning, children begin to communicate in a context where they realize the importance of regulating their lives. In this phase, children begin to make communication choices based on a host of factors related to themselves, those they are talking to, and the circumstances of their interaction. In this phase of development, children are able to make appropriate meaning choices. From this viewpoint, the entire process of learning how to mean is a process in acquiring personal powers. Success in learning how to mean will precipitate successful development of personal powers.

SUMMARY

The two opposing theoretical views of meaning, the structural and the functional, have different focuses. The structural perspective is concerned with an examination of the "underpinnings" of meaning, while the functional approach consists of exploring the dynamics of meaning. Whereas the structuralists examine objects and phenomena as referents of meaning, the functional approach examines the process of meaning. In *Learning How to Mean* M.A.K. Halliday argues that both the product of meaning and the process of meaning must be examined simultaneously.

As background for Halliday's functional approach to meaning, Vygotsky's explanation of the development of the thought-language relationship was examined. Children's use of language changes dramatically as they age: young children's language reflects a more dependent relationship on others, while older children use language in the process of self-regulation. The older child is able to control the environment through language.

Before infants reach their first birthday they use sounds to communicate what they need (the instrumental function of language), to ask someone for something (the regulatory function), to relate to others (the interactional function), to express feelings (the personal function), to ask questions and discover things (the heuristic function), and to show their curiosity about their social world (the imaginative function). As children move into the second phase of meaning, they are able to use language to elicit action or a response from others (the pragmatic function) and use language for learning (the mathetic function). The striking difference between phases 1 and 2 is that in the first phase all functions are used separately, while in the second phase they are combined. In the third phase of meaning development children communicate through the ideational and interpersonal functions; usually, these functions are used simultaneously. In this final phase children make choices about what to say, based on knowledge of the situation gained from adults' social and cultural expectations of them. They know certain scripts for behavior, and they have schemas for approaching various communication situations.

REFERENCES

HALLIDAY, M.A.K., *Learning How to Mean: Explorations in the Development of Language*. New York: Elsevier, 1975.

VYGOTSKY, LEV S., *Thought and Language*, trans. E. Hansmann and C. V. Vakar. Cambridge, Mass.: M.I.T. Press, 1962.

PART III

THE CHILD'S COMMUNICATION SYSTEM: NONVERBAL DEVELOPMENT

Researchers struggle to find order amidst chaos in their study of the human being's use of nonverbal communication. Although theorists suggest that we follow rules in our use of nonverbal codes, they have not yet presented explicit statements of such rules. And although language experts have suspected that nonverbal cues constitute a significant portion of a message, traditional theories have given very little importance to such cues. Often, tone of voice and body movement are discussed as cues that simply enhance or clarify the verbal message. However, recent studies argue that nonverbal language has a far more important function in communication than merely dressing up words. Scientific study in selected areas of nonverbal communication has extended over many years. Nonverbal communication of emotions through intonation patterns is certainly not a new area of study. Moreover, the examination of gestures dates back to ancient theories of speechmaking. Yet the concerted effort to study nonverbal communication as a *system*—one that is described by sets of rules for the communication of information, attitudes, and feelings—has been undertaken only in recent years.

A second condition that helps explain the chaos in the study of nonverbal communication is the lack of an established system of coding and classifying the meaningful nonverbal units in a person's communication. Although we have numerous systems for classifying the sounds, words, and sentences of our language, established methods for classifying our "winks, blinks, and nods" are just now being developed. Thus, we are striving to find a science of nonverbal communication.

A third condition that accounts for our caution in studying nonverbal communication is our lack of knowledge concerning the basis of nonverbal language. At the present time experts do not agree about the nature of children's acquisition of nonverbal language. Some scientists argue that the biological-endowment hypothesis works well in explaining verbal-language development but falls short in accounting for nonverbal development. Is the nonverbal system a totally learned system, based on environmental conditioning? Or do infants have innate capabilities to use facial, vocal, and bodily cues? We know very little about the relationship of nonverbal communication to the human mind. As we begin to discover that human emotions are predictably related to neurological and physical processes, we are beginning to see new avenues for research in the physical communication of emotions. With greater understanding of the human brain and the relationship of the brain to the communication process, we will be in a better position to examine the course of nonverbal-communication development in children.

With these qualifications in mind, we approach the study of nonverbal-communication development in children. Chapters 8–10 are based on *what we believe to be true* about nonverbal communication in children and adults. We will explore recent theories and scientific investigations that have helped explain how children communicate by using their body, their voice, and the space around them. Although there are presently no specific methods for examining the whole of nonverbal development, there are three research directions that describe the existing body of knowledge.

1. The science of kinesics, which deals with bodily communication, offers an approach that is very compatible with studies of verbal language. This approach involves the analysis of gestures, movements, and positions of the body according to a progression closely akin to that in verbal language development; the result is an attempt to isolate "kines," "kinemes," "kinemorphs," and even a "kinegrammar." Analyses are mainly of adult communication, but a few studies do attempt to account for the emergence of nonverbal cues in infants and children.

2. Scientific study of prosody in speech has attempted to account for the relationship of features of the voice, such as pitch and loudness, to meaningful cues in our messages. Experts in the study of prosody are beginning to examine the emergence of prosodic features in the speech of young children.

3. The science of proxemics, which deals with our use of distance (and touch) in communication, offers still another direction in nonverbal-language study. Based on research with adults, proxemic theorists have established norms of proxemic behavior—actually, distance "conventions" in communication. The direction of proxemic research in children's language development has been to examine the emergence of such conventions in children's communication.

Part III examines children's communication through the channels of body motion, the voice, and space. Although the discussion in Chapters 8–10 is not as sophisticated as our study of verbal communication in Part II, it should provide an overall perspective of the development of children's non-verbal communication.

CHILDREN'S BODY LANGUAGE

As adults we have been taught that first impressions are crucial in social and business interactions. Our physical appearance, which includes our posture, bodily movements, and dress, is considered to be a most important persuasive tool in conveying a positive first impression. Apparently, we believe that initial messages sent by our bodies are more immediate than initial messages sent with our words.

Going beyond first impressions, we know that the meaning underlying a person's message is often communicated with arm movements, eye blinks, and smiling faces. We include a chapter on children's body language because of its supreme importance in most communication situations. Chapter 8 discusses body language in terms of two major types of movement: arm and hand gestures and facial expressions, especially smiling. Information on development in each of these areas suggests that important changes take place in nonverbal communication from birth throughout the elementary-school years.

THE VOICE COMMUNICATES!

One of the first channels of communication available to the infant is the voice. Infants communicate vocally and understand basic vocal messages. Tone of voice, or prosody, is based on the pitch, loudness, pausing, and tempo of a message. Children have practice in communicating meaning vocally from the time they become social beings.

As children come closer and closer to acquiring the adult communication patterns of their culture, they learn to vary aspects of their voice in accordance with ideas, moods, and feelings. Children learn that others will understand their tone of voice even if their verbal message seems unclear. Although it may take children longer to understand the meaning of prosodic variations in the voices of others, particularly in terms of emotional communication, the importance of such learning cannot be deemphasized simply because of its slower development.

As teachers of children, we must be very aware of vocal communication and its development in children. Chapter 9 focuses on children's development of prosody, in terms of pitch, loudness, pauses, and tempo.

CHILDREN'S COMMUNICATION IN SPACE

Edward Hall, the founder of the study of proxemics, insists that one of the most nagging barriers to effective communication between cultural groups is interpersonal spacing in communication. Hall has observed marked differences in the communication patterns of adults from different cultural and subcultural groups, such as differences in distance between speakers, shoulder orientation, eye contact, and other proxemic variables. These differences are apparently the product of cultural learning. If we are to achieve more effective communication among social and cultural groups, we must understand proxemic conventions and how they develop in children. Exploratory studies with children suggest that proxemic conventions develop throughout children's elementary-school years. In their early years, children use a very small "space bubble" in their interactions with others.

The messages we send with our bodies do not exist in a vacuum: they emerge in a personal space around us—our "communication territory." These proxemic messages are important because they indicate our feelings, likings, and judgments. We know that children are in the process of learning to act and talk in space, but we have only basic information about children's spatial behavior. The purpose of Chapter 10 is to explore children's development of proxemic communication in four distance zones outlined by Hall. We will find that proxemic differences among children are related to sex and ethnic background.

8

the body language of children

A child's first communication experiences with other children are considered *acted conversations* by child psychologist Jean Piaget. Acted conversations are cryptic because they rely heavily on gestures and bodily demonstrations rather than words.[1] To understand what young children are talking about, we must notice their pointing, bobbing, and waving movements. Children's gestures often tell us more about what they are "really saying" than do their words. In fact, it's virtually impossible to interpret utterances such as the following without watching a little finger pointing to a car or a head bobbing toward the playhouse:

"This does that."

"That goes there."

"Make that thing do it this way."

The dialogue of an acted conversation lends that quaint character to children's speech. There is no question about it: young children talk with their bodies.

Acted conversations depend almost totally on body language, whereas verbal conversations—which emerge later, according to Piaget—present a more balanced picture of the verbal and nonverbal channels of communication. For younger children communication is synonymous with movement:

[1]Jean Piaget, *The Language and Thought of the Child*, trans. M. Gabain (New York: Meridian Books, 1955), p. 94.

their arms, legs, and heads seem to be in a constant state of motion as they work, play, and talk with others. Younger children depend on gestures and bodily movement for a *direct statement* of their message. With the acquisition of verbal language, gestures and movements take on the different role of *complementing the verbal message.*

How do children learn to "talk" with their arms, their faces—their entire bodies? Ray Birdwhistell, a leading scholar in the field of *kinesics*, the study of body-motion communication, insists that all children acquire such a communication system as they learn their native language. In fact, membership in a social or cultural group depends on mastery of the nonverbal-communication system—body motion and voice—as well as the verbal system.[2] Initially, children get to know their new friends through obviously physical contacts. A poke in the eye, a tug on the ear, and a finger in the nose are simply the child's way of saying hello and learning more about you. Children rely heavily on their bodies in discovering the world around them:

> Children, before they are taught the inhibitions of our society, explore their world by touch. They touch their parents and cuddle into their arms, touch themselves, find joy in their genitals, security in the texture of their blankets, excitement in feeling cold things, hot things, smooth things and scratchy things.[3]

The communication of young children is also very physical. The message of a two-year-old boy might involve standing at the cookie jar, pointing, and uttering a gruntlike sound. If he gets a cookie—or even if he doesn't, for that matter—communication probably took place if someone was around. We assume that as the child becomes verbally adept he relies less and less on nonverbal communication. That the child becomes proportionately more verbal as he ages does not and should not suggest to us that the nonverbal channels of communication become either nonexistent or unimportant. In fact, all adult speakers constantly engage in body-motion communication, and although some of us may "move" more than others, all of us would be lost without this form of language.

CHILDREN AND MOVEMENT

Imagine yourself a parent trying to keep a two-year-old child inactive for ten days. A pediatrician gave this order to a friend of mine following her little girl's surgery. The thought of keeping an active, rambunctious child relatively motionless for such a long period of time seemed impossible—and it was. The young child understood her mother's orders to

---

[2]Ray Birdwhistell, *Kinesics and Context: Essays in Body Motion Communication* (Philadelphia: University of Pennsylvania Press, 1970), p. 7.
[3]Julius Fast, *Body Language* (New York: M. Evans, 1970), pp. 79–80.

be still, but her compliance lasted about thirty seconds. From a child's point of view living is synonymous with moving. Restrictions in movement are frustrating for anyone, especially young children. According to psychoanalytic theory, a child's reactions to bodily restrictions reveal the human drive, based on an urge called *motility*, to be free to move at will.

"Jim Thorpe, the famous four-star athlete, is said to have imitated each move in a baby's active day. He gave out, exhausted, after four hours. The infant continued for eight or more."[4] The child moves constantly. He engages in movements that serve no visible purpose aside from the sheer experience of movement—crawling, running, bouncing, jumping, and whirling. Many of these activities are rhythmic and seem to provide the child with great satisfaction and pleasure. If the activity is blocked, the child inevitably becomes restless or angry.

Motility, the spontaneous movement of the skeletal musculature, is considered an urge in the same sense as the oral, excretory, and genital urges. Bela Mittelmann, a noted authority on psychoanalytic study of the child, explains that there are identifiable parts of the body that communicate a sense of urgency.[5] During the second and third years of life the child experiences rapid development of motor skills. Many of the child's motor activities can be considered spontaneous releases of emotions, feelings, and reactions. The so-called urge to be bodily free is at its peak in preschool years and steadily declines after five or six years of age. After the child is ten years old, the motor urge remains at a consistent low. Dr. Mittelmann relates the decline of the motor urge to the rise of children's preference for verbal activity to motor activity.

WHAT IS BODY LANGUAGE?

All of us know that a wink, a smile, or a frown may tell someone how we feel; words are not always necessary. Others can tell that we are uncomfortable by watching our fidgeting, bodily tension, and wandering eyes. Body language can be defined as any reflexive or nonreflexive movement or position used to communicate an emotional, attitudinal, or informational message to someone else. Let's explore this definition in detail.

Body movements (for instance, waving and winking) and positions (for example, hunched shoulders and wide-open eyes) are the basic categories of body language. Although any movement or position during communication is capable of message value, not all motion necessarily communicates. For example, we could conclude that our friend's wrinkled brow is a sign of her

---

[4]T. Berry Brazelton, *Infants and Mothers: Differences in Development* (New York: Delacorte Press, 1969), p. 158.
[5]Bela Mittelmann, "Motility in Infants, Children, and Adults," *Psychoanalytic Study of the Child*, 9 (1954), 154.

dissatisfaction with our presence, but we could be wrong. Maybe her wrinkled brow is simply the result of her attempt to keep light out of her eyes as she is talking.

Body movements and positions can be considered either *reflexive* (involuntary) or *nonreflexive* (voluntary). An involuntary motion often studied by kinesic experts is pupil dilation—the widening of the pupil in the eye. It can tell your opponent in cards that your hand is good. Research also indicates that the male's pupil dilates twice as much as normal when he is shown a picture of a nude woman. Supposedly, he is communicating his excitement. Pupil dilation has been used as a measure of students' reactions to critiques of their speeches by a video-taped critic-teacher. When the teacher made positive statements about their speeches, the students' pupils dilated. These studies suggest that the eyes communicate messages of excitement, arousal, and pleasure. Are we conscious of our pupils dilating? Probably not. Facial twitches, eye movements, and shoulder orientation are body-language cues that we send involuntarily to others.

Nonreflexive movements or positions seem to be more within our control in communication; however, their interpretation is often more difficult. Because we can control some of our movements when we are communicating, we can deceive the person to whom we are talking. A smile to an employer may be well within our control: we want him to receive a positive message. Maybe our real feelings for him at that moment are not positive, but let's assume that we don't want him to see our true feelings. Instead, we put on a kind of act with our body language, hoping he will believe it. In this case the body-language message is inconsistent with our feelings. In other instances our controlled movements, verbal language, and thoughts can all be on the same wavelength.

The agreement of body language with verbal language is a crucial point. When verbal and nonverbal messages are in agreement—let's say both are very positive—few problems arise in interpreting the communication. But what if the verbal message contradicts the nonverbal message? Which message should we believe? For centuries psychoanalysts have tried to resolve the problem of patients who seem to be saying one thing but meaning something else. Psychoanalysts approach the problem by attributing the contradictory messages to a conflict between superficial (deceitful) feelings and true feelings. Often, the verbal channel conveys the superficial feelings and the nonverbal channel the true feelings. According to one nonverbal theorist, the role of the psychiatrist, then, is "to help the client separate the wheat from the chaff."[6] This is done by analyzing the nonverbal channel to determine the person's underlying feelings and attitudes.

We can use verbal language to communicate many different types of

[6]Albert Mehrabian, "Communication Without Words," in *Communication: Concepts and Processes*, ed. Joseph DeVito (Englewood Cliffs, N.J.: Prentice-Hall, 1971), p. 108.

messages. The range of messages communicated by body language is somewhat more limited, however. We can use our bodies to refer to objects or events (deictic gestures), to mimic certain movements or events (pantomimic gestures), and to communicate semantic and relationship information (facial expressions and arm movements). In many cases these nonverbal messages are not as clear-cut and well defined as our verbal messages. Yet this greater potential for ambiguity cannot diminish the supreme importance of body language in communication with others.

Body language includes movements of *a part of the body*, such as a nod of the head or a raising of the eyebrows, and movement of *the entire body*, such as overall body tension or jumping up and down. Movements and positions are usually related to emotional messages. Your pleasure in seeing someone you haven't seen in a long time may result in a visible expression of that emotion. Body motion can also communicate your attitude toward another person: how much you like him ("liking" messages) and how important you perceive him to be ("status" messages). Research has indicated, for example, that extreme bodily tension may communicate "You're a high-status person" or "I don't like you." In addition, our body language can answer questions: "How much?" (a little or a lot), "Which way?" (up or down), and "How big?" (tiny or gigantic).

Experts in kinesics stress the importance of cultural and environmental differences in understanding body language. Body language is culture-bound, and a body motion may communicate two entirely different messages to members of two different cultural groups. To complicate matters, a body motion may not even convey a particular meaning. If there were always a one-to-one correspondence between *motion* and *meaning*, we could simply learn "body words" (movements or positions always associated with a particular meaning) and a "body grammar" (patterns of movements and positions that communicate meaning in "body sentences"). According to Bird-whistell, the aim of kinesic research is to uncover the movements and combinations of movements that generally convey meanings. After decades of research, however, a *body language* has been difficult to isolate. Although we are fairly confident that we have discovered the morphology and grammar of verbal language, exploration into the morphology and grammar of body language is certainly in its infancy.

To get an idea of the nature of kinesic research, let's use the example of the eyelids. It's been found that the human eye can distinguish eleven different positions of the eyelid. Only four of the eleven appear to be used by Americans in their communication: (1) "overopen" (wide-eyed), (2) "slit," (3) "closed," and (4) "squeezed." The eleven possible positions are called *kines* and the four meaningful positions (to Americans) are called *kinemes*. Kinemes are like phonemes: they are the building blocks of nonverbal messages, just as phonemes are the building blocks of verbal messages. Kinemes are defined differently for different "speech" communities: one culture may have four kinemes of eyelid position, and another may have as many as five or six.

In addition to kines and kinemes, there are *kinemorphs* and *kinemorphemes*. Kinemorphemes are "body words," defined by a movement or series of body movements whose total effect is a minimal meaning unit. *Social kinesics* is the study of bodily movements that accompany spoken language and appear to convey social meaning. Research indicates, for example, that bodily movements vary when the message refers to "he" as opposed to "they," something that happened in the past versus something that will happen in the future, and something "over" rather than something "under." Posture—specifically, the carriage of the pelvis—is a dead giveaway of gender. The messages we send with our bodies are patterned and structured like our spoken language—thus, the meaningful phrase "body language."

Our discussion of body language in children focuses on two major types of body movement: hand and arm movements, generally referred to as gestures, and facial movements, especially smiling.

HAND AND ARM GESTURES

Most accounts of children's development of gestures suggest that as children become more verbally "proficient" they rely less on gestures. Some even claim that children virtually drop gestures from their communication repertoire as they age. More recent studies of gestures suggest, however, that while some types of gestures decrease in frequency as the child ages, others increase and continue to function effectively with the child's verbal language. In this section three categories of gestures are explained in terms of developmental information:

1. When children point to objects or places to refer to "this," "that," or "over there," they use *deictic gestures.*

2. *Pantomimic gestures* are used to mimic or copy aspects of an object or event children see or feel, as when they show you how they might have looked when they first walked, or when they communicate the surprised look a friend had when he found a dollar bill.

3. Arm and hand movements that add semantic or relational information:

    a. *Semantic modifiers:* When children use gestures to illustrate size or shape or to show emphasis, contrast, or amendment of the content, they are using gestures semantically.

    b. *Relational gestures:* These are gestures that children use to communicate their feelings about their relationships with those they talk to. Relational gestures can convey feelings such as affection, hostility, and cautiousness.[7]

---

[7]For a further discussion of these three categories, see MerryAnn Jancovic, Shannon Devoe, and Morton Weiner, "Age-Related Changes in Hand and Arm Movements as Nonver-

Developmental information, though not complete in any one category, tends to indicate that deictic and pantomimic gestures are important for young children but decline with verbal development. Semantic and relational gestures, however, tend to increase in frequency with verbal development.

deictic gestures

When children point and refer with their hands and arms, they are using deictic gestures. Likewise, when children point and refer with words, they use deictic verbal language. The deictic gesture is the most elementary form of movement in communication because a most elementary form of information (direction, place, or movement) is being transmitted.

The basis of the deictic gesture is pointing. The development of pointing takes the following direction, according to Catherine Murphy and David Messer:

1. The baby reaches and grasps objects that are attainable.
2. The baby reaches for an object that is not attainable, and this reach is interpreted as an indicator gesture by others. In this sense, adults seem to transform the reach into the gesture.
3. The infant is continually exposed to adults' pointing, the more conventional indicator gesture, and begins to intentionally communicate through pointing herself.[8]

This three-step process, heavily influenced by the thinking of psychologist Lev Vygotsky, illustrates the profound effect adults have on the child's nonverbal language. The pointing gesture seems to begin solely in the mind of the adult, only later becoming a means of communication for the child.

Based on Murphy and Messer's research with one- and two-year-olds, two generalizations can be made with regard to the child's acquisition of pointing. Both stress the critical role the mother's behavior seems to have in the infant's acquisition of this type of communciation. First, the mother's pointing is accompanied by some type of verbalizing. More commands are used in talk to one-year-olds and more descriptive language (about an object being pointed to) in talk with two-year-olds. Second, infants learn to follow pointing, and seem to understand some types of pointing gestures earlier than others. For example, they follow pointing *away* before they follow the more abstract gestures of pointing *across* and pointing *forward.*

bal Communication: Some Conceptualizations and an Empirical Exploration," *Child Development,* 46 (1975), 922–28.

[8]Catherine Murphy and David Messer, "Mothers, Infants and Pointing: A Study of a Gesture," in *Studies in Mother-Infant Interaction,* ed. H. Rudolph Shaffer (New York: Academic Press, 1977), pp. 325–54.

The fourteen-month-old child is capable of following a variety of pointing gestures, and may even be able to estimate the direction and angle of the object pointed to. The nine-month-old infant, however, seems able to follow only a general point to an object "out there."

When young children first use pointing gestures of their own, they do not employ the simultaneous glancing used by adults. Most important, they do not seem to check to see whether or not their gesture has been understood or viewed. The child's lack of sensitivity may be based on an underdeveloped meaning of the gesture or on a rather strong assumption that the adult will follow the pointing.

Children must acquire a system called *deixis*, which allows them to refer to proximal/nonproximal contrasts, such as "here" versus "there" and "this" versus "that." The verbal system of deixis takes several years for the child to master. "Pointing with words," on the other hand, grows directly out of children's ability to point with their fingers. Children begin pointing from a very early age, and continue to rely on pointing for explaining much of what they mean. As they add the deictic words to their language and gestures, the gestures become less critical to the communication of ideas. According to a study by Eve Clark and C. J. Sengul,[9] once children learn to elaborate the deictic utterances in which they pick out objects and events they can dispense with deictic gestures altogether.

Most children use at least one deictic word by two and a half years of age, though they do not seem to realize that pairs of words, such as "here" and "there," are capable of communicating contrast. When they attempt to contrast two objects, they do so by pointing to each one in turn.[10] Children have no deictic contrast between "here" and "there" or between "this" and "that" until about age five or six. The verbal system probably requires heavy reliance on gestures through the preschool years, and it is well into the elementary-school years before children produce language that does not include deictic gestures. Comprehension of deictic contrasts may develop by age five or six, though production seems to follow this age.

Another type of deictic gesture involves reference to more specific objects and events. After examining two preschoolers' verbal and nonverbal language, a theorist proposed three distinct stages in the development of such gestures:

1. *Parallel encoding:* at this stage children seem to rely heavily on the gesture, though they may incidentally use words. Both words and gestures are used simultaneously:
   a. "I want crayon." (grabs crayon from brother)

---

[9]Eve V. Clark and C. J. Sengul, "Strategies in the Acquisition of Deixis," *Journal of Child Language*, 5 (1978), 457–75.
[10]*Ibid.*, p. 459.

b. "Doggie sleepin'." (points to dog lying down)

c. "See dat." (points to toy)

2. *Verbal complementation:* the nonverbal message or gesture is somewhat ambiguous, though the verbal message seems to clarify the meaning:

a. "Make it go." (hands other a favorite car)

b. "That's my daddy." (points to picture)

c. "Someone knockin'." (points to door)

3. *Substitution of verbal forms:* most of the information is carried verbally, while the gestures seem only to add redundant information:

a. "My eyes have sleep in them." (rubs eyes)

b. "He hit me hard." (pounds fist into palm)

c. "It went round and round." (makes circles with arm)[11]

pantomimic gestures

One of the most elementary approaches to the study of children's body language examines children's pantomimic gestures. Studies of such gestures define them as self-contained communication segments and examine them in isolation. Gestures of greeting (such as indicating "hello" with a waving hand) would be considered, for example. Obviously, there are limitations to this kind of study. Most body language accompanies verbal and vocal messages and does not stand alone as a communicator of meaning. In short, our gestures—in fact, all of our body motions—*accompany* the messages we convey in our words, our language structure, our voice, and our use of space. The study of "isolated gestures" does, however, lend some insight into how children learn what theorists have called nonverbal "emblems"—that is, nonverbal segments of communication that can stand alone and signal meaning to an observer.

To study the development of pantomimic gestures in children, Geraldine Michael and Frank Willis examined children's ability to transmit and interpret twelve frequently employed gestures.[12]

1. Go away.

2. Come here.

3. Yes.

4. No.

5. Be quiet.

6. How many?

7. How big?

[11]Ernst L. Moerk, *Pragmatic and Semantic Aspects of Early Language Development* (Baltimore: University Park Press, 1977), pp. 190–99.

[12]Geraldine Michael and Frank Willis, "The Development of Gestures as a Function of Social Class, Education, and Sex," *Psychological Record,* 18 (1968), 515–19.

8. Shape (for example, round or square).
9. I don't know.
10. Good by.
11. Hi.
12. Raised hand for attention.

These twelve gestures were the ones observed most frequently in direct observation of children from four to seven at play and in the classroom. The children in the study were interviewed individually. They were asked first to transmit each of the twelve pantomimic gestures and then to interpret the same gestures when communicated by the interviewer. To elicit the gesture "Come here," for example, this instruction was used: "If you had to be quiet and you were over there (pointing away) and you wanted me to come to you, what would you do?" Children were judged on their accuracy in transmitting and interpreting the twelve gestures. The study posed the following basic questions:

1. Are older children (in this case first graders) better in transmitting and understanding gestures than younger (preschool) children?
2. Are girls or boys better in transmitting or interpreting gestures?

Children with one year of school (about six years of age) were better in both transmitting and interpreting the gestures than children of preschool age. The older children's longer exposure to communication in peer groups—communication that includes nonverbal messages and signals—probably explains their ability to send and receive gestural messages more accurately. Boys scored better than girls in interpreting the gestures, but the authors could only guess why this happened. They suggested that because boys are slower to acquire verbal language (a questionable assumption), they develop nonverbal language more rapidly. Conclusions regarding sex comparisons are almost impossible to draw.

During their preschool and early elementary years, it seems that children acquire a repertoire of pantomimic gestures capable of communicating a number of different ideas. Their ability to understand these gestures in others develops by first or second grade.

semantic and relationship gestures; the body language of gender communication

Gestures that communicate important semantic information, such as gestures of emphasis, and gestures that convey information about relationships between persons develop steadily in the growing child. These gestures show a steady rise from preschoolers to older children. Surprisingly, however, detailed studies on the development of these types of movement are sparse. But with increased attention to their importance, it is likely that major research projects will study the development of nonverbal relational and semantic messages in children. The study of relational and semantic gestures has only recently been pursued with adults; developmental inquiries will emerge soon, no doubt.

One interesting line of research in the area of relational gestures examines the body language used by children to communicate gender. No one wants to raise a child who doesn't know what sex he or she is. Very early in life, according to Germaine Greer, both boys and girls are taught strategies of coyness and shyness. Eventually, these strategies are reserved for little girls; little boys are shocked out of them. Inevitably, the little boy must "break his umbilical cord with mother; little boys are encouraged to get out of their mother's way, and they eventually 'want to' and are encouraged to do this. Little girls are not."[13] According to Greer, little girls are punished for wandering too far from home, whereas little boys are urged to wander and to explore the unknown in groups with other little boys. Little girls must stay home like little mommies and do their household chores.

Children acquire gender behaviors in their homes. Elementary-school teachers continue parental training in the classroom by rewarding and punishing children for their "appropriate" and "inappropriate" gender behaviors.[14]

the basis of gender role

According to Dr. Benjamin Spock, "babies in the last half of the first year discover their genitals the way they discover their fingers and toes, and handle them in the same way, too."[15] Although a one-year-old boy does not know that he is a boy, he becomes aware, long before he enters school, that he is "sexed," and he behaves accordingly.

The child's awareness of being masculine or feminine is not simply an outgrowth of being male or female. The child's sex (male or female) is an inborn variable based on physiological parameters, mainly the reproductive organs. Gender (masculine or feminine) *may* or *may not* be inborn in the child. Many psychologists consider gender a learned variable, one based on the child's experiences with parents and others he or she encounters. But

[13]Germaine Greer, *The Female Eunuch* (New York: McGraw-Hill, 1971), p. 68.

[14]Support for this statement can be found in Teresa Levitin and J. D. Chananie, "Responses of Female Primary School Teachers to Sex-Typed Behaviors in Male and Female Children," *Child Development*, 43 (1972), 1309–16.

[15]Benjamin Spock, *Baby and Child Care* (New York: Pocket Books, 1968), p. 372. © 1945, 1946, 1957, 1968 by Benjamin Spock, M.D. Reprinted by permission of Simon & Schuster, Inc., Pocket Books Division and the New English Library, Ltd., England.

studies by Harry Harlow (University of Wisconsin Primate Laboratory) dealing with chimpanzees and their acquisition of gender roles suggest that gender is inborn. Monkeys reared with "cloth mothers" behave in typical sex-typed ways: male monkeys behave in typically boyish fashion, whereas female monkeys wouldn't think of playing in such roughhouse ways. The monkeys in this study had no parental models to copy, yet they developed appropriate sex-typed behaviors. Future research with human beings is clearly necessary: we can't answer questions on the origin of human gender behavior with studies of primates. Yet such studies indicate that the previously "settled" issue of gender as a learned set of behaviors must be examined more carefully.

Medical studies reveal that gender role is well established by the second birthday, about the time children begin to string words together. Children develop this role from their second year on. Let's examine the factors affecting the development of gender role.

acquisition of gender role

According to Jerome Kagan, there are at least three kinds of experiences that affect the degree to which children regard themselves as masculine or feminine:

1. the child's identification with mother, father, sibling, parent-surrogate, or peers
2. the child's acquisition of bodily and verbal behaviors that define masculinity or femininity
3. the child's perception that others regard him or her as possessing appropriate sex-typed characteristics.[16]

As background for our discussion of the body language of gender display, let's discuss these three kinds of experiences.

An identification is a belief that some attributes of a model—perhaps a parent, sibling, or peer—belong to the self. If a six-year-old boy identifies with his father, he believes he exhibits characteristics of his father and regards himself as masculine. A boy's motivation to identify with his father is based on his desire to command the attractive goals (such as strength and power) that are possessed by his father. The child assumes that if he possesses some of the physical characteristics of his father, such as the way he walks and carries himself, he might also command his desirable psychological properties, such as power, respect, and love. The child behaves as if he believes in the argument that things appearing alike on the outside are alike on the inside.

[16]Jerome Kagan, "Acquisition and Significance of Sex Typing and Sex Role Identity," in *Review of Child Development Research*, ed. M. Hoffman and L. Hoffman (New York: Russell Sage Foundation, 1964), pp. 145-51.

Of primary importance in the child's acquistion of gender role is the ability to imitate or copy the bodily behavior of the same-sexed parent. The important "test" of the child's gender-role behavior occurs when the child enters social groups, particularly school. Consider the following case.

> A boy with a minimally masculine father will confront the societal standard for masculinity when he enters school. Since his overt behavior will be less sex typed than that of his peers, he will perceive a discrepancy between his actions and those of "other boys." He will be tempted to conclude that he is not masculine because his behavior does not match that of the male peer group, and because he may be the target of accusatory communications implying that he is not masculine.[17]

The result of this child's experience is that his gender role is challenged and thus weakened.

Compare the above test situation with that of a boy who has extensive practice in copying the very masculine behavior of his masculine dad. Not only does this boy identify with his father, he also succeeds in copying the masculine behaviors of his father. When he encounters peers with masculine behaviors similar to his own, he perceives the similarity. Similar test situations occur for girls. The traditional signals of feminine behavior—submissiveness with boys, inhibition of aggression, cultivation of personal attractiveness, and so on—become the bases for the girl's comparison of herself with her peers.

gender identifiers

A primary means of communicating gender role is through a kind of body language called gender display. Ray Birdwhistell has studied the communication of gender and has discovered gender identifiers in adults that are also present in young children. Birdwhistell's studies located the emergence of gender communication at about eighteen months to two years of age—about the same period in which gender is determined in children. Although the preschool child may have intellectual difficulties realizing that her gender is a constant and unalterable phenomenon of her world, her body clearly indicates that the matter of gender has been decided.

Working with informants from seven different cultures throughout the world, Birdwhistell found that each culture has stereotypes of feminine and masculine behaviors, stereotypes that can be "acted out." Bodily movements and positions are an important part of this "acting." Birdwhistell's investigations pointed out that young children mature "into" gender behaviors and that as they grow older they mature "out of them."

---

[17]*Ibid.*, pp. 147–48.

The gender display of Americans was found to be accomplished through three gender cues, two exhibited in posture and one in facial expression:

1. In sitting, males tend to cross their legs with the thighs at a ten-to-fifteen-degree angle apart, whereas females tend to cross their legs with the thighs, lower legs, and feet together. Similarly, men tend to stand with their arms alongside their trunk at a ten-to-fifteen-degree angle; women stand with their arms directly beside their trunk. This distinction is called the *intrafemoral angle and arm-body angle.*

2. Females carry their pelvis forward in what is called an anterior roll (the bottom is pulled forward) whereas males carry their pelvis back in a posterior roll. This distinction is called the *flexibility of the pelvic spinal complex.*

3. Males open and close their eyelids in a relatively continuous fashion; female eyelid movements are much more variable. Unless there are accompanying signs of sleepiness or drowsiness, men are judged "effeminate" if they disobey this "rule" of *eyelid movement.* [18]

Gender cues may differ from culture to culture, but these three supposedly remain constant for most Americans.

the child's acquisition of gender identifiers

There have been few studies of the child's stage-by-stage acquisition of the body language of gender communication. Probably the most revealing of such studies have involved analysis of films of young children. In one of his studies Birdwhistell used slow-motion film to study gender identifiers in infants and children. He concluded that children begin to display these identifiers in their second year. [19] For example, a female of fifteen months had learned to communicate, bodily, that she was a southern, upper-middle-class female. She held her pelvis in an anterior roll and kept her arms alongside her trunk. A twenty-two-month-old boy in the same study was filmed in a spread-legged position and rolled his pelvis posteriorly. On the basis of this study and other slow-motion-film analyses of infants and children, Birdwhistell located the emergence of the body language of gender as early as the second year. He insists, however, that further research is necessary if the acquisition process is to be described in detail.

gender communication: changing identities?

Birdwhistell suggests that children in today's society have some difficulty in learning gender behaviors, primarily because of the sexual revolution. He finds no evidence that men in Western European society are be-

[18]Birdwhistell, *Kinesics and Context,* pp. 43–44.
[19]*Ibid.,* pp. 47–50.

coming weaker or that women are becoming stronger. Other observers maintain that children are not having difficulty in acquiring their gender role; rather, they are acquiring gender roles that are not defined as specifically as before. What may trouble parents is whether this "blurring" of genders is merely a fad their children are going through or a permanent state of affairs.

Further study of the body language of gender communication may reveal a shift in children's communication from traditional gender cues to a more modern set of cues. One implication of children's development of gender communication is this: adults must understand the process of this development in children as well as the "norms" of the community. Our reactions to children's gender messages must not be dictated solely by traditional conceptions of gender roles.

FACIAL MOVEMENT

Different portions of the face (such as the brows and forehead, the eyes, and the lower face) help in communicating emotional messages. A study comparing these portions of the face revealed some major findings about facial communication that relate to children's acquisition of it:

1. The portion of the face that by itself best predicted emotions (the emotions studied were happiness, sadness, surprise, anger, disgust, and fear) was *the eyes*. They ranked first (73 percent). The lower face, including the mouth, was next (67 percent), and the brows and forehead were third (49 percent). Of course, the total face was the best predictor of emotion (88 percent).

2. Some emotions could be almost perfectly predicted by either the eyes or the lower face: happiness and surprise were the best examples. Other emotions, such as fear and disgust, were not well predicted by any of the facial areas.[20]

From these findings we can offer two practical suggestions, to children as well as adults, for interpreting the emotional messages of others. First, in mainstream American culture, looking at a person's eyes is the best way to "listen effectively." Though the entire face is the best predictor of how people feel, the eyes are the single most informative portion of the face. Second, in interpreting more complex emotions, such as fear or disgust, we must view as many nonverbal cues as we can, because one facial area alone is not effective in communicating such subtle messages.

Our examination of facial movements centers on three interesting areas

[20]Paul Ekman, Wallace Friesen, and Dilvan Tomkins, "Facial Affect Scoring Technique: A First Validity Study," in *Nonverbal Communication*, ed. Shirley Weitz (New York: Oxford University Press, 1974), pp. 34–50.

of investigation with children: (1) smiling—types of smiles and their development in children; (2) facial recognition—interpreting emotions in faces; and (3) facial cues and physical attractiveness—how adults react to children.

smiling: forms and functions

In a classic study in the fields of psychology and child development, L. Alan Sroufe and Everett Waters examined infants' smiles and laughter from their earliest stage, the spontaneous smile (called that because of its unknown origin), to their maturity at about one year of age.[21] They studied infants' smiles from many perspectives: physiological, psychological, contextual, cognitive, affective, and social. Smiling and laughter are components of what they call the *tension-release mechanism* because they occur in a context involving stimulation, tension, smiling and laughter, and a release activity. Let's explore a brief example. A mother wears a mask and approaches her child playing. The infant sees her, ceases her ongoing activity, becomes quiet, and stares intently at the masked person. When she realizes the person is her mother, her face brightens, she smiles or laughs, and then she reaches. The reach and smile may occur simultaneously, but the reach never precedes the smile. The researchers suggest that the tension-release process for this child is as follows: incongruous stimulus→appraisal of that stimulus→recognition→SMILE→reach. A motor behavior, in this case the reaching, terminates the tension-release mechanism from which smiling originates.

The researchers do not suggest that infants' smiles serve only this role; they explore the social interpretations of smiling as well. As the infant gets older, the smile becomes primarily a social behavior, serving well as a greeting. The researchers suggest that smiling's social function complements its tension-release function. While the smile allows the baby to remain oriented toward novel stimuli, it also signals well-being and encourages others to continue providing interesting events for which she can again smile. Sroufe and Waters also suggest that the smile probably helps establish turn-taking patterns in interactions between babies and those who give them care.

N. G. Blurton Jones examined the literature on children's smiling behavior and posed several generalizations that are worthy of our consideration.[22] First, he suggests that *social interactions* are the major context for children's smiling, whether in play groups, in talks with their mother, or in their greetings to others. Second, children who smile a lot have mothers who smile a lot, which indicates that this nonverbal behavior seems to be a

---

[21]L. Alan Sroufe and Everett Waters, "The Ontogenesis of Smiling and Laughter: A Perspective on the Organization of Development in Infancy," *Psychological Review*, 83 (1976), 173–89.

[22]N. G. Blurton Jones, "Non-Verbal Communication in Children," in *Non-Verbal Communication*, ed. R. A. Hinde (New York: Cambridge University Press, 1972), pp. 282–83.

product of the child's environment. The most interesting aspect of children's smiling is how they use it with their peers. One study shows that children low in the peer-group pecking order smile more when they initiate conversations with high-status peers than the high-ranking children do with the lower-status peers. On the other hand, children high in the pecking order tend to smile in response to smiles more often than other children.

Smiles are not of one type. A surprising number of studies have confirmed that the vast bulk of smiles can be classified under three major categories:

1. *Upper smile:* The mouth corners are drawn up and back, the upper lip is raised, exposing the upper teeth, and the lower teeth are covered. This is the most common smile.
2. *Closed smile:* The mouth corners are pulled up and back but the upper and lower teeth are covered.
3. *Broad smile:* The mouth corners are pulled up and back, exposing both upper and lower teeth.

Usually, these three smiles are associated with three functional settings:

1. Upper smile: group interactions and greetings
2. Closed smile: solitary play
3. Broad smile: active play

One study examined the development of these three types of smiles in preschool-aged children.[23] Observations were made of seventy-five boys and seventy-five girls in five nursery schools. Their smiles were counted, analyzed, and tabulated for their type (one of the three) and "person-context" (male peer, female peer, teacher, observer, or "child only"). The results of the study indicate a consistent and steady rise in children's use of the more common smile, the upper smile. The average number of upper smiles per hour for children increased from twenty to over thirty. The closed- and broad-smile types did not show significant increases, however.

The most interesting result of this study is that the older children become, the more selective they seem to be in their use of the upper smile. Boys reserve the social (upper) smile for fellow boys by age four, almost never using it with girls. Girls become selective too, though not as much as boys.

facial recognition and interpretation

How do children develop the ability to recognize other children's faces? In a study of first, second, third, and sixth graders of different sexes,

---

[23]J. A. Cheyne, "Development of Forms and Functions of Smiling in Preschoolers," *Child Development*, 47 (1976), 820–23.

races (black and white), and school types (segregated and integrated), researchers found that children's ability to recognize faces increased markedly from first through third grade.[24] After third grade improvement was only slight, however. Findings on racial differences were most interesting. When the children were given pictures of their own race, the black children were better able to recognize faces than the white children. Further, the black children did better at recognizing white children's faces than the whites did with blacks' faces. The researchers offer experience as a possible explanation, suggesting that black children may have greater exposure to whites (say on TV and in person) than whites have to blacks.

As children progress through their elementary-school years they become more adept in interpreting emotions communicated facially and bodily. The exact nature of this development has not been specified, but we do know that with experience children become better decoders of emotion conveyed in body language. Certain emotional messages cause young children extreme difficulty, however; we talked briefly in Chapter 1 about contradictory messages such as joking and sarcasm. Studies have indicated that elementary-school children have trouble resolving the role of a smiling face in such messages. They tend to pay much greater attention to the negative intonation of the voice and judge the conflict message to be extremely negative (more negative than adults would judge it).

Three researchers explored the evaluative connotations of smiles in parents' communications to their children.[25] Interactions between children and their parents were video-taped in the families' homes. One purpose of the study was to examine the positiveness of the mother's smile in comparison with the father's smile. Based on previous studies, the authors' prediction was that the fathers' smiles would be accompanied by more friendly, approving statements than the mothers' smiles. The prediction was supported: the fathers' smiles had a greater positive meaning for children, whereas the mothers' smiles were accompanied by messages that could be positive, neutral, or even negative. Apparently, Mom's smile doesn't "mean as much" as Dad's. It was suggested that mothers employ smiling as frequently as they do to soften the more negative messages they often send to their children. The result of this may be that mothers' smiles become less meaningful to children.

What are the implications of this study for children's communication development? First, children must learn to evaluate the smiles in their parents' communication to them. The task appears to be far simpler when the father smiles: Dad's smile can be associated with a friendly, approving

[24]Saul Feinman and Doris Entwisle, "Children's Ability to Recognize Other Children's Faces," *Child Development,* 47 (1976), 506–10.
[25]Daphne Bugenthal, Leonore Love, and Robert Gianetto, "Perfidious Feminine Faces," *Journal of Personality and Social Psychology,* 17 (1971), 314–18.

message. But understanding Mom's smile may be more difficult for a child. The mother's smile may be associated with a variety of messages, not all of them positive, friendly, or approving. The "public smile" of the middle-class mother presents additional problems, according to the authors. It is possible that she tries to meet middle-class expectations of being a good mother. To soften the blow of a more critical message, or to communicate submission or compliance, she may smile to fit the role of the loving mother. What happens, however, is that children may have difficulty understanding what the *real message* is. And that's a tough job for anyone.

A second set of implications concerns children's perceptions of the facial expressions and smiles of their teachers, in the classroom or elsewhere. If children assign different meanings to the smiles of males and females, then this behavior could extend into the educational setting. Quite possibly, the male teacher's smile may be a strong tool in the communication of pleasure or satisfaction with the children's performance. On the other hand, the female teacher may be at a disadvantage because her smile may be assigned more general meanings by the children. Children's reactions to encouragement provided by teachers of both sexes should be studied more closely if we are to see whether there are some significant differences.

facial cues and physical attractiveness

Children judged as attractive are also judged as more pleasant, intelligent, and honest than children who are rated as unattractive. Theorists who write about person perception say that we cluster our trait judgments like this in forming impressions of others. W. J. Livesley and D. B. Bromley agree with other researchers that people use a number of cues to make inferences about mental and personal qualities of others. They suggest that people seek to unify and organize these impressions toward a simple judgment.[26] Appearance plays an important role in person perception by establishing a set of characteristics about the other, including age, sex, and social class.

Elementary-school teachers were asked in a study for their reactions to children who were supposed to have committed a misdeed.[27] All data in the case studies of the children were alike, except that one set of files had pictures of attractive children and the other set, unattractive children. The teachers viewed the children and their misdeeds in very different ways. In general the unattractive children were judged negatively and described as brats, troublemakers, and those who pick fights. The attractive child com-

---

[26]W. J. Livesley and D. B. Bromley, *Person Perception in Childhood and Adolescence* (New York: John Wiley, 1973), p. 31.

[27]Chris Kleinke, *First Impressions: The Psychology of Encountering Others* (Englewood Cliffs, N.J.: Prentice-Hall, 1975), pp. 4–6.

mitting the same misbehavior was judged as usually charming and well mannered; the explanation for her misdeed was that she had "a bad day and goofed." The child's face in a picture seemed to make a difference in these case studies, suggesting that punishment for misdeeds may somehow be related to the configuration of the child's face!

In another study children from nine through fourteen were interviewed on what features they thought made someone "good-looking."[28] A tabulation of their responses indicated that a broad range of facial cues contribute to that judgment. Three quarters of the children referred to the other's face in explaining the attractiveness, the hair was mentioned in over half of the responses, and the eyes (47 percent), teeth (47 percent), and mouth (40 percent) were also mentioned frequently. While previous writers stress the importance of physical cues in only the initial phases of interaction for both children and adults, this study insists that the physical variables continue to be important for the older children, even after significant periods of interaction.

body language and personal powers

An effective use of body language in communication, as well as the understanding of the messages communicated in the body language of others, are important in children's development of powerful communication. Though kinesic messages are not always related to the content of our communication, they are related to the relational messages we communicate. In other words, our effectiveness in communicating and understanding human feelings is at the heart of effective body language.

From the standpoint of sending messages with body language, several of the basic competencies of Dr. Burton White are dependent on effective body cues—communicating affection or hostility to peers, communicating affection or hostility to adults, and showing pride in one's accomplishments. Without an adequate repertoire of postural, facial and gestural cues, children's communication of these messages is certainly not as effective. The subtleties of their relational communication are intricately related to their effectiveness as physical communicators.

From the perspective of interpretation of the relational messages of others, children's awareness and decoding of the body language cues of others will determine whether or not they are understanding their important relationships with others. Since kinesic communication contains much about what others think about them, and how they are viewing them in communication, it is important that children interpret these messages accurately.

[28]Robert E. Kleck, Stephen Richardson, and Linda Ronald "Physical Appearance Cues and Interpersonal Attraction in Children," *Child Development*, 45 (1974), 305–10.

For children to develop the necessary personal powers to function as autonomous individuals, they must learn to function effectively in their interpersonal relationships with others. They must learn to take care of themselves, while still relying on others when necessary. What better criterion is there for effective functioning in interpersonal relationships than effective use of body language? Whether in communication with children's peers, family members, or relatives, there is a back-and-forth flow of messages being communicated through body language. Children must become aware of these messages and interpret them correctly if they are to get along with the important persons in their lives.

SUMMARY

Young children communicate in a very physical manner. They may point, poke, and wave in an effort to be understood. Often, their body language is a direct statement of their messages. As children develop verbal skills, the bodily channel of communication becomes more entwined in the total communication process. Body language includes all reflexive and non-reflexive movements and positions of the body that communicate emotional, attitudinal, and informational messages. Just as children must learn the syntactic rules of their language, they must also learn the patterns of bodily movements that communicate messages to others.

Kinesics, the science of body motion, involves the study of bodily movements in communication. Ray Birdwhistell has studied body motion cross-culturally and has derived a notation system for recording bodily behavior in communication. He stresses, however, that elements of a body language, such as "body words" and a "body grammar," are yet to be defined.

Two categories of body language are critical in children's development of kinesics: hand and arm movements and facial movements. The first category consists of at least three types of gestures: deictic gestures, pantomimic gestures, and semantic and relational gestures. Deictic gestures involve pointing to objects and places "mentioned" in the child's message. With greater experience in expressing deixis through words, children begin to use fewer pointing gestures. Pantomimic gestures, rather self-contained movements that signify something (such as a greeting or a size gesture), develop steadily in children from preschool to early elementary years. The pantomimic gestures play a far less important role in children's communication than the semantic and relational gestures. To illustrate the semantic and relational area of body language, we explored the emergence and development of gender communication and identified key movements and positions displayed therein. Both medical studies and communication studies suggest that children begin to communicate their gender by the time they use language—that is, around their second birthday. Communication of gender by Americans is accomplished through posture, eye behavior, and the angle of arms and legs to the body. Two-year-olds have acquired some of the bodily cues that communicate gender, and during their preschool years they practice the body language of gender display. In the elementary-school years, the child matches his or her gender display against that of peers.

Studies of facial communication have found the eyes to be the most important single area of the face in the sending of emotional messages. Of course the entire face is the best predictor of an emotional message. Smiling is an important nonverbal message for young children, though study of its functional usage shows variation among children. Factors such as the child's age, the status of the child in the pecking order, and identity of the other person affect the frequency and likelihood of the child's smiles. More specific examination of smile types shows that children develop the social smile, or upper smile, in which the upper teeth show when the corners of the mouth are turned up. Children seem to interpret smiles in different ways, depending on who uses them. For example, they often do not assign the smile of the mother the same meaning as the smile of the father. Studies of physical attractiveness in children suggest that facial configuration somehow affects all sorts of judgments. For example, elementary-school teachers rate misdeeds of children differently if their pictures show attractive faces rather than unattractive faces. The attractive child is given all types of excuses for the misdeed, such as "She had a bad day." The unattractive child is often judged as a brat, a spoiled troublemaker, or a pest, however. Children seem to agree with adults in giving the face a primary role in portraying attractiveness: in a study of older elementary-school children, facial cues were mentioned most frequently as contributing to "good looks."

SUGGESTED READINGS

BIRDWHISTELL, RAY, *Kinesics and Context: Essays in Body Motion Communication*, Chap. 1. Philadelphia: University of Pennsylvania Press, 1970.

BLURTON JONES, N. G., "Non-Verbal Communication in Children," in *Non-Verbal Communication*, ed. R. A. Hinde, pp. 271–96. New York: Cambridge University Press, 1972.

CLARK, EVE, and C. J. SENGUL, "Strategies in the Acquisition of Deixis," *Journal of Child Language*, 5 (October 1978), 457–75.

JANCOVIC, MERRYANN, SHANNON DEVOE, and MORTON WEINER, "Age-Related Changes in Hand and Arm Movements as Nonverbal Communication: Some Conceptualizations and an Empirical Exploration," *Child Development*, 46 (1975), 922–28.

MEHRABIAN, ALBERT, "Communication Without Words," in *Communication: Concepts and Processes*, ed. Joseph DeVito, pp. 106–114. Englewood Cliffs, N.J.: Prentice-Hall, 1971.

9
the child's voice communicates

The voice is a powerful channel for communicating ideas and feelings, both obvious and subtle. We demonstrated this generalization dramatically in a modest experiment with fifth-grade children. The children sat in front of a television monitor and watched a "TV teacher." The teacher delivered short messages to them, and after each one the children told us what the teacher was "really saying." Some of the messages constructed for the children's viewing were contradictory messages in which the verbal (words), vocal (voice), and bodily (face) channels were not saying the same thing. In one instance the teacher said, "You did a real good job, children!" with a big smile on her face but with a negative, sarcastic voice. How would the children resolve a conflict message such as this one?

The children studied the TV teacher carefully, their eyes opened wide and their bodies motionless. When she finished her sarcastic message, and before we had the chance to ask the children what they thought of it, they gave away their feelings: they stuck out their tongues at the television monitor. The teacher's smiling face didn't help to ease the pain of the message. Incidentally, adults probably focus some attention on the positive facial and verbal channels in resolving a sarcastic message; their reactions to sarcasm, although still negative, are significantly less so than young children's reactions. The teacher's voice was an extremely powerful element in the children's interpretation of her words: her voice was negative, the children heard this, and they didn't like it. "Her voice was nasty," said some of the children, and so they interpreted the message to be a nasty one. What better way is there to strike back at a nasty message than to stick out your tongue at its sender?

Children pay close attention to the voices they hear. In terms of content the voice communicates a lot to children, even very young children. This is not surprising, because children understand and convey ideas and feelings in the voice before they do so verbally. Babbling is not a practice period for children's acquisition of speech sounds; it is simply a period in which infants exercises their vocal apparatus, making sounds for the sake of making sounds. Infants are not "careful" to make only those sounds that occur in the speech of adults around them. Instead, they produce a variety of sounds, many of which are totally foreign to their native language. The adult speech they hear has little to do with the *content* (sounds) of their babbling, but it has a great deal of bearing on the *form* of that babbling.

It is during the period of babbling that children begin to experiment with the intonation of their language. Sometime between six and twelve months children learn to ask questions, express anger, and communicate excitement—not with words but with sound patterns. Infants communicate their needs and feelings by means of the intonation patterns in their voice. A nine-month-old boy who babbles a question, complete with a rising intonation contour, deserves an answer. He is experimenting with the communication of meaning through the prosodic features of the voice. According to Phillip Lieberman, the child's crying and babbling contain the same signals that serve the linguistic function of intonation in adult speech.[1] Apparently, infants first develop the *form* of human speech by acquiring the prosodic features of speech. Then, they "plug in" the *content* when they acquire verbal language. They use both aspects of their language—form and content—to communicate meaning to others. Just as an eighteen-month-old girl can communicate her needs with two-word sentences, the nine-month-old boy communicates his needs with rising and falling pitch patterns in his crying and babbling. The speech of a three-year-old child contains the basic elements of human speech: pitch, pause, loudness, and tempo.

An account of children's development of communication would be incomplete without a discussion of the voice—how children use their voices to send messages and how children interpret the vocal messages of others. Before we explore these issues we must define the key terms used in the study of the voice.

Prosody, sometimes called "the music of our speech," is the earliest dimension of language to be used and understood by young children. "From infancy to old age it will continue to be the critical marking that makes one's speech peculiarly his own."[2] The prosody of our speech is flexible, varying

---

[1]Phillip Lieberman, *Intonation, Perception, and Language* (Cambridge, Mass.: M.I.T. Press, 1966), p. 41.
[2]Mildren F. Berry, *Language Disorders in Children* (New York: Appleton-Century-Crofts, 1969), p. 128.

with our moods, thoughts, and feelings. The elements of prosody—pitch, pause, loudness, and tempo—are varied to produce meaningful signals in our messages. Because these elements interact with each other in intricate ways, the vocal channel in communication is exceedingly complex.

To place prosody in its proper perspective in the vocal system, let's compare three types of vocal signals:

1. rising pitch at the end of a question (prosodic feature)
2. whisper or giggle (paralinguistic feature)
3. yawn or cough (nonlinguistic feature)[3]

These three signals all originate in the vocal channel; they differ mainly in their degree of linkage to the verbal channels. Prosodic features, such as the rising pitch pattern at the end of a sentence, are tied directly to words and sentences. In a sense, intonation is "nested in" the verbal channel. The paralinguistic features, such as giggles and whispers, are linked more loosely to the verbal channels. Often, such features are totally separate from the content of our speech. The nonlinguistic features are even more removed. The linkage of coughs, sneezes, and throatiness to the verbal channel is minimal. Figure 9.1 illustrates the three-part division of voice characteristics. In brief, the three aspects of voice can be defined as follows:

1. *Prosodic features:* the pitch, pause, loudness, and tempo of our voice during communication, features that interact to produce variations in "melody" that communicate meaning
2. *Paralinguistic features:* the manipulations of the voice, such as giggling or breathiness, that are a part of the stream of speech and that may signal our "mood"
3. *Nonlinguistic features:* voice quality (determined in part by characteristics that act as a background for speech) and vocal reflexes (for example, sneezing and yawning)

PROSODIC FEATURES

This chapter considers the first set of features in the network of the voice: prosodic features. Our primary concern is with *variations in the voice* that contribute to the meaning of our messages. The prosodic features are the features linked most directly to the verbal message, and consequently they vary more than paralinguistic features and nonlinguistic features. For example, a person may have a raspy voice (a nonlinguistic feature) that characterizes his speech. As a permanent background characteristic, this raspiness may not communicate a particular message. Paralinguistic features involve some degree of variation in the voice, especially in the case of vocal

[3]David Crystal, *Prosodic Systems and Intonation in English* (Cambridge: Cambridge University Press, 1969), pp. 128–31.

STRONG   1. *Prosodic Features*

          a. pitch: the direction of tone change (rising or falling) and range of tone (high to low) in the voice

          b. pause: the filled hesitations ("um," "ah," repeats) and silences in our speech

          c. loudness: the overall volume in the voice, as well as changes in volume (stress)

          d. tempo: the overall rate in speech, as well as internal changes in rate (speeding or slowing down within phrases, sentences, and messages)

   2. *Paralinguistic Features*

          a. vocal qualifiers: whispering, breathiness, falsetto, resonance

          b. vocal qualifications: laughing, giggling, sobbing, crying

   3. *Nonlinguistic Features*

          a. voice quality: the permanent background characteristics of the voice that help identify a person's voice (for instance, as harsh or throaty)

          b. vocal reflexes: uncontrollable sneezes, coughs, yawns, and snores

WEAK

degree of linkage to verbal channels (vertical axis label, STRONG at top, WEAK at bottom)

Figure 9.1. *Aspects of the voice: prosodic, paralinguistic, and nonlinguistic features.*

qualifiers. Whispered speech or breathy speech helps communicate a feeling or mood, but these features are applied to our messages more generally; variation *within* messages is not characteristic of paralinguistic features.

Variations in the prosodic features of a child's message can help shape the meaning in his message, a characteristic of adult communication. Consequently, we must take a careful look at children's production and comprehension of prosodic variations. We don't have a comprehensive statement of how children acquire the prosody of their language. We do have some evidence that the more grammatical aspects of prosody, such as the pitch contour at the ends of sentences, seem to come naturally to children. Children learning English typically employ downward pitch contours at the ends of sentences.

A knowledge of babies' intonation patterns and prosodic variations can be extremely helpful to those who must care for an infant. Many inexperienced caretakers will automatically interpret a baby's cry as a signal that he is hungry, but studies have shown that only one particular cry pattern communicates hunger. That pattern contains the following prosodic clues: a moderately pitched, loud cry, a regular rhythm, and brief pauses so that the infant can catch his breath. The regularity of the pattern is probably the best clue for identifying the hunger cry. Other cries have different prosodic patterns. For example, the pain cry is very high-pitched and consists of long, drawn-out squeals. The fatigue cry is lower in pitch, varies in loudness, follows a generally slower pace, and contains telltale grunts and sucking noises.

What about those aspects of prosody that are related more closely to the communication of how we feel and what we think and believe? Research in this area is quite limited, even for adults. Most studies simply describe the voice patterns in children's and adults' speech. For example, pitch changes in children's voices have been studied very thoroughly. We can also read detailed accounts of how adults use pauses in speech. But theories that explain *why* we pause when we do are sketchy. Recent research focuses on how children learn the meanings associated with various intonation patterns.

In this chapter we will discuss the information that is currently available on aspects of the child's voice during communication. The result is a rather tentative picture of vocal communication and its emergence. After defining the four major prosodic features of the human voice—pitch, pause, loudness, and tempo—we will explore how they are involved in the development of the child's voice.

pitch

The pitch of a person's voice is the product mainly of the vowel sounds in speech. Pitch is a psychological entity, dependent on the fundamental frequency of vocal-fold vibration in the production of a vowel sound. In children's cries, babbling, and eventually their first words, the pitch of their voices depends on the high or low tone of these vocalizations. Just as a musical note played on a clarinet has a fundamental frequency and distinguishing overtones, the human voice producing a vowel has a fundamental frequency and distinguishing overtones (the latter are called *formants*). The perception of pitch in a human voice is based on the fundamental frequency of the voice.

pause

It is perfectly normal, for a number of reasons, for a person's speech to be interrupted. At the end of a phrase or sentence we pause to signal the end of an idea for our listener. Often, we pause to make a person wait for the important word(s) forthcoming or to stress the importance of words just spoken. In other instances we pause to select just the right word. During these pauses we might remain silent, we might use "ah" or "um" to fill the pause, or we might repeat a phrase or word and then continue.

Most of the studies on pauses in speech have been conducted from the speaker's viewpoint; little attention has been devoted to the effects of pauses on listeners. Consequently, pauses have been categorized according to their encoding characteristics in terms of the speaker's behavior. Pauses have traditionally been placed in two major categories:

1. *Unfilled pauses:* silences in the stream of speech; they are not filled with any type of verbal activity. They occur at *normal junctures* in a message (such as at the end of a sentence) and at *decision points* in a message (for instance, before a new idea or a difficult word).

2. *Filled pauses:* portions of our speech that are filled with "excess" verbalizations: (a) an elongated vowel ("ah," "uh," or "eh"); (b) a repeat (saying a syllable, word, or group of words again within an utterance); and (c) a false start (starting a phrase or sentence and then starting a second time by repeating an initial syllable, word, or group of words).

Research on pauses in speech (or *hesitation phenomena*) has attempted to link each type of pause with a particular mental or emotional activity. For example, silence perhaps reflects thinking or a decision, and a repeat or an "uh" may reflect a speaker's anxiety in communicating. Clear-cut correlations of this type have not emerged from the investigations. Many researchers conclude that hesitations are *predictable* in one case—at the end of phrases and sentences—but are highly unpredictable in another sense— placed in a difficult communication situation, some persons use repeats, others use elongated vowels, and still others simply remain silent. The demands of the situation may be the same for all of them, but the manner in which anxiety or thinking is communicated by hesitations seems to vary with the individual.

Emphasis on interaction between persons rather than on speaker-centered activity has resulted in a more complex set of categories for analyzing sound-silence patterns in conversations. Consider these five concepts offered for the study of pauses in the communication of children and adults:

1. *pauses:* intervals of joint silence (by speaker and listener) bounded by vocalizations of the speaker

2. *switching pauses:* intervals of joint silence during the switching of the role of speaker (in other words, silence between two persons' messages)

3. *vocalizations:* segments of uninterrupted speech or sound by the speaker

4. *speaking turns:* the back-and-forth sharing of the role of speaker

5. *simultaneous speech:* overlapping speech; a switching pause may be missing.[4]

---

[4]These concepts were proposed in J. Jaffe and Stanley Feldstein, *Rhythms of Dialogue* (New York: Academic Press, 1970).

Combining traditional categories of pauses—filled pauses, for example—with this more recent framework seems to produce a more complete system for analyzing pauses in speech.

loudness

Loudness is the psychological correlate of the intensity (or amplitude) of our speech. The loudness of a person's voice is primarily the product of the intensity of the voiced stream of air in vowel production. Psychoacoustic research has indicated that the perception of loudness is also based on the frequency and the duration of a sound. But generally speaking, the greater the intensity of the sound the greater its loudness.

Loudness in speech can be considered from two points of view. One is the overall *loudness level* in a person's message. Often we find ourselves talking very loudly to another person. This may happen when we're excited or angry, for example. In these instances our voice is loud in relation to our level of loudness in normal conversations. At other times we may use a soft voice throughout a conversation, perhaps to communicate a sense of urgency. In both cases we are talking about the overall loudness level we select for a message. From a more detailed point of view, loudness can be varied within a phrase, a sentence, or a message in order to communicate meaning. We usually call this type of loudness variation *stress*. We may stress certain words by uttering them louder or softer than the words surrounding them. In short, loudness has two prosodic dimensions: the general loudness level we select for our utterances and the variations in loudness within our utterances.

tempo

The tempo of our speech also has two dimensions. The first and more general dimension is the overall *rate* of our speech. Rate is measured most easily as the number of words spoken per time segment. The second dimension of tempo is an internal one: the speeding up or slowing down of the rate of speech within phrases or sentences. The most important question regarding tempo, of course, is whether *conventions in speech rate* correlate with specific meanings. Not much is known, however, about internal variation in speech rate—that is, how we speed up and slow down our rate of speech within phrases, sentences, and oral paragraphs and how such internal changes in rate affect our communication of meaning.

The foregoing descriptions of pitch, pause, loudness, and tempo provide a background for our discussion of the prosodic characteristics of children's speech. Our next task is to explore children's development of these prosodic features in their speech.

THE DEVELOPMENT OF PITCH AND INTONATION IN CHILDREN'S SPEECH

In an experiment that confirms infants' early communication by means of pitch,[5] a ten-month-old boy and a thirteen-month-old girl were observed as "they conversed" with one parent and then the other. Their babbling was recorded and electronically analyzed. Each child sat in the lap of the mother and then the father and played with a pet—the boy with a dog and the girl with a cat. With the fundamental frequency of the child's conversation as the measured variable, it was found that the infants' pitch was higher with the mother than with the father. Further, the pitch levels the infants used in their conversations with their parents were lower than the pitch levels they used in solitary babbling or when they were crying. Lieberman concluded that infants are able to "control" pitch because of their acute perception of the fundamental-frequency differences in the voices of their parents. Since both children in this study were not yet communicating verbally, it seems that vocal communication (specifically, pitch) emerged first.

Intonation—the pitch patterns, or contours, in our speech—is a key element in children's language learning. Ben Blount and Elise Padgug examined prosodic, linguistic, and paralinguistic cues in the speech of English-speaking and Spanish-speaking parents in an effort to find the most common features in their speech to their children.[6] *Exaggerated intonation* turned out to be the most common feature in both languages, and accounted for about 21 percent of the cues in the parents' speech. The voice plays a role in all but one of the top six features:

1. exaggerated intonation (21 percent)
2. breathiness of the voice (9 percent)
3. high pitch (8 percent)
4. repetition of an utterance or a short series of utterances (7.7 percent)
5. lower volume (7.2 percent)
6. lengthened vowels (7.1 percent)

The first and third features reflect the key role of pitch and intonation in parents' speech to their children. It seems likely that parents use pitch to communicate a great deal about the flow and quality of language and com-

[5]Cited in Lieberman, *Intonation, Perception, and Language*, p. 45.
[6]Ben Blount and Elise Padgug, "Prosodic, Paralinguistic, and Interactional Features in Parent-Child Speech: English and Spanish," *Journal of Child Language*, 4 (February 1977), 67–86.

munication patterns. The second and fifth features involve the intensity of the voiced stream of air during vocalization and the resulting loudness of speech. Though an explanation was not offered on why parents adopt this breathy, soft manner, the answer is perhaps that they are attempting some type of adaptation of their voice to the tinyness of their listener. Although other categories included semantic, grammatical, and interactional features that were thought to be present in adults' speech to children, the results indicated that at least for very young children prosodic features are much more prevalent as helpful cues. The authors suggest that prosody takes on a less important role in parents' speech to older children.

Traditional accounts of the role of intonation in children's speech have assumed a rather clear and straightforward position:

1. Children acquire pitch and intonation patterns very early in their development of language.
2. Pitch plays a major role in children's early sentences, especially in the communication of yes/no questions—for example, "You will help me with the picture?"

More recent writings in the area of intonation and child language development take a more complex view of intonation and its role. The authors use terms such as "intonation groups" and "tone patterns," and say that in any utterance there is a nucleus, or main stress, along with varying use of pitch contours. In a study by A. Cruttenden of children's acquisition of intonation in particular types of utterances—the children communicated reports of football scores for "home" and "away" teams—developmental differences were noted for older children (seven through ten years).[7] Cruttenden found that even the ten-year-olds have things to learn. Let's examine this study in greater detail.

Cruttenden agrees with traditional writings on the subject of intonation that a three-year-old child can use rising and falling pitch contours effectively. Yet the ten-year-old child is still learning the meanings of rather intricate intonation contours. How can we infer anything about language acquisition from a study of children decoding football-score reports that contain complex intonation patterns? Cruttenden argues that these patterns match the intonation patterns of complex syntactic structures in English, such as the following:

1. "The best person to do it would be the person who knows how best." (The falling-to-rising nuclear tone in the first part of the sentence signals a further intonation group to follow.)
2. "John gave Bill seven but Peter gave Jane six." (This is an utterance with two nuclei, or two stressed events.)

[7]A. Cruttenden, "An Experiment Involving Comprehension of Intonation in Children from 7 to 10," *Journal of Child Language*, 1 (November 1974), 221–31.

Obviously, these sentences contain complex grammatical patterns that young teenagers must learn to use and understand.

Earlier learning of intonation is certainly important too. Pitch contour becomes critical when children learn to ask yes/no questions, around the age of three. Because the interrogative intent is not yet communicated in the order of the words in their sentences, rising pitch is important in the questions asked by children from three through six:

"I can push it now?"
"We are going to Grandma's house tomorrow?"

The interrogative pitch contour is relatively simple when compared with the more complex contours the child must learn for effective communication. Cruttenden outlined two of the more complex but important pairs of concepts that children must master, with the aid of pitch contours, in their acquisition of language:

1. *Similarity/Difference:* the similarity or dissimilarity of events or things can be indicated by like or contrasting pitch contours.

2. *Expectedness/Unexpectedness:* upward and downward pitch sweeps can signal unexpected or expected events.[8]

Other concepts requiring pitch patterns for their effective communication are finality/nonfinality, doubt/certainty, and subordination/superordination. How children learn these complex intonation patterns requires investigation.

In conclusion, intonation development involves a host of complex processes of sorting out and expressing in the vocal aspects of speech. We know that parents typically exaggerate intonation in their speech to young children, apparently believing that this will help children understand them better. It is likely that this practice plays a major role in children's development of intonation, a critical component in their oral communication.

pitch changes in the child's voice

A number of voice changes take place between birth and puberty, and probably the most dramatic is an overall lowering in the pitch of the voice. Research with children has indicated, however, that pitch does not simply decrease steadily from birth to puberty. Although a child's voice does exhibit a gradual decrease in pitch between about two and twelve years of age, the

---

[8]*Ibid.*, p. 222.

pitch changes that take place in the first few years of life and at the onset of puberty are much more dramatic, complex, and difficult to explain.

A study of infants from birth to five months of age revealed a rather complex trend in pitch change, as measured by the fundamental frequency of the voice. Sheppard and Lane recorded crying and vocalizing of infants in controlled settings.[9] Fundamental-frequency recordings were made by complicated electronic equipment attached to a plexiglass "air crib" installed in the infants' homes. The results of the study indicate that during the infant's first month of life the fundamental frequency of his voice lowers steadily. Beginning in the second month, the pitch changes direction and rises steadily until about four months, when it levels off.

Both the initial drop in pitch and the secondary increase in pitch after the first month were explained first by the physiological development of the infant and by acoustical principles related to such development. During the first month the vocal folds increase in area, thickness, and length. These physiological changes explain the initial drop in pitch of the infant's cries. Pitch change shortly after the first month is apparently explained by the child's ability to increase subglottal pressure. These terms are simply a fancy way of saying that growing children can cry louder and with greater force; it's not easy to tune out the piercing cry of a two-and-a-half-month-old infant. Because the physical and respiratory strength of older infants has increased drastically, the fundamental frequency of their vocalizations increases as well. Both of these factors—the change in vocal folds and the build-up of subglottal pressure—account for the pitch trends in early infancy.

The pitch trends of the first five months can also be explained by the different functions vocalizations serve at different ages. Infants' cries are reflexive and communicate their needs for sleep, food, comfort, and activity. As infants approach three months of age they have greater control over their vocalizations and cries. Now they can signal, to some extent, their needs and feelings for others. Researchers have called these later vocalizations *motivated vocalizations*. This change in function, then, may help explain the dramatic change in pitch of the older infants' vocalizations.

The pitch of a two-year-old's voice is only slightly lower than that of an infant's voice.[10] Once children begin to use sentences in communication, however, their pitch begins to drop in a slow and steady fashion. There is a downward pitch trend through infancy and early childhood years. A short time before puberty the second period of dramatic change in pitch of children's voices takes place. For boys the period is commonly called the

[9]W. C. Sheppard and H. L. Lane, "Development of the Prosodic Features of Infant Vocalizing," *Journal of Speech and Hearing Research*, 11 (1968), 94–108.
[10]Robert McGlone, "Vocal Pitch Characteristics of Children Aged One to Two Years," *Speech Monographs*, 33 (1966), 178–81.

"change of voice." Here for the first time boys' and girls' voices begin to take on characteristic differences. The pitch of girls' voices also drops, but the change is not as noticeable as it is with boys.

The pitch range of children's voices has also been studied. The total range of frequencies for a newborn is about five tones—a very restricted range. The range expands in the child's preschool and early elementary years, so that by seven years of age it has doubled. But during the early teens the pitch range increases only to eleven tones. Consequently, children's pitch range is relatively stable by the end of the early elementary-school years.

We know a great deal more about the pitch of children's voices as they age than we know about how children learn to use pitch variations in communicating. Most explanations of the development of pitch and intonation in children's speech assume that from the babbling period on, infants are able to use pitch variation to signal their needs and feelings. By the time children have acquired the basic syntactic structures of their language (around three to four years of age) they have also acquired the ability to use intonation along with these structures. Their progress in the use of intonation patterns to communicate meanings is a relatively unexplored area in children's speech development. Recent studies have begun to focus on children's comprehension of intonation patterns, but more research is required for a decent understanding of the developmental process.

PAUSES IN CHILDREN'S SPEECH

The study of children's use of pauses or hesitations has been confined largely to the observation of children in their later elementary-school years.

By the time children reach school age, their speech contains filled and unfilled pauses that are almost adult-like. Further, their pausal patterns are fairly well set. To illustrate these generalizations, let's review a study of hesitation in children.

children's hesitation

Research with adults has indicated a strong relationship between the type of speaking activity and the frequency of pauses or hesitations. When adults were given a cartoon from the *New Yorker*, for example, and asked to describe or interpret it, there were more hesitations in the interpretation condition.[11] When our speech is somewhat automatic, as in description, we

---

[11] Frieda Goldman-Eisler, *Psycholinguistics: Experiments in Spontaneous Speech* (New York: Academic Press, 1968), pp. 50–59.

make little use of hesitations, except for the ones that are necessary to indicate grammatical information (for instance, the end of a sentence). But when our speech requires thought, as in interpreting the meaning of a cartoon, then pauses of various types (both filled and unfilled) increase in number and frequency. It has been suggested that pauses of this nature reflect decision points within our speech.

Levin and his research team investigated pauses in children's speech during two different conditions: children were shown three physical demonstrations and asked to *describe what they saw* and *explain why it happened.*[12] Levin predicted that pauses would be greater in the condition of explanation, as studies with adults had indicated. The children ranged in age from five to twelve. The study found that the number and duration of pauses was greater in the explanation condition than in the description condition, as predicted. The children hesitated with many more filled pauses (such as "ah," "um," and repeats) and silences when they were trying to explain why something happened. Let's take one example. The children were shown two balloons of different sizes and colors. One was filled with air and the other with helium. The researcher released both, and of course the helium balloon rose to the ceiling while the air-filled balloon landed on the floor. The researcher asked "Why do you think that happened?" after the children described the event. Here are some of the children's answers:

"The red one goes up." (color answer)

"The small one goes up and the big one falls down." (size answer)

"The one that goes up is lighter than air." (scientific answer)

Whether the children's answers to the "why" question were correct or incorrect, hesitations were greater in these answers than in the answers given in the description condition.

The research team also examined children's development of pause as a prosodic feature. They compared pausal patterns in the speech of children ranging from five to twelve years of age and found no significant differences. This finding supports our generalization that children's pauses are well established by the time they enter school.

Studies investigating the communicative uses of pause (such as to emphasize a point) are greatly needed in order that prosodic development may be more fully explained. Experience in listening to children tells us that from the time children use multiple-word sentences they use pauses that are characteristic of adult speech. Young children may simply imitate the filled

[12]Harry Levin, Irene Silverman, and Boyce Ford, "Hesitations in Children's Speech During Explanation and Description," *Journal of Verbal Learning and Verbal Behavior*, 6 (1967), 560–64.

pause "um" in about the same way they imitate a new word. It appears almost as if children feel grown-up when they engage in that pensive "ah" or "um" before they answer our questions. Ask a four-year-old boy to help with a chore, and he may pause, wrinkle his brow, and respond just like an adult: "Well, um, I guess I could help." Obviously he has heard that hesitation pattern before.

pauses in children's communication

When we focus on conversations or interactions rather than on vocalizations, a different picture of the development of pausal phenomena emerges. One way to assess children's conversational effectiveness—an adult's too, for that matter—is to see if they match their *pauses* and *switch pauses* to those of the person they are talking with. This aspect of pausal development is far more complex in many ways than the rather specific study of hesitation phenomena. In talking about children's development of socialization, researchers refer to *conversational congruence*—the matching of pauses and switch pauses mentioned above. Some researchers say that children who have mastered conversational congruence have learned empathy; such children are often rated as warmer, more effective communicators.

In a study of children from five to seven years,[13] pause and switch-pause durations for older children (6.4 to 7.2 years) significantly matched those of their conversation partner. For the younger age group (5.4 to 6.1 years) only the switch-pause durations matched. These results were offered as evidence for the development of conversational congruence in young elementary-school-aged children. Even more convincing evidence was offered when the researchers examined the younger children's performance in the two sessions in which data were gathered for the study: the younger children improved significantly in their pause-congruence scores from the first to the second session, which suggests that they did better with more experience in the task. Though they did not reach the criterion for pause congruence by the end of the second session, their improvement was noteworthy.

Other measures of pauses in communication are *vocalization time* and *floor-holding time*, or the total time a person remains as the speaker though silences may be interspersed. These measures allow us to examine in a more global way the phenomenon of pause in children's communication development. Consider the following results of a study of young children and their mothers.[14]

---

[13]Joan Welkowitz, Gerald Cariffe, and Stanley Feldstein, "Conversational Congruence as a Criterion of Socialization in Children," *Child Development*, 47 (1976), 269–72.
[14]H. Rudolph Schaffer, Glyn M. Collis, and Gayle Parsons, "Vocal Interchange and Visual Regard in Verbal and Pre-Verbal Children," in *Studies in Mother-Infant Interaction*, ed. H. Rudolph Schaffer (New York: Academic Press, 1977), p. 297.

age group	vocalization time		floor-holding time	
	child	mother	child	mother
one-year-olds	0 min 50 sec	1 min 19 sec	3 min 55 sec	6 min 04 sec
two-year-olds	1 min 20 sec	1 min 58 sec	4 min 02 sec	5 min 58 sec

These data suggest two important patterns that should be considered by anyone interested in children's development of prosody, and in particular, communication timing. First, mothers' sensitivity to their children is especially apparent in the consistent patterns of floor-holding time for the two age groups. While the mothers do use more vocalization time with the older children, they leave a lot of time "blank." In other words, mothers engage in excellent matching behavior—what we referred to earlier as conversational congruence. Second, the amount of time children vocalize seems to increase from age one to age two, though their general pattern of floor holding time seems to remain constant. In short, children seem to increase their vocal fluency in a context of extreme sensitivity by their mothers to communication factors.

nonfluency in children's speech

Parents and teachers are rarely concerned when children use filled pauses infrequently in their speech. But they are concerned when children speak with frequent repetitions of sounds and syllables: they know there is a problem called stuttering and they dread considering what they are hearing.

Recent advice from speech pathologists has helped clarify the problems of nonfluency and stuttering.[15] First, most experts agree that most children go through a period (or periods) of nonfluency, during which their speech includes repetitions and pauses. The result is often disturbing to our ears because we like to hear "fluent" speech, especially from our own children. Given the fact that most children go through periods of nonfluency, how can we spot the problem that deserves professional attention? Here is where the advice of speech pathologists becomes invaluable for parents and teachers. The majority of beginning stutterers show excessive syllabic repetitions; some even employ blockages (complete stops in speech in an effort to "get a word out"). The problem is cyclic in nature: periods of complete fluency alternate with periods when speech is so filled with repetitions that communication is hindered and we become concerned. Young children

---

[15]Our discussion of nonfluency in young children is based primarily on the approach of Joseph Sheehan in *Stuttering: Research and Therapy* (New York: Harper & Row, 1970). Another presentation that might be helpful in understanding beginning stuttering is Charles Van Riper's *The Treatment of Stuttering* (Englewood Cliffs, N.J.: Prentice-Hall, 1973), Chap. 14.

showing these symptoms usually do not realize what they are doing. They are not aware of their nonfluency, and so they do not worry about it or react to it. As you will see in our guidelines for helping the child with nonfluencies, this lack of awareness is a "plus" for recovery.

The problem. It is important to realize that the problem does not reside within the child. Although the child's speech reveals the problem, the members of the family constitute the major portion of the problem. According to a noted expert in stuttering therapy, "The stuttering child is the parents' symptom. . . . He is a statement about them—and they are quite correct in regarding it as unflattering."[16] Although such parents may behave no differently from another set of parents with a child who is fluent, the fact remains that their behavior has precipitated the nonfluency problem. Children with nonfluencies are products of their environment. If pressures and expectations are unreasonably high, they may respond with nonfluency. Consider this analogy and its conclusion.

> Putting the pressure on a child is like driving across a railroad crossing without looking. Most of the time you can get away with it. But the gain is not worth the risk. The parents of stutterers were probably not behaving conspicuously worse than others. They just got caught at it.[17]

The traditional advice to parents and teachers is this: "Ignore the problem and it will go away." This advice is based on the fact that most children who go through periods of nonfluency "recover" without professional assistance—the number of such children is estimated to be 80 percent. This advice works for the majority of children. But what about the unlucky 20 percent? According to Sheehan, the best advice is this: "Leave the child alone and treat the parents." "Leave the child alone" is advice quite different from "Ignore the problem," yet most experts in speech pathology today agree with Sheehan that the best approach is to treat the parents of children with nonfluencies.

Treatment. The onset of stuttering or nonfluency in young children falls principally between the ages of two and seven years, with peaks at three years and five years. As we have noted, about 80 percent of children recover spontaneously but 20 percent do not. Our suggestion to teachers and parents is that we not play the odds. If a child demonstrates the symptoms of beginning stuttering, the parents should be counseled by a speech and language clinician. The therapist may suggest a number of changes; one might be to make a hectic household a more relaxed one. The thrust of treatment is this:

[16]Sheehan, *Stuttering*, p. 304.
[17]*Ibid.*

reduce parental pressures on the child. The following suggestions for parents and others concerned with helping the child who is nonfluent are some of those given in an approach employed at Northwestern University.

1. Reduce pressures on the child at home and at school. Evaluate expectations for performance in view of the child's age and abilities. Avoid imposing too many pressures to perform. The pressures experienced by a given child may not be obvious at first. Look for events that seem to precipitate frustration or uncertainty in the child.

2. "Quiet down" your speech with the child. Speak at a slower rate, talk more softly, and avoid complicated language.

3. Don't demand a lot of speaking from the child. Avoid creating an atmosphere that includes pressure to talk. It's often helpful for each parent to create a "special time" with the child where the child knows he has their attention. A short period of time, one with each parent, seems to relieve the need for constant attention.

4. Be consistent in your discipline. All who care for the child must make some decisions about what limits are tolerable (for instance, at mealtime, bedtime, and playtime, and in getting dressed). *The Magic Years: Understanding and Handling the Problems of Early Childhood* by Selma Fraiberg (published by Scribner's) should help parents decide what limits and goals are reasonable.

5. Avoid rushing or hurrying the child. Make certain that enough time elapses between activities and that you are not rushing from place to place. When the child's fluency increases, time demands can be increased in small proportions.

6. Treat the child normally in most respects. Try not to give the child the impression that she is "special" or "different" from other children. For example, if the child's misbehavior requires discipline, respond in a calm but firm way so that additional pressure is not imposed. If class activities require talking in front of the class or reading aloud, don't exclude the nonfluent child. Rather, be sure that the child has ample time and that others do not interrupt. In general, help relieve pressures but without being obvious.

7. Never call attention to the child's speech. When speech is nonfluent, don't comment on the nonfluency and don't tell the child to slow down, think about his speech, or say it again. When the child's speech is fluent, don't praise the fluency. In a word, avoid any comments on the child's speech whatsoever.

8. Don't call the young child with nonfluencies a "stutterer." It is most likely an inappropriate label. Often, when neighbors and peers hear this label, they talk about it, possibly in the child's presence. Calling attention to the problem through such a label can be very detrimental to the child's fluency. After all, the child is usually unaware of the nonfluencies, and this label can cause concern in him and harm his normal process of developing fluency.[18]

These eight suggestions can help parents and teachers begin to understand the problem of nonfluencies in children's speech.

Our discussion of nonfluencies in children's speech has clearly indicated a problem deeper than the prosody of the child's voice. On the surface the nonfluencies of the beginning stutterer appear to be prosodic problems.

[18] Diane Hill, Director of the Primary Stuttering Program in the Speech and Language Clinic at Northwestern University, offered these suggestions.

But further investigation reveals that what we previously thought of as "pausal problems" are not simply that. Sheehan urges us to consider stuttering a role-conflict problem and not a voice problem. According to this perspective, our discussion of nonfluency has taken place in a context (a chapter on voice) that is not very appropriate.

TEMPO AND LOUDNESS IN CHILDREN'S VOICES

Albert Murphy has made the following statement about children's development of prosodic features in communication:

> By the age of four or five years, the child is communicating with the use of his entire being. His manner of speaking, loudness level, inflections, quality of voice, rate of utterance, talkativeness or taciturnity, attitudes, and vocal spontaneity or inhibitions all combine to give an impression of his developing personality.[19]

The prosodic features of tempo and loudness are well established in children's vocal patterns by the time they enter kindergarten. While current theorists might quarrel with Murphy about the five-year-old's mastery of inflections, few would argue with him about the other aspects of prosody—rate and loudness.

One area of communication study that should highlight the importance of children's development of effective tempo and loudness cues is the study of inconsistent messages. In a study in which aspects of the voice were carefully analyzed in tandem with other communication factors, *vocal spontaneity*, or the naturalness of a person's delivery, was singled out as being related to voice credibility.[20] In speech, words are typically slurred together, the speed of talking is variable (fast to slow) but the overall rate is rather fast, the rhythm is somewhat jerky, and there are sudden pitch changes. Most of these are characteristics of tempo, and they suggest that a natural, lively flow of speech is perceived as believable by others. This should suggest to us a flaw in the advice that many parents and teachers in the past have given to children learning their language: be more careful in how you talk, be deliberate in your speech, and slow down. This advice is probably important for someone who speaks too quickly to be understood at all, but probably ineffective for the child who becomes very excited when she talks and allows the tempo of her speech to show this.

[19]Albert T. Murphy, *Functional Voice Disorders* (Englewood Cliffs, N.J.: Prentice-Hall, 1964), p. 33.

[20]Daphne Bugenthal, "Interpretation of Naturally Occurring Discrepancies Between Words and Intonation: Modes of Inconsistency Resolution," *Journal of Personality and Social Psychology*, 30 (1974), 125–33.

While children may develop their speaking rate early in their acquisition of language, their ability to understand speech depends on the speaker's use of a tempo that is appropriate to the difficulty of the message content. Adults seem to know that overall rate of speech is important to consider when they talk to children, and they seem to slow down their speech quite naturally when they talk to younger children. One study systematically examined the effects of adults' rate of speech on children's comprehension of easy and difficult sentences.[21] The study found that a slower speaking rate definitely made it easier for eight- and nine-year-olds to understand both easy and difficult sentences. For six- and seven-year-olds, however, the slower rate seemed to help only in the understanding of the easy sentences. Maybe the difficult sentences were so overpowering to the younger children that a slower rate couldn't be helpful. The implication of this study is important: the tendency of adults to slow down their speech to children, especially in communicating difficult directions and explanations, is a valid technique that may also come naturally. In any case, we should be aware of how helpful our rate of speech can be to children when they try to understand our messages to them.

CHILDREN'S INTERPRETATION OF CONFLICT MESSAGES

The conclusion to a discussion on the importance of voice in communication might effectively end just as it began—with a consideration of contradictory messages. When adults are given messages whose vocal, visual, and verbal channels are not in agreement, which channel is most important in resolving the conflict? For example, adults watching and listening to the following message would agree that it is one of pleasant sarcasm and not extreme criticism:

"You're a real winner!"   (verbal)
smiling face   (visual)
sarcastic voice   (vocal)

Adults are capable of understanding the important role of the voice in communicating sarcasm, but at the same time, they are aware of the subtleties of meaning in the smile and use of words. Children react to sarcasm in a predictable fashion: they rate it very negatively. It is not until some time

[21]Nickola Nelson, "Comprehension of Spoken Language by Normal Children as a Function of Speaking Rate, Sentence Difficulty, and Listener Age and Sex," *Child Development*, 47 (1976), 299–303.

later—often the teens—that children correctly resolve the conflict in sarcasm and other contradictory messages.[22]

If the intonation of a person's voice is convincing in the communication of a contradictory message, then the content of the message is virtually disregarded.[23] The voice has the greatest weight in the resolution of ambiguity among the channels of communication, except when the person speaking uses a voice that is not spontaneous, but is deliberate and polished. In this case, studies show, the role of the voice is diminished because the person "weighs his words."

COMMUNICATION POWER: VOCAL EFFECTIVENESS

The child must learn to use her voice effectively in the communication of various messages. She must convince her friend she's sorry, explain directions carefully, and communicate urgency in her plea for help. Her voice is paramount in her communication of an effective apology, set of instructions, or request. A child's personal power rests on her ability to take care of her own needs, and the voice must work along with other verbal and nonverbal channels in communicating just the right message.

A second dimension of communication power that concerns the voice is the child's understanding of the relationship messages sent by others. Since people use their voices to communicate their feelings toward others, children must learn to read these messages. They must learn to assess how others feel about them and how others characterize the relationship. "Does he like me?" "Is he my good friend?" "Does he trust me now?" Answers to questions like these can be formed with the help of cues drawn from a careful listening to the human voice.

The communication talents closely related to the effective use of the voice deal mainly with the communication of emotion and relationship. Probably the most important of these talents are the expression of affection and hostility (to children and adults) and the display of pride in one's accomplishments. To increase their personal power, children must be effective in sending and receiving messages that deal with feelings and relationships.

SUMMARY

Prosody, the music of our speech, is the earliest dimension of language to be employed and understood by infants. The elements of prosody—pitch, pause, loudness, and tempo—vary with our moods,

---

[22]Daphne Bugenthal et al., "Perception of Contradictory Meanings Conveyed by Verbal and Nonverbal Channels," *Journal of Personality and Social Psychology*, 16 (1970), 617–55.

[23]Bugenthal, "Interpretation of Naturally Occurring Discrepancies Between Words and Intonation," p. 131.

thoughts, and feelings and with the information in our utterances. Infants begin to experiment with intonation during the babbling period. Their babbled utterances contain some of the prosodic features of the full-fledged sentences that adults use.

To follow the development of prosody in children, we examined the four prosodic variables—pitch, pause, loudness, and tempo—and then reviewed studies of children's progress in developing each of them.

Children rely heavily on pitch to communicate yes/no questions. In their preschool years they show an increased familiarity with intonation patterns that communicate emotions and information. During their later elementary-school years children acquire the intonation contours of the more complex syntactic structures in their language. Children's acquisition of pauses, switch pauses, and vocalization timing also shows a pattern of steady development toward adult norms. Children learn, for example, that they must match their pauses and switch pauses to the speech of the person they are talking to; this talent is called conversational congruence, and it seems to be developed by the age of seven. Studies indicate that though children seem to establish their own tempo patterns by the time they enter school, the speaking rate of others is critical in their understanding of others' messages. It is easier for children to understand both difficult and easy sentences if the speaker employs a slower rate of speech.

SUGGESTED READINGS

BERRY, MILDRED F., *Language Disorders in Children*, pp. 128–35. New York: Appleton-Century-Crofts, 1969.

MENYUK, PAULA, *The Acquisition and Development of Language*, pp. 54–64. Englewood Cliffs, N.J.: Prentice-Hall, 1971.

WELKOWITZ, JOAN, GERALD CARIFFE, AND STANLEY FELDSTEIN, "Conversational Congruence as a Criterion of Socialization in Children," *Child Development*, 47 (1976), 269–72.

10
children and communication through space

The following discussion took place in a second-grade classroom after the teacher had presented some pictures and information on animals' spacing patterns.

Teacher: Animals are fun to watch. Have you ever noticed what an animal does when you come very close to him? Sometimes, if you try to get too close to an animal, he might run away or get angry and snap at you. Has this ever happened to you?

Terry: My cat runs away whenever I get close to her—I don't think she likes it when I sneak up on her.

Kenneth: If I go near my neighbor's dog, he growls at me. He scares me, so I don't get too close to him.

Carol: I can get real close to my dog—he never seems to move. All he does is curl up in the corner of our kitchen and sleep. If I yell at him, then he'll bark a little.

Teacher: The reason why animals run away, growl, or bark at you is because maybe you've done something to them that bothers them. You know, an animal has a "bubble of space" around him. If you get inside this bubble, the animal reacts. He might run away, bark, or try to attack.

Children: (verbal and nonverbal signs of understanding)

Teacher: Do you think that *you* have little bubbles of space around yourselves?

Children: (giggles)

Teacher: Of course you wouldn't bark or growl at someone, but you might react in another way. Do you think that if someone came very close to you—came inside your bubble—that you would like it?

Kenneth: If my sister comes too close to me I just pop her one![1]

[1]This and the following discussion between a teacher and her second-grade students is

The teacher was trying to discuss principles of *proxemics*—interpersonal spacing in communication—with her second-grade class. The aim of the discussion was to understand that humans as well as animals have "territories" that they defend in their day-to-day encounters with others. This territoriality is a characteristic of people as well as animals, according to recent anthropological findings. The teacher was attempting to draw a parallel between the territorial behavior of animals, which the children could easily observe, and territorial behavior in human beings, probably a more difficult observation for seven-year-olds. Her conclusion was that the concept of human territoriality was somewhat difficult for young children to understand. Apparently, the lesson produced more giggles than fruitful discussion.

For the most part children thought the topic was silly. They said it was foolish to compare themselves to their dogs or cats and they could only laugh at such thoughts. The teacher perceived this reaction, and so she shifted the discussion to another proxemic principle:

Teacher: Sometimes we have a space or place we call our own. We might have a special chair at the kitchen table that we like to sit in, and so we call it "our chair." If anyone else sits in it, we remind him it's ours—that he shouldn't sit there. Or, we might have a special place in our house or our apartment that's "our place." Do you have a territory—a space or place—that you call yours?

Kenneth: I have my own room, where I can sleep and play.

Teacher: Good! That's a good example.

Kenneth: And I don't let my brother and sister come into my room either—unless I give them permission.

Children: (giggles)

Teacher: How about your own chair at the dinner table? Do any of you have your own special chair?

Children: (laughter)

Teacher: Think about it for a minute. Don't you usually sit in the same place for your meals, or do you sit in a different chair each time?

Bob: I do. I always sit in a chair closest to the back door, so that when I'm done eating I can run right out the door.

Children: (laughter)

Teacher: Is that chair "your territory"?

Bob: I guess so.

Children: (giggles)

Teacher: What would you do, Leslie, if you walked into our classroom one morning and someone else was sitting in your desk?

---

based on a study by Linda Schiff, for which I was the thesis director: "A Study of Proxemics for Elementary Education," (Master's thesis, University of Illinois at Chicago Circle, 1973).

Leslie: (indignant) I'd tell him to move—he's in the wrong desk!

Children: (giggles)

Teacher: What if he didn't get up right away? Would you tell him it was "your desk"—that he invaded your territory?

Leslie: Yeah, and if he didn't move, I'd kick him out!

Children: (uproarious laughter)

The teacher obtained much better results when she asked the children to talk about their territories in terms of objects. They seemed to understand the proxemic principle better in relation to their own bodies.

WHAT IS PROXEMICS?

The teacher and her second-grade class were discussing principles of proxemics. More specifically, proxemics has been defined by its major theorist, Edward T. Hall, as "the study of how man unconsciously structures microspace—the distance between men in conduct of daily transactions, the organization of space in his houses and buildings, and ultimately the layout of his towns.[2] Hall has written two revolutionary books on proxemics—*The Hidden Dimension* and *The Silent Language*. As his definition indicates, the study of proxemics encompasses more than what we might call "interpersonal spacing"—how people position and space themselves when they talk to one another. In fact, proxemics includes spacing in our homes, offices, neighborhoods, and cities. Proxemics concerns a broad range of topics, from how we use interpersonal space to communicate our trust in a friend to how city planners space houses, streets, and natural resources to communicate a feeling of peace and tranquility in a city.

Our concern in this chapter, as was the teacher's concern in her classroom discussions, is with the human use of space in interpersonal communication. The teacher was attempting to make her children aware of the crucial proxemic principle that human beings are territorial beings. Each of us has a personal space that surrounds us, according to Hall; when someone unexpectedly invades this space we react in a number of different ways, depending on how well we know that person, the circumstances of the "invasion," and several other important factors. Certainly we don't growl, bark, or bite a person who invades our territory. But we do react to territorial invasion in rather interesting and observable ways: we might show signs of tension, our eyes might open wide or look up, we might squirm a little, or

---

[2]Edward T. Hall, "A System for the Notation of Proxemic Behavior," *American Anthropologist*, 65 (1963), 1003–26.

we may even move away. All of these reactions illustrate the discomfort we feel when someone gets too close to us.

Hall's research demonstrates that all animals have a protective sphere, or "bubble," that they keep around themselves. Enter that bubble, and the animal will either flee or attack. Some animals have smaller bubbles than others, usually because of their size and relative power in the animal world. For example, a smaller animal, such as a lizard, has a smaller bubble than a larger animal, such as a bear. The powerful lion has a bubble far larger than its size would indicate, primarily because of its power in the jungle.[3] In addition, Hall found that for different kinds of activities animals exhibit different and predictable spacing patterns among themselves.

In attempting to correlate this kind of animal behavior with human communication behavior, Hall found striking similarities. Human beings, like animals, have a personal space they defend in their day-to-day encounters. If another person comes too close to us, we will react in some manner, probably a visible one. If someone stands too close to us on a relatively empty bus, we may pull away, wondering if the person had a motive. If a stranger sits very close to us in church, we might move away, hoping the person doesn't notice what we have done. In some instances there's not much we can do. In a crowded elevator someone may be right on top of us, and because the person is a stranger we don't like the invasion. But since there's nowhere to go in a crowded elevator we employ other proxemic techniques to alleviate our discomfort: we look up or down, we stare at the floor numbers in the elevator, or we even pull our arms close to our body.

If given some type of instruction on the subject, adults can recognize their territoriality. Children acquire territoriality at some point in their development of communication. Young children are typically considered as cuddly, close little people. Do children have to learn spacing patterns? Why do children find the notion of territoriality so amusing when it relates to themselves?

Hall argues that the conventions of proxemic space in communication with others are learned at a very early age. Children learn to use space in their communication much in the same way they learn to use words. Recent research in proxemics suggests that young children display some of the proxemic patterns in communication that are typical of adults from a comparable ethnic background. For example, children use different spacing patterns in communicating with males and females—an adult pattern. Just as a child's grammar and vocabulary increase in size and complexity through the first years of life, the child's proxemic communication becomes increasingly complex, adapting to situations and other persons.

---

[3]Edward T. Hall, *The Hidden Dimension* (New York: Doubleday, 1969), pp. 10–15.

Before we examine the available information on children's development of proxemic communication, it is important that we examine proxemic research with adults. In other words, our starting point will be the interpersonal spacing patterns of adults, both male and female, of several ethnic backgrounds and social-class groups. Our "communication territory" is divided into four zones, each serving a particular function and regulated by a specific set of rules. We will discuss these zones as well as interpersonal-spacing differences attributable to sex and cultural group. Following a brief summary of the results obtained with adults in each area of investigation, we will examine these results in light of studies with children. However, there are very few studies dealing with children's interpersonal-spacing patterns. Consequently, our generalizations regarding children's development of proxemic-communication patterns are tentative and must be examined in greater detail in the course of more extensive research.

ZONES OF TERRITORY

adults' proxemic zones

Edward Hall has described four distance zones (the *zones of territory*) that constitute the space in which people communicate under a number of circumstances.[4] Hall proposed these zones following observations of middle-class adults, mainly natives of the northeastern seaboard of the United States, a high percentage of them with professional backgrounds. His studies indicate that each of these four proxemic zones contains a "near" and a "far" phase.

1. *The intimate zone:* In the near phase of the intimate zone (zero to six inches) another's presence is overwhelming. This is the distance for love-making, wrestling, comforting, and protecting. In the far phase of the zone (six to eighteen inches) the head appears very large and some features appear distorted. Within this distance people converse intimately with each other.

2. *The personal zone:* In the near phase of this zone (one and a half to two and a half feet) physical features are very apparent. Holding hands is done in this zone. In the far phase of the zone (two and a half to four feet) physical contact is not easily engaged in, but another person is clearly seen. People might discuss personal problems in this zone.

3. *The social zone:* In the near phase of the social zone (four to seven feet) touching is not possible. Personal business and social gatherings are characteristic of this zone. The far phase of the zone (seven to twelve feet) allows total vision of the other person's body. Formal business is typical of communication in this zone.

4. *The public zone:* In the near phase of the public zone (twelve to twenty-five feet) the body of another person is visible but details of the face are not. Formal styles of language are

[4]*Ibid.*, Chap. 10.

appropriate. A speaker addressing an audience is an example of communication in this zone. In the far phase of the public zone (over twenty-five feet) details of facial and bodily movement are extremely difficult to see. This distance occurs between an important public figure (for instance, a political personality) and an audience.

Those who write about proxemics have argued that the zones of territory cannot be generalized to all segments of our society. They stress that the classification system is based on a sample of our population certainly not representative of all human beings. Omitted were the young, lower socio-economic groups, nonprofessionals, and many other groups. Yet studies presenting distance standards appropriate for these groups are not available. In fact, few studies have been conducted to test the validity of Hall's zones of territory for other social, cultural, age, and economic groups.

Many students today argue that Hall's zones of territory are not appropriate for their own communication: they are far too large. For example, at social gatherings they prefer to communicate within much closer distances than Hall's scheme provides. They suggest that a distance of over three feet does not seem right for discussing personal issues with another person. Yet as we have noted, research supporting a different set of distance standards for younger communicators has not been reported. A study conducted on our campus did indicate the need for further research with different age groups.[5] Our study placed college students (eighteen to twenty-five years of age) in an interview situation in which the topics were of a personal nature. We predicted, on the basis of Hall's scheme, that a personal interview in the intimate zone would be a "failure." Interviews were conducted in both the personal and intimate zones.

Although students fidgeted more in the intimate-distance interview, they did not object to such a distance, nor did they evaluate the interviewer negatively—even though she sat nose to nose with them. These results surprised us. We predicted that the extremely close interview (six to eighteen inches) would be perceived by students as an invasion of their personal space. Yet students said they liked it, they were not uncomfortable, and they didn't think something was wrong. Although their physical behavior (for instance, turning away, twisting their shoulders, and showing tension) gave away the fact that they were at least unconsciously uncomfortable, they didn't seem to mind the close proximity. In fact, many of the students suggested that interviews should become more intimate communication situations in which desks, tables, and distance do not separate the two persons involved.

Further examination of the zones of territory characteristic to different

[5]Diane Shore, "The Effects of Close Proximity in a Dyadic Interview Situation" (Master's thesis, University of Illinois at Chicago Circle, 1971).

age groups in our society might reveal that with age comes more "distant" communication. Also, with today's emphasis on close and truthful communication perhaps a territorial description of humans will be fashioned that differs drastically from Hall's scheme, which was derived some years ago. Of great importance to us is an understanding of children's proxemic zones and an answer to the question of how children acquire the distance conventions of a social group. Research with children should hold the key to a better understanding of our interpersonal-spacing behavior.

children's territories

Watch preschoolers and young elementary-school children as they play and work in various school and playground settings. Their proxemic patterns are striking: they stand and sit *very close* to one another and to their teachers. Children seem to interact in the intimate zone. Waiting in lines, little children are "plastered together" when they seem to have a lot of room to spread out. When children can play in a large sandbox, they sit on top of one another, leaving a large area of the sandbox virtually untouched. Walking up stairs together is done body to body. Children seem to enjoy games that involve a lot of physical contact, touching, tagging, and lying on top of each other. Indeed, children touch, hug, and hold each other a lot when they play and talk. This observation led us to the following conclusion:

> *Children frequently engage in what proxemic experts would view as communication in the intimate zone, touching and holding those they communicate with.*

How big is the personal zone for children? Shawn Scherer used a unique photographic measurement system to obtain estimates of the distance between young children playing and talking on their school playgrounds.[6] In parks adjacent to the schoolyards yet distant enough so that a tripod-mounted camera was inconspicuous to most of the children, an experimenter took pictures of children having conversations. Estimates of the distances between the children were then calculated. Though the study focused on socioeconomic-class and subcultural comparisons, the results of the distance calculations were striking: most conversations took place at a distance of between six and fifteen inches, a rather small area. The lower-class children interacted at distances of about six to eight inches, while the middle-class children were between ten and fifteen inches apart. A general

[6]Shawn E. Scherer, "Proxemic Behavior of Primary School Children as a Function of Their Socioeconomic Class and Subculture," *Journal of Personality and Social Psychology,* 29 (1974), 800–805.

estimate for all children is about *ten inches*. Let's place this estimate in perspective.

Research with adults suggests that in our personal conversations with others we interact at a distance of one and a half to four feet, the average being about two feet. With this in mind, consider again the children's average of only ten inches. While children are physically smaller than adults, and while this might lead us to expect that their smaller distance average is in proportion to their bodies, difference in size does not account for the dramatically different averages. We must conclude that children typically work, play, and talk close together. We can make this generalization:

Children's personal zone is smaller and narrower than that of adults; in fact, children communicate at distances of only inches.

HOW CHILDREN LEARN THE ZONES OF TERRITORY

In a Chicago suburban school we conducted a study dealing with principles of proxemics and elementary education.[7] The study examined second-grade children's awareness of the four zones of territory outlined by Hall. Two methods were employed:

1. Children were shown a series of "absurd pictures" in which communication was taking place at an inappropriate distance. For example, a girl was telling a secret in the personal zone instead of the intimate zone, or two persons were talking intimately from a social distance. The children were told that there was something "silly" about the picture and were asked to identify what it was.

2. Children were presented groups of three pictures, each group containing pictures of similar communication situations. Two of the three pictures were alike in terms of proxemic distance and one was different. Other features of the pictures (such as the persons in them, their dress, and their bodily positions) were the same. The children were asked to find the picture that was different, much in the same way that *Sesame Street* asks children to play the "same-different" game.

The results of our study indicated that seven-year-old children were aware of proxemic absurdities in both the intimate and personal zones (they said that "distance was silly"). In addition, they were fairly good at isolating the "different" picture in the groups of three that illustrated the intimate and personal zones. However, the pictures illustrating the social and public zones caused difficulties for second graders. Our study also reported a three-day instructional program and its results. In this program researchers attempted to see whether children would benefit from proxemic instruction,

[7]Schiff, "A Study of Proxemics for Elementary Education."

part of which focused on explanations and role-playing of communication activities in the four zones. After three days of instruction children still experienced difficulties with questions on the social and public zones. Although their overall test scores were significantly better following the instruction, the children found the intimate and personal distances easier to talk about than the social and public ones.

To explain why the second graders had difficulty with the social and public zones, we presented a number of possible explanations, including the following major ones:

1. Children talk with others in much closer proximity than adults do. Children hug, cuddle, and generally stay close to others when they communicate. Since their communication typically occurs in the closer zones, children would be more aware of deviations from these norms, as in pictures with a "distance absurdity."

2. Children have more experience with activities and situations that occur in the closer proxemic zones than in the social and public zones. For example, they tell secrets, talk with friends, and play close to another child, but they do not often attend social gatherings or present talks in front of large audiences. The closer zones appear to be more relevant to their experiences than the social and public zones. Experience, then, may explain the differences in awareness.

Our results provide some data for speculation on children's acquisition of the zones of territory. Our study suggested that children learn the "rules" for the zones in a step-by-step fashion. They may become aware of human-distance behavior in the intimate zone first, because from infancy they are closely involved in touching and other activities in that zone. Children become aware of the personal zone next, when they begin to socialize, attend school, and engage in personal activities with their peers. Communication in the intimate and personal zones is probably well developed by the early elementary-school years. As children begin to experience more organized social situations, such as working in groups, they begin to form rules for the social zone. Finally, with experience in formal settings, as in talking to an audience, children develop an awareness of distance in the public zone.

In addition to learning the proxemic zones, children must also learn proxemic "conventions" typical of adult communication.

Further study of children's interpersonal spacing has taken three directions:

1. the comparison of boys and girls
2. the comparison of children from different cultural and social-class groups
3. the comparison of elementary-school children of different ages (usually first graders through fifth graders)

This focus on *comparisons* stems from the abundance of research with adults along this line. Research with adults has indicated that proxemic patterns vary according to sex and cultural group. The impetus for such research has come from Hall: he argues that cultural groups differ so radically in their interpersonal-spacing patterns that misunderstandings can arise between them. Further, Hall claims that males communicate less directly (at a greater distance and with less direct shoulder orientation) than females. Several studies have been conducted to gain experimental support for these assertions. Although they do not agree in their findings and conclusions, we are able to draw a number of generalizations. Some support Hall's theory and others do not.

SEX DIFFERENCES IN PROXEMIC PATTERNS

Studies of interpersonal spacing with adults have found that almost without exception males differ from females in their *directness* (shoulder orientation) in communication. Two important focal points for studying interpersonal spacing in communication are:

1. The distance (in feet and inches) between the participants.
2. The shoulder orientation (also called the *proxemic axis* or the *communication axis*) of the participants. Axis measurements are usually based on the "clock position" of the shoulders—for example, 12:00 indicates parallel shoulders in face-to-face communication. In most conversations we do not use a 12:00 (twelve o'clock) shoulder orientation, for it would be extremely direct, almost as to confront the other. Generally, we use a position that involves about a 2:00 (two o'clock) angle between the shoulders, so that participants are placed next to each other somewhat indirectly.

Stanley Jones found that sex differences in interpersonal spacing were consistently demonstrated across subcultural groups in New York City—blacks, Puerto Ricans, Chinese, and Italians.[8] In all cases women faced each other more directly than males did in their communication. Perhaps the difference stems from females' greater affiliational needs, greater desire for emotional involvement, and higher degree of interest in nonverbal feedback, or a combination of these factors. Other studies have supported the finding that females communicate with a more direct shoulder orientation to each other than males do. However, differences in proxemic distance between males and females have not been found.

sex differences in interpersonal spacing of children

Stanley Jones and John Aiello conducted two studies on the interpersonal-spacing patterns of young children, hoping to draw generaliza-

[8]Stanley Jones, "A Comparative Proxemics Analysis of Dyadic Interaction in Selected Subcultures of New York City," *Journal of Social Psychology,* 84 (1971), 35–44.

tions regarding acquisition of the proxemic conventions found in research with adults. In a study of first- and second-grade children from three cultural groups—Puerto Rican, black, and white—they found that white boys stood farther apart than white girls but that this difference did not occur with the Puerto Ricans and the blacks.[9] This sex difference in communication distance may be acquired at an early age by white middle-class children because of the greater emphasis placed on appropriate gender roles in their homes. The shoulder-orientation results were not as easy to interpret, however. In fact, they were inconsistent with adult norms: girls exhibited less direct shoulder orientation than boys.

In a second study, this time with black and white first, third, and fifth graders, Jones and Aiello found that boys were less direct than girls in their shoulder orientations to each other.[10] These results fit the adult norms rather well.

Sex differences in interpersonal spacing begin to emerge sometime after the first grade and are most obvious around the fifth grade. Differences in shoulder orientation between boys and girls are more pronounced with fifth graders than with either first or third graders. The directness of shoulder orientation in fifth-grade children is comparable to that of adults. There are no clear-cut differences in communication distance between children based totally on sex.

sex differences in children's interpersonal spacing: what do they mean?

That very young white middle-class children "learn" sex differences in communication, as demonstrated in their proxemic patterns, may illustrate the greater emphasis placed on gender display by their culture. Further, studies indicate that proxemic conventions typical of males and females in any cultural group are exemplified by young boys and girls belonging to that group. The major difference between boys' and girls' interpersonal spacing lies in the degree of "directness" of communication. Sometime in children's early elementary years they will demonstrate proxemic patterns of communication typical of adults in their cultural group that are of the same sex. As Hall suggests, these patterns emerge early. If boys or girls deviate from these interpersonal-spacing patterns, this may cause difficulties for them. Teachers must be aware of developmental trends in proxemics in order to cope with these difficulties.

[9]John Aiello and Stanley Jones, "Field Study of the Proxemic Behavior of Young School Children in Three Subcultural Groups," *Journal of Personality and Social Psychology*, 19 (1971), 351–56.
[10]Stanley Jones and John Aiello, "Proxemic Behavior of Black and White First-, Third-, and Fifth-Grade Children," *Journal of Personality and Social Psychology*, 25 (1973), 21–27.

CULTURAL DIFFERENCES IN PROXEMIC PATTERNS

Hall suggests that the way people position themselves when they talk may cause misunderstanding, particularly when the participants are of different cultural or subcultural groups. What may seem an appropriate distance or orientation for one cultural group might be too close for another cultural group. Put members of different cultural groups together, and misunderstandings due to interpersonal spacing may easily arise. The insistence of a person from one cultural group for close proximity might be interpreted by someone from another cultural group as a hostile or pushy gesture. The proxemic differences in communication, such as those between blacks and whites, are acquired early in life. According to Hall, these proxemic conventions are permanent barriers to effective intercultural communication.

Studies comparing cultural groups in terms of interpersonal spacing have in many instances supported Hall's generalizations.[11] For example, Arabs interact more closely than Americans, and members of Mediterranean cultures interact more closely than people in North European cultures. In other instances experimental support has not been obtained, as in a study comparing the interpersonal spacing of Latin Americans with that of North Americans. Since most of these studies were conducted in very controlled laboratory conditions, however, the results must not be taken too seriously. "Native" cultural behavior patterns don't happen as naturally when researchers record, observe, and measure from all angles a person from another country.

The Jones study comparing Italians, blacks, Chinese, and Puerto Ricans was conducted on the streets of New York City. Jones found no significant differences in communication distance or communication axis among the subcultural groups, although he predicted such differences on the basis of Hall's writings. Since his study was conducted under natural conditions in poverty neighborhoods in New York City, Jones suggested that his lack of support for Hall's generalizations may have been due to the overriding factor of poverty, not culture. In other words, a "culture of poverty" might be a more important factor in explaining proxemic patterns than the specific cultural origin of the persons communicating.

Hall's writings have suggested that lower-class blacks and middle-class whites differ in communication distance, primarily because blacks seem to

[11]See, for example, R. Forston and C. Larson, "The Dynamics of Space," *Journal of Communication*, 28 (1968), 109–16 (Latin Americans and North Americans); K. B. Little, "Cultural Variations in Social Schemata," *Journal of Personality and Social Psychology*, 10 (1968), 1–7 (Mediterranean and North European cultures); and O. Watson and T. Graves, "Quantitative Research in Proxemic Behavior," *American Anthropologist*, 68 (1966), 971–85 (Arabs and Americans).

become more "involved" with one another than do whites. Research studies comparing blacks and whites have produced mixed results, however: in one case Hall's predicted difference was supported and in another case the opposite was true. In terms of shoulder orientation, results are more consistent: blacks exhibit a less direct shoulder orientation in communication than whites.[12]

cultural differences in children's interpersonal spacing

Studies comparing children of various cultural groups have produced varying results as well. For example, some studies have found that black children interact at a closer distance than white children,[13] but others have found that distance distinguishes black and white children's communication only at a younger age (for instance, in first grade but not in fifth grade).[14] As we mentioned earlier, Hall argues that cultural differences in interpersonal spacing are acquired early in a child's life, and that these patterns remain with children as they grow older. For example, the studies conducted by Jones and Aiello support Hall's claim that children of different cultures exhibit proxemic differences from an early age:

1. Black children faced each other less directly than white children, especially in the earlier grades.
2. Black children stood closer to one another, especially in the earlier grades.
3. By the fifth grade interpersonal spacing of black children and white children differed only in shoulder orientation, not in distance: black children were less direct in shoulder orientation than white children.

Clearly, we need further studies of proxemic differences based on cultural background. Understanding the roles that communication distance and axis might play in differentiating children's communication will enhance our understanding of the communication problems of children and adults from cultural backgrounds different from our own.

social-class differences in children's interpersonal spacing

Scherer noted in his study of children's proxemic behavior in schoolyards that the variable of social class was significant in explaining the

---

[12]Albert Scheflen, "Non-language Behavior in Communication" (Paper presented at the annual meeting of the New York Chapter of the American Academy of Pediatrics, Elmsford, N.Y., October 1969).

[13]See, for example, J. C. Baxter, "Interpersonal Spacing in Natural Settings," *Sociometry,* 33 (1970), 444–56; and F. N. Willis, "Initial Speaking Distance as a Function of the Speaker's Relationship," *Psychonomic Science,* 5 (1966), 221–22.

[14]For instance, Jones and Aiello, "Proxemic Behavior"; and Aiello and Jones, "Field Study of Proxemic Behavior."

differences in the children's interpersonal spacing. Two schools were studied in Toronto, one in a lower-class neighborhood and the other in a middle-class neighborhood. The results from the two schools were dramatically different. The lower-class children, both black and white, interacted at close distances from one another—six to eight inches on the average. The middle-class children of both races communicated with each other at far greater distances—between ten and fifteen inches on the average. While Scherer did note that black children exhibited slightly closer distances than whites, the differences were not statistically significant. In fact, Scherer suggested that if Jones and Aiello had controlled for more social-class-related factors in their studies of elementary-school children, the cultural difference they found may have been less prominent. Scherer's study leads to this generalization:

> *Children from lower-class neighborhoods interact at closer distances than children from middle-class neighborhoods.*

The reasons for this difference can only be speculated upon, but those offered by Scherer resemble those offered by Jones in his 1971 study of various New York subcultural groups—crowding and closeness in poverty homes and neighborhoods.

implications of cultural and social-class differences in children's interpersonal spacing

Once we are able to isolate the proxemic differences in children's communication that appear to be due to cultural and social learning, we will be in a far better position to help students communicate effectively with others. The few proxemic studies reported to date have revealed rather striking differences in children's communication. According to the Jones-Aiello studies, the major cultural difference between black and white children is in the directness of shoulder orientation, or communication axis: in communicating, black children face each other less directly than white children. The distinctive patterns of communication behavior reflected in this difference are acquired as early as the first grade, and they seem to remain beyond that level. Thus, communication axis may be a persistent barrier to effective communication among blacks and whites from childhood on.

With regard to social-class differences in interpersonal spacing, a more consistent pattern seems to have emerged, with adults as well as children. Lower-class children interact at closer distances than middle-class children, and this difference seems to be a rather dramatic one for both white and black children. While it is difficult to lend a valid interpretation to these findings without further investigation, we could speculate either that (1) middle-class children learn greater communication distances more quickly than lower-class children, or that (2) lower-class children will always communicate at closer distances than middle-class children.

DEVELOPING PERSONAL POWERS: PROXEMIC AWARENESS

It is important for children pursuing independence to gain an awareness of the role of proxemic factors in their communication with others. Often, children's feelings about persons or events are conveyed most effectively through their posture—how directly they face people or how close they stand to them. Children who are aware that they communicate messages in these ways are more aware of the effects of these messages on others. They know that closeness can be an important factor in convincing a little sister they care about her. They know that keeping away from another person says something in a powerful way to that person.

In addition, the competent communicator knows that others communicate messages in their closeness and distance, too. Reading postural cues and assessing physical closeness can only help children as they attempt to understand what others are saying about them and to them.

The communication talents that require proxemic awareness in their effective implementation are gaining and maintaining the attention of adults in socially acceptable ways. Children who are aware of proxemic conventions will communicate their need for attention and help without invading the other person's space; they will know that an appropriate use of their body in space will be beneficial in communicating this need.

For children to move from the domain of other-regulation to self-regulation, they need to incorporate a communication code that both expresses self and adapts to others. While children must be able to employ the appropriate proxemic conventions in their communication, to show a level of maturity that reflects a level of independence, they must also be capable of responding appropriately to the proxemic messages of others. Human use of space in communication is critical to our feelings about the effectiveness and appropriateness of the interaction, and children acquiring communication power learn the importance of space in their communication.

SUMMARY

The study of human territoriality is in its infancy. How people communicate in space is a relatively new science of human behavior. There are many unanswered questions concerning adult proxemic behavior, and new studies must be designed to answer these questions. Of even greater importance is how children acquire the rules of communication in space. When we understand more about a child's acquisition of proxemic behavior, our understanding of adult norms will be more meaningful: the standards and conventions employed by adults will then have a developmental basis. The few studies of children's interpersonal spacing that have been conducted indicate that certain patterns of proxemic behavior are learned in the early elementary grades. Children's personal space seems to be very small—possibly averaging about ten inches, compared with the adult average of about two feet. Young children (for instance, second graders) are most aware of communication distance in the "closer" zones—the intimate and personal zones. Their understanding of communication conventions in the social and public zones may depend on social and public communication experiences in their elementary-school years. It seems likely that children acquire spacing behavior in a zone-by-zone fashion, beginning with the intimate and personal zones.

Studies comparing the proxemic behavior of elementary-school children from various ethnic backgrounds have indicated that certain proxemic patterns are well established by the first grade. For example, sex differences in shoulder orientation are evident in the communication of white middle-class first graders. For black and Puerto Rican children sex differences are slower to emerge. This difference might be explained by the greater emphasis placed on appropriate gender display in white middle-class homes.

Concerning ethnic differences in interpersonal spacing, a number of proxemic patterns distinguish blacks' and whites' communication in early elementary-school years, yet the only proxemic difference in the communication of black and white children to remain beyond the fifth grade is communication axis. We suggested that this "directness" variable may pose a barrier to effective communication between the groups, for it is a difference that seems to begin in childhood and remain throughout adult years.

Social class has been offered as an alternative to ethnicity in explaining proxemic differences in children. Specifically, lower-class children have been found to communicate at closer distances than middle-class children.

Though further studies will have to be done on the development of proxemic conventions in children, we can safely conclude that proxemic patterns continue to emerge throughout the elementary-school years.

SUGGESTED READINGS

BAXTER, J. C., "Interpersonal Spacing in Natural Settings," *Sociometry*, 33 (1970), 444–56.

JONES, STANLEY, and JOHN AIELLO, "Proxemic Behavior of Black and White First-, Third-, and Fifth-Grade Children," *Journal of Personality and Social Psychology*, 25 (1973), 21–27.

SCHERER, SHAWN E., "Proxemic Behavior of Primary School Children as a Function of Their Socioeconomic Class and Subculture," *Journal of Personality and Social Psychology*, 29 (1974), 800–805.

PART IV
COMMUNICATION
DEVELOPMENT

Part IV offers an approach to learning that can help children become more effective communicators. Chapters 11–13 integrate verbal and nonverbal aspects of communication into a model of instruction that centers on the *communication situation* and has as its objective the development of communication competencies. Thus far we have discussed children's communication in three areas:

1. the forces affecting communication development (Part I)
2. the stage-by-stage development of morphology, syntax, and semantics in children's communication (Part II)
3. children's development of body language, voice, and proxemics in communication (Part III)

The final part of this text offers a classroom approach to communication instruction that aims to foster effective communication in day-to-day situations.

Studies in children's language development have been extremely helpful in explaining why a child's language develops as it does. We can trace the stages of development in any channel of communication, whether we are talking about syntax or body language. We know that children acquire the basic rules of their language before they enter kindergarten. But the rules of language are not all that children must acquire in order to communicate effectively. Children must also learn that language is a tool; when used creatively and appropriately it can serve them well. Consider the eight-year-old boy who always waits until his dad has eaten dinner and is relaxing with the newspaper before he asks permission to do something. Or how about the child who waits until Grandma is around (she can't refuse her grandchild anything) to ask for a new toy? These children have learned something about language that has little to do with sounds or syntactic patterns. Instead, they have acquired rules or strategies for dealing with communication situations.

"Children learn when to speak, when to be silent, when to use ritual language, when to use baby talk, when to use polite forms and when to shift language in a multilingual community."[1] While children are mastering the grammatical rules of their language, they are also learning usage rules—rules that apply to the communication situation at hand. Courtney Cazden suggests that when we consider the relationship between language structure and language use, for purposes of instruction, we might see a paradox.[2] To resolve the paradox, she cites a quotation from the Duchess in *Alice in Wonderland*: "And the moral of all that is—'Take care of the sense, and the sounds will take care of themselves.'" Cazden suggests that a variant of the Duchess's moral applies here: take care of the *use* and the structure will take care of itself. In other words, if instruction centers on how children can use language effectively in a variety of communication situations, the children will easily develop the more complicated aspects of language structure. Consequently, Part IV focuses on the communication situation and offers instruction on communication strategies children must acquire in order to participate effectively in their interpersonal relationships.

Often, the effectiveness of a communicator is not related to the use of an extensive vocabulary, careful articulation of speech sounds, or perfect grammatical phrasing. Instead, it is based on the *appropriateness* of what we say. The message must be appropriate to the person, the setting (time and place), the topic being discussed, and the task at hand. The competent communicator carefully weighs the *factors of the communication situation:*

1. *participants:* the person(s) involved in communication
2. *setting:* the time and place of the communication event
3. *topic:* the subject matter of communication
4. *task:* the goal or purpose of communication

Because the competent communicator weighs the factors of the situation well, she can *bargain:*

---

[1]Dan Slobin, ed., *A Field Manual for Cross-Cultural Study of the Acquisition of Communicative Competence* (Berkeley: University of California Bookstore, 1967), p. 10.
[2]Courtney Cazden, "Two Paradoxes in the Acquisition of Language Structure and Functions" (Paper presented at the Conference of Developmental Sciences, CIBA Foundation, London, January 1972), p. 5.

"Mommy, if you let me have one more cookie, I promise I'll eat all my vegetables for dinner!"

The competent communicator can *manipulate:*

"You're the best Dad in the whole world. . . . Can I stay up late and watch TV with you, Dad?"

The competent communicator can *comfort:*

"I'm sorry you don't feel good, Mom. Why don't you rest for a while on the couch? You've been working too hard. I'll be real quiet. OK?"

Competent communicators certainly know the rules of language structure; more important, they know how to use language as a tool in everyday situations.

Chapters 11, 12, and 13 discuss the communication situation, the communication framework, and communication competencies, respectively. Let's look a little closer at each of these topics.

THE COMMUNICATION SITUATION
AND COMMUNICATION STRATEGIES

Children learn to adapt their communication to important parameters of the communication situation: participants, setting, topic, and task. Principles of effective conversation are also important. For example, "Say just enough but not too much" is a relevant guideline children must learn. According to another approach to the communication situation, the coorientational view, we must learn to give explicit attention to the process of interaction with our communication partner. For instance, we must be able to say, "You know, we aren't agreeing in this conversation at all." Children acquire communication strategies for use in given communication situations. They learn to adapt their strategies to listeners so that they have communication power.

THE COMMUNICATION FRAMEWORK

Children learning any language acquire a certain perspective about the process of communication. They must become acquainted with the axioms of communication, such as "You cannot *not* communicate" and "Messages have content and relationship components." The second part of this chapter explains the five functions of communication and then discusses them in developmental terms. These five functions provide the raw materials for the content of communication.

COMMUNICATION COMPETENCIES

In their struggle to become competent communicators children learn a set of communication competencies, such as those outlined by Burton White. The instructional framework for the development of these minimal communication competencies is based on four components: (1) building an adequate repertoire of communication strategies, (2) using appropriate selection criteria in choosing among alternatives, (3) implementing one's communication choices, verbally and nonverbally, and (4) evaluating communication choices from the perspectives of self (for example, Did I accomplish my purpose? Did it work out the way I wanted it to?) and the other person (for instance, Did my friend understand? Does my friend feel okay about what happened?). A set of minimal communication competencies targeted for fourth-grade children is presented and explained in this chapter. The conclusion relates this competency framework back to the basic premise of this text—that communication is the child's power play.

11

the communication situation and communication strategies

A CHILD'S PLAY

cast of characters:

Mommy . . . . .the mother
Jimmy . . . . .the four-year-old son
Witnesses . . . . .the throng of shoppers

Act 1, Scene 1
Today is a shopping day. Jimmy and his mother are going to the department store together to buy a winter jacket for Jimmy. Unfortunately, both Jimmy and his mom are exhausted from the night before. Jimmy had a difficult time falling asleep and kept his mother hopping with frequent and persistent demands for one more glass of water, one more trip to the bathroom, and one more hug and kiss. As they pass through the toy department, which happens to be en route to the children's-clothing department, Jimmy spots a shiny red truck that looks interesting. He suggests to Mom that he wants it, no, *needs* it. She informs him (somewhat tensely) that first they are going to buy the jacket and if he's well behaved she will consider the truck on the way out. Sorry Mom, Jimmy decides that he won't try on *anything* until he has the truck. Mommy says (somewhat *more* tensely) that she is too tired to put up with any more nonsense, that he knows better (really?), and that

Consulting Author: Royce Rodnick Gardner.

maybe they won't buy the winter jacket, which means Jimmy will not be able to play outside with his friends when it is cold (come on Mom, who's kidding whom?). Undaunted, Jimmy notes that there are now many people who seem to be observing this scene and he remembers that the strategy of tantruming in front of strangers can be pretty persuasive. He cries, he whines, and he falls to the floor, refusing to budge. Mom is becoming increasingly nervous. Everyone appears to be looking at her (critically?) and at Jimmy (sympathetically?). Is there anything left to do but relent and buy the truck? She does so, and happy little Jimmy willingly toddles off to be outfitted for the jacket.

This scene is not an unusual example of a child's shrewd analysis of a communication situation. Jimmy knows his mother pretty well. He can predict her behavior in many situatuions, on the basis of his past experiences with her, and he can manipulate his behavior (as in making a fuss in public) to accomplish a particular goal (getting a new toy). Sometimes his strategies work and sometimes they don't. In either case the child is learning, through success or failure, a great deal about his own and others' behavior in important communication situations.

Jimmy has made some sound decisions about his verbal and nonverbal language choices on the basis of his analysis of the communication situation:

1. *Participants:* His mother does not wish to have a nagging child embarrass her in front of others.
2. *Setting:* The department store in daytime has many onlookers to witness his distress.
3. *Topic:* The truck, the subject matter of his communication, is in full view; everyone can see how much he wants it.
4. *Task:* A strong desire for the truck is both obvious (his message is clearly stated) and understandable (a boy needs a truck, right?).

The communication strategies that Jimmy employed reflect a fairly high level of communication mastery. His nonverbal choices were more than adequate for accomplishing his goal. Jimmy won. His mother's language choices, which were also based on the people, setting, topic, and task of the communication situation, may have been the best she could make under the circumstances. While she probably knew that giving in to a misbehaving child is good neither for establishing behavioral rules nor for maintaining her self-esteem, she may have felt lost in trying to cope with Jimmy. So she gave in. She weighed the factors, analyzed her choices, and decided to buy the truck. Buying the truck is not necessarily a losing communication choice, but it does seem to be a weak one in this situation because the mother had warned her child of the consequences of his behavior. She may not have seen the choice of simply saying, "Yes Jimmy, I see you want it, but I am angry you have acted this way. You are throwing a tantrum, and I don't like it. Let's come back if you can calm down."

Ideally, participants in a communication situation develop a mutual goal and a mutually satisfactory way to accomplish the goal. The thrust of this chapter is a discussion of the nature and importance of the communication situation and the significance of how a situation is perceived by the participants. Each communication situation asks us to make certain appropriate language choices, verbal and nonverbal. Consequently, this chapter deals with two major topics: (1) the communication situation, seen from four basic perspectives, and (2) communication strategies and their importance in comunication power.

THE COMMUNICATION SITUATION

There are a number of ways to define the communication situation. We can gain greater insight by considering all these approaches, since each allows us to see the communication situation from a slightly different perspective. Three approaches view the communication situation as evolving from somewhat implicit assumptions persons have about the rules of an interaction and their roles in it. A fourth approach considers the communication situation to emerge from explicit assumptions persons share about the roles, rules, and purposes of a communication encounter. These are the four approaches:

1. *the dramatic view*, which pictures the communication event in performance terms
2. *the categorical view*, which classifies situations according to the types of language that are appropriate in them.
3. *the parametric approach*, which examines how the variables of participants, setting, topic, and task affect our communication choices.
4. *the coorientation approach*, which views successful communication as a process that is mutually defined by the participants.

the dramatic view

Anthropologist Ervin Goffman has suggested that we can interpret all social behavior as if it were a dramatic performance.[1] He finds that most of us have a highly developed ability to play successfully the roles demanded of us at any moment. Most of us do not have the tools of the professional actor at our command, and we rarely have a script that indicates what we should say. We don't have the rehearsal time to practice the most effective tone of voice or bodily movement, nor is the setting of the scene always one with which we are familiar or in which we are comfortable. We might know the roles of the characters—for example, mother, child, and teacher—but we cannot always

---

[1]Ervin Goffman, *Presentation of Self in Everyday Life* (New York: Doubleday, 1959).

predict the best way to deal with these roles or the persons behind them. Yet we do acquire "acting techniques" that allow us to cope with others.

As we saw in our play, four-year-old Jimmy has already begun the process of discriminating among the acting techniques available to him, such as crying, asking for water, and throwing a tantrum. He has mastered a few roles, such as the "good boy" and the "bad boy," and he has some knowledge of the appropriate setting in which to play these roles. If he were home alone with Mommy, the tantrum technique and its associated "bad-boy" role might not work. But even without the skills of the professional actor, Jimmy possesses, as do most children, a very powerful tool: the use of both verbal and nonverbal language, which aids him in coping with the communication situations he encounters.

A child's ability to role-play is often uncanny. Many times a mother is left wondering where her child picked up a certain expression, a particular body movement, or a strangely familiar tone of voice. She may think it's cute or she may shudder at the thought that the child is imitating her. Early in life a child realizes that individuals are different and have different roles. Consider the case of Maria and her awareness of roles. Her learning begins with her observations of her immediate family. For example, she realizes that her father expresses his love differently than her mother does. To be tossed into the air and caught with a hug is Daddy's way. Mommy shows her love by worrying about whether she's eating her vegetables and by making certain that she's dressed warmly enough. Maria knows that Grandma never scolds her, but her older sister sure knows how to yell when she accidentally spills milk on her schoolbooks. She observes that different persons react differently to her. Perhaps she also learns that she responds differently to different persons. Her messages of hunger, anger, and illness are reserved for her mother. She saves the exciting story about the jet airplane she saw flying right over her house for Daddy's ears alone. Maria allows Grandpa to hug and kiss her, but her older brother better not try it. Children must learn how to use their language in real situations with real people. Different persons have different roles, and children's communication must be adapted to these roles. Maria, a five-year-old girl, has a good start in learning the importance of roles in communication.

Whereas professional actors must use their abilities to portray *other* persons, our young social actors must use their abilities to learn about other persons so that they can portray *themselves* in the most successful and rewarding ways. This requires that children be given opportunities to observe other individuals and to talk about how they function within their roles. Children must be encouraged to experiment with their language and analyze the results. The end product of their efforts is a repertoire of language strategies that enables them to deal successfully with characters and scenes they encounter in day-to-day communication "performances."

the categorical view

We can view the communication situation in the same manner in which we examined grammatical structures. Just as we reviewed the child's development of grammatical categories (Chapter 6), we can study the child's communication development according to categories of usage. The goal of communication learning is communicative competence, the ability of persons to perceive and categorize the social situations of their world and to differentiate their way of speaking accordingly.[2] Communicative competence, like linguistic competence, involves a categorization process in acquisition. Just as children learn syntactic rules that tell them how to categorize and order words in sentences, they acquire a knowledge of how and when to use various sentences to express feelings and ideas in their interpersonal relationships.

Children learn various categories into which communication events can fit. For example, a child may have a category of "be quiet" situations—those times and places when she knows she must be silent. She may also have a category of "be polite" situations, in which she finds it more advantageous to be the "good girl" rather than the "bad girl." These two categories might look something like this:

"be quiet" category

1. Mom has a headdache.
2. Mom doesn't realize that it's past my bedtime.
3. I don't want the teacher to call on me in class.
4. I am being scolded by my father.
5. My friend has told me a secret.
6. I am in church.

"be polite" category

1. I am talking to an older person.
2. I am asking for a favor.
3. Someone has given me a gift.
4. We are eating dinner.
5. I am talking to my teacher.
6. I am asking for permission to do something.

The child forms such situational categories because she is able to perceive similarities and differences in others' reactions to her behavior. Through a trial-and-error procedure the child is able to build mental labels for situations that are alike and require an appropriate type of behavior from her to insure a pleasant outcome. Consequently, categories emerge. Here are three more possible categories:

"be forceful" category

1. I'm sure my idea is a good one.
2. I'm encouraging a friend to do something.

"be careful" category

1. I'm talking to my teacher about schoolwork.
2. I'm giving directions.

"be concerned" category

1. My friend has a problem.
2. Something was accidentally broken.

[2]Dell Hymes, "On Communicative Competence," in *The Mechanisms of Language Development*, ed. R. Huxley and E. Ingram (London: CIBA Foundation, 1970), p. 84.

Situational categories help steer the child in an appropriate direction of behavior. New situations are added to a category as the child encounters and classifies them. The child can generalize what she knows about a category already developed—for example, "I should be polite to persons in high authority, such as the doctor and my teacher"—to new situations—"I should be polite to the principal of my school."

Appropriateness, a key term in the study of communication situations, is determined by (1) the culture of the child and (2) the parameters of the situation. A culture will dictate norms that a child must learn in order to become an "exemplary member" of that culture. Further, the four parameters of a communication situation (participants, setting, topic, task) have a strong bearing on the child's verbal and nonverbal language choices in that situation. We can now define *communicative competence* as

the mastery of an underlying set of appropriateness rules—which are determined by culture and situation—that affect the verbal and nonverbal choices in communication events.

For any one communication situation, the more language options available to the person, the more likely the choice will best fit the demands of the situation. The verbal and nonverbal options selected for use in the situation can be called *communication strategies*. Ideally, the strategies selected (the particular ways of speaking or acting, such as being quiet, being forceful, or being polite) are appropriate to the culture and the situation.

The third view of the communication situation focuses on its four parameters. Before explaining these parameters, let's momentarily examine the role of a culture on the person's communication behavior. Most anthropologists assume that an individual who is a member of a culture must operate by the norms of that culture. At the core of this assumption are the premises that (1) all behavior is rule-governed and (2) the culture determines the appropriateness of various behaviors by establishing certain rules of behavior for its members. In their attempt to become members of their culture, children must learn their culture's rules of communication appropriateness. Through exposure to accepted practices in their culture, children generalize rules for appropriate behavior in a multitude of situations, such as playing and talking. Sports may be the most important play activity for children in one culture; music or games may be highly valued in another culture. Rules about children's behavior in communication situations (for instance, "Never talk to someone you don't know") also vary from culture to culture.

A young child of the dominant culture in America, for example, is taught that it is polite to address a person by his name—and in some cases a title, such as Mr., Mrs., or Dr. Further, it is socially acceptable to inquire about a name: "Whom were you named after?" A Navajo child, on the other hand, would not dare ask about somebody's name or make a comment about it. Anthropologist Edward Hall warns us that in Navajo culture this would be a rude and unacceptable procedure.[3]

Because cultural norms are so important in determining what is appropriate communication behavior, it is imperative that teachers become familiar with the cultural norms and practices of their students. The task is not too difficult if the teacher and students share basic cultural values. But if the teacher is a young white woman from a middle-class, Protestant background and her students are of a different race and background, she must learn about the cultural practices that are important to her students.

the parametric approach

Those who have stressed the importance of studying the communication situation agree that the basic units of analysis are the participants, setting, topic, and task. These four parameters *define* the communication situation and help determine the appropriateness of verbal and nonverbal language. Let's discuss the four parameters and illustrate them with examples.

Participants are those persons engaged in the communication event. We can describe the participants according to age, sex, culture, education, status, or any other attribute relevant in a particular culture. There are far simpler ways to talk about the participants in a conversation. Instead of perceiving a person's sociological attributes we often perceive people in this way:

"He's my father." (Better watch out.)

"She's my best friend." (Anything goes.)

"He's my teacher." (Be careful.)

Children's perceptions of another participant in a communication situation are based on their perception of that person's role in their lives. Children may speak differently with their teacher, a high-authority person, than they do with their brothers or sisters. This is probably because children see a teacher as a person continually evaluating them, making judgments, and affecting their school "careers." With a brother or sister, however, there is less fear of negative evaluation—or any kind of evaluation, for that matter. Such perceptions play an important role in how children talk to others.

Children's self-images, their feelings about themselves, also affect

[3]Edward T. Hall, *The Silent Language* (Greenwich, Conn.: Fawcett Publications, 1959), p. 24.

their communication choices. If children feel pretty good about themselves, or, conversely, if they have doubts about themselves, this will probably be reflected in their verbal and nonverbal language. Furthermore, children use language differently when speaking to someone they believe thinks highly of them (their best buddies, for example) than they do when they are sure they are perceived negatively (by the principal who just last week warned them that their behavior in class had better improve).

The place and/or time of the communication event is the *setting*. Children must learn that the setting involves rules that govern the type of language that they can use. Upon entering school children quickly learn that all sorts of things they took for granted at home cannot be done at school. What mother ever made her children raise their hand before asking a question? Imagine the frustration children must feel at being told to sit up straight and fold their hands instead of being able to talk and play freely with other children. Many children have been warned by a teacher, "Save that type of language for home—we don't speak that way in school!"

Timing can also be an important consideration for language usage. Most children have heard rules such as "There will be no crying at the dinner table—save it for after dinner" or "Don't bother Daddy until after he's read the newspaper—then he'll play with you." Timing is also involved in an occasion such as a funeral or a birthday party. There are certain conventions of behavior and communication that are appropriate on such occasions. For example, we know that silence is often the best form of communication at a funeral. On the other hand, children know they should communicate their birthday greetings to a friend when attending his party.

The *topic* is the subject matter, or referent, of speech. The familiarity, potency, and degree of interest the topic has to someone will affect his language choices in a communication situation. If you were called upon to give two spontaneous lectures—one on children's communication development and the other on computing square roots—your two lectures would probably exhibit drastic differences in your use of language. Although you would certainly be fairly articulate and confident discussing the former topic, you might appear inept mumbling what little you can recall about how to compute a square root. From your standpoint children's communication is a far more familiar topic.

Sex is a potent topic in many cultures. Some cultures dictate that children should not be exposed to a topic that has any sexual overtones. After all, "the superego of the child might be affected." Yet, if it is much too early to send the children to bed and the juicy gossip can't wait, the adults might use euphemisms in talking about the topic. They may spell certain words or names, whisper, or lower their voices.

A perceptive teacher will discover that her students' language gives pretty good clues as to how interested they are in a particular subject.

Falling asleep, doodling, and inattention are, of course, obvious signs of boredom or confusion. Questions, alertness, smiles, and frowns are usually positive signs of students taking an interest in a topic. Clues that tell us the degree of interest others have in our topic will affect—should affect—how we talk about the topic.

Task refers to the reason or objective for an individual's communication. If we are analyzing children's speech, we must ask this question: What are they trying to accomplish in communicating? Teachers or parents often tend to assume that "poorly behaved" children's objective is to annoy them. If they were to evaluate the children's communication situations more carefully, perhaps they would realize that "poorly behaved" children may be communicating a need for extra attention and that their goal in behaving poorly is to have someone notice them, even if the strategy is a negative one.

Frequently, adults are criticized for integrating the slang expressions of the times into their speech. They are accused of trying to be "with it" but failing miserably. Perhaps this is an unfair accusation. Their task might be a desire to show they are willing and anxious to communicate with their children, but their strategy might not be the most effective one for accomplishing this task.

A frequent objective of both younger and older children's communication is to avoid the bedtime hour, a task for which they may have many strategies. Toddlers use the familiar strategy of throwing a special toy out of the crib only to cry for someone to come in and pick it up. There is also the popular "I'm thirsty" routine, which most mothers know only too well. Older children often use the excuse of "just remembering" that there is homework left unfinished or that their teacher gave them an assignment that required an extra hour of TV watching! If a parent sees through the routine and comments, "That tactic won't work this time," the parent is engaged in *coorientation*, the subject of our next approach to the communication situation.

the coorientation approach

Most of our communication behavior is spontaneous activity. We do not consciously choose every word that we utter, nor do we think all the time about what every part of our body is doing. When we speak to another person we assume that we are being understood, that we are acting appropriately, and that we share some mutual reason or goal for talking. These assumptions about communication behavior generally remain implicit, or out of awareness, unless participants become aware that there is a conflict between communication goals, or confusion or discomfort on the part of one or both of them. Robert Craig and Bonnie Johnson suggest that at this point there is a moment of realization in which participants become *explicitly* aware of the interaction and attend to their own and the other's behavior in an effort to make sense of the encounter.[4] This conscious attempt to make sense begins the *coorientation process*, in which participants begin an explicit effort to probe and question the assumptions of the interaction. Remarks such as "What do you mean by that?" "Have I understood you correctly?" and "I'm confused" are indicators that persons are attempting to interpret their own communication and that of another person. Coorientation is a way of resolving conflict, a cooperative effort to identify a joint goal.

At the beginning of the chapter we observed a four-year-old's persuasive strategy of tantruming to get his own way. We viewed Jimmy's strategy pretty much from his perspective and called it a success. Frankly, it appears that Jimmy was a smart little boy who roped his mom into buying the truck. But his mother may have been trying to coorient her perspective of the situation with Jimmy's. She may have recognized Jimmy's symptoms of fatigue, as well as her own. In order to accomplish what was really their mutual goal—to get the errand done and go home—she satisfied Jimmy's immediate goal (the truck). To be honest, she was buying some peace and quiet with the truck so that she could get things done. This is something parents often do, though psychologists are quick to point out that the strategy may do more harm than good by rewarding undesirable behavior.

There are times, then, when effective communication depends upon the participants' mutual ability to coorient their perspectives of the communication situation. Moreover, the coorientation process explains why we tacitly agree to follow certain norms of communication behavior. These norms generally insure that our mutual goals for talking will be accomplished. Paul Grice has outlined four such norms:

1. *Quantity:* say just enough—not too little and not too much.
2. *Quality:* don't say something that you believe to be false, or speak about something for which you lack evidence.
3. *Relevance:* make your contribution relate to the topic and the situation.
4. *Manner:* be clear about what you want to say, and be as brief as possible.[5]

When we agree to follow these criteria we indicate a desire to take each other's perspective into account during the exchange and in general to cooperate with each other to accomplish our communication goals.

How do children learn communication norms, and how do they develop the coorientational perspective? Recent studies have indicated that as

[4]Robert T. Craig and Bonnie M. Johnson, "Coordinating Definitions of the Situation: A Communication Perspective," unpublished manuscript, University of Illinois, Chicago Circle, Chicago, Il., 60680.
[5]H. Paul Grice, "Logic and Conversation," *Syntax and Semantics: Speech Acts*, 3 (1975), 41–58.

children get older they practice the rules of conversational cooperation and adjust their speech to the person they are talking to.[6] Children learn to adjust the number and length of their utterances so that they correspond with those of their partner. They also learn to use similar patterns of pausing. That they learn to adjust in such technical ways suggests that children are aware of the coorientation process on a very unconscious level.

Children learn to express concern when they encounter confusion in communication situations, but it is not until they are older that they are capable of *metacommunicating*, or talking *about* their confusion. Young children do not appear to have the skills for effective coorientation, though studies have not been conducted to define these skills and examine their progressive development throughout childhood. We do know that young children are able to comment about a communication situation that bothers them:

"Huh? I don't get that."

"You sure are talking like you're big stuff."

"Wait a minute, you're not the boss of me."

Rarely do they comment on their own behavior, however. They relate the confusion or disagreement they may feel about the other person's communication. Only when they are older are they able to converse about the confusion or status disagreement reflected in the three preceding examples. Studies are needed to explain more fully the process of children's development of coorientation skills.

In summary, when there is a conflict of goals or some confusion about the norms of an interaction, there is a greater need to discuss, probe, and interpret exactly what is happening in the situation. This is the process of coorientation. There are times when participants need to render the dramatic, categorical, and parametric perspectives of a communication situation secondary to the coorientational perspective. Coorientation is also reflected by participants who follow communication norms in order to avoid conflict and accomplish a mutual goal. The focus on effective communication choices leads to the second major topic of this chapter: communication strategies that represent verbal and nonverbal choices appropriate to the communication situation.

---

[6]See, for example, Catherine Garvey and M. BenDebba, "Effects of Age, Sex and Partner on Children's Dyadic Speech," *Child Development*, 45 (1974), 1159–61; M. Shatz and R. Gelman, "The Development of Communication Skills: Modifications in the Speech of Young Children as a Function of Listeners," *Monographs of The Society for Research in Child Development*, 38 (1973), 55; and Joan Welkowitz, Gerald Cariffe, and Stanley Feldstein, "Conversational Congruence as a Criterion of Socialization in Children," *Child Development*, 47 (1976) 269–72.

COMMUNICATION STRATEGIES

The language choices children make, based on their awareness of the communication situation, are influenced heavily by their past experiences in similar situations. In addition, the strategies at their command *change* as they develop. The more strategies a person has for a particular situation, the more likely it is that she has just the right one to employ. Our discussion of communication strategies has two focuses:

1. the origin and development of communication strategies
2. the effect of communication strategies on communication power

the origin and development of communication strategies

Communication strategies emerge in a number of ways. A child may discover a strategy at random, while playing or talking by himself. A strategy can originate from observation of an important communication model. A child may also learn a communication strategy from direct teaching by an important communication model. Let's briefly examine these three basic strategy-learning approaches.

1. The random-learning approach. A communication strategy can begin in the random behavior of a child. Picture little Matt, only five months old, lying in bed, rhythmically banging his head against the headboard. He's not hurting himself. In fact, he seems to enjoy the rhythm of his head moving back and forth. His mother hears the banging and enters the room, very upset to see and hear Matt engaging in this potentially harmful behavior. She picks him up to comfort him, certain that he might hurt himself. Matt, not understanding his mother's concern, continues to bang his head the next day. After all, it feels pretty good. His mother comes running into his room again. About a week later Matt is in his crib, feeling a bit uncomfortable and fussy. His mother has not given him the attention he wanted all day. Crying has not worked. Matt begins knocking his head, not so innocently this time. He moves harder and louder than he ever did when it was for his own enjoyment. Predictably, Matt's mother comes to his rescue with the much-wanted attention. A communication strategy is born! So, in random learning a child engages in a particular behavior, receives a positive response, and probably makes a mental note of the wonderful feeling that accompanied the response to the behavior. If the response to that same or similar behavior is continually satisfactory, a child may incorporate such behavior into his repertoire of communication strategies.

2. The observational-learning approach. Strategy learning takes place when children observe important communication models. For example, three-year-old Max observes his seven-year-old brother, Bobby, interacting with his friends in various ways. When Bobby does not get his way with his smaller friends he resorts to shoving and grabbing. When the friends are older or bigger, Bobby is much more likely to negotiate a deal by trading something he has or suggesting they take turns. Max is learning a great deal about getting along with friends from watching Bobby. Children probably gain most of their knowledge about communication strategies from observing mothers, fathers, sisters, brothers, and peers. They observe strategies put into action by others, and may include these strategies in their own thinking about a situation. If they have an opportunity, and feel comfortable, they may try the new strategy. If it seems effective, they may add it to their repertoire. From observing others, children also learn sex-role stereotypes related to language. They learn, for instance, that it is okay for Dad to swear and use rough language (because he's a man), but that it is inappropriate for Mom to use profanity or for profanity to be directed at her (because she's a woman). One study demonstrated that elementary-age children learn certain sex-role patterns of speech. Part of the children's development of communication competence consists of "learning what it means to talk like a lady."[7]

3. The Tutorial Approach.   This approach consists of children receiving direct advice from important persons regarding their communication. Very young children may require more explicit feedback in order to make sense out of their communication behavior. For children to develop appropriate communication strategies, formal instruction in conjunction with what they normally integrate from their social experiences within their family and culture may be necessary. Children are anxious to become productive social members of their family, peer group, and school system. Therefore, they usually welcome knowledge of such strategies as how to ask for things in a polite way, how to answer a telephone, how to address grownups, how to ask for information, and how to disagree. In some instances we directly teach children these strategies. There is good reason for explicitly indicating to children communication strategies that are expected, desired, and enjoyed.

Before children enter school they have mastered many communication strategies that are successful for them in countless communication situations. Certainly, however, they have the potential for acquiring many more. In interviewing mothers for their interpretations of their children's strategies, we found something that was initially surprising to us: older children (seven to eleven years) used fewer communication strategies than younger children

[7]Carole Edelsky, "Acquisition of an Aspect of Communicative Competence: Learning What it Means to Talk Like a Lady," in *Child Discourse*, ed. Susan Ervin-Tripp and Claudia Mitchell-Kernan (New York: Academic Press, 1977), pp. 225–43.

(one to four years) in situations such as trying to extend the bedtime hour.[8] We had thought the number of strategies would be greater for the older children. After careful consideration of the data, however, we realized that our older children probably had a more finely tuned system than the younger children for selecting an effective strategy. The older children did not have to try out a number of approaches, hoping one of them would work; this was the case for some of the younger children. The older ones *knew* what would work. If our concern is to help students in their relations with others significant to them, then the goals of communication instruction should be to *increase the child's repertoire* of communication strategies for dealing with these critical situations, and to develop for children a *set of criteria* for selecting the most effective and appropriate strategy for a particular situation.

Examples of communication-strategy development. Studies show that we can plot a steady development of children's listener-adapted communication throughout the elementary-school years. These studies illustrate children's mastery of persuasive strategies. Let's begin by considering a study of this development from six through twelve years of age.[9] We will use two examples from the study to explain the five stages of development proposed by the researchers. One example is how children would talk to a friendly versus a selfish-seeming peer in trying to get a toy; the other is their strategies in asking a blind versus a seeing florist for some flowers. The five stages are excellent milestones to consider in children's development of persuasive strategies.

Stage 1 is characterized by nonadaptation and a naive perspective. In this early stage of development children seem unable to verbalize about the relevant characteristics of the situation and listener they must account for in their communication. Though children have experience in adapting messages from their early years, children as old as six are not skilled in talking about these characteristics. So, to both the friendly and the selfish buddy the children's message was the same: "Can I play with the truck?" No special adaptation was attempted for the blind florist either: "I'd like those flowers please" (perhaps pointing to a special bunch of flowers in the window).

In *stage 2* characteristics are perceived but there is no adaptation. Children are able to talk about relevant listener characteristics, but their relation to communication tasks is not accounted for in the children's communication choices. While the children may have mentioned the importance

[8]Royce Rodnick and Barbara Wood, "The Communication Strategies of Children," *Speech Teacher*, 22 (1973), 114–24.

[9]Jesse Delia and Ruth Anne Clark, "Cognitive Complexity, Social Perception, and the Development of Listener-Adapted Communication in Six-, Eight-, Ten-, and Twelve-Year-Old Boys," *Communication Monographs*, 44 (1977), 326–45.

of the selfishness of the peer and the blindness of the florist, their communication to each did not reflect these perceptions.

Awareness of characteristics and a prediction of failure typify *stage 3*. Children see the relevance of certain characteristics to the communication situation. However, their lack of control over the communication code leads them to predict failure for any attempts they might make. This stage seems to be important in children's development because it shows their profound sensitivity to the consequences of the situation: if they do not adapt, they may fail. Some of the eight-year-olds were careful to point out, as they offered rather nonadapted responses, that "this probably won't work, but. . . ." Children in this stage seem to feel ill-equipped to select the best communication strategies.

Stage 4 is characterized by undifferentiated adaptation. Children are able to respond to listener characteristics with global, or undifferentiated, strategies. They use minor, general adaptation techniques rather than elaborated, differentiated ones. To the friendly peer they might ask, "Can I play with your truck?" and to the selfish one, "Can I play with your truck, pretty please?" The strategy in the latter case is a simple, global one of being polite through tone of voice and use of "pretty please." To the blind florist the children may have said, "I'd like the ones in the front window—the yellow ones." Such attempts show a general sensitivity to parameters of the communication situation.

In *stage 5* children exhibit differentiated adaptation. They use refined and elaborated strategies and approaches in adapting their communication. Note this increasingly elaborated progression:

"Can I play with the truck, please?" (stage 4)

"Can I use your truck for a few minutes?" (stage 5, modest aim)

"If you let me use your truck for a while, I'll give you something of mine to play with." (stage 5, more elaborate)

One of the more interesting adapted messages cited by the researchers is one that a child gave to an angry man when trying to retrieve a ball in his yard:

"Excuse me sir, my ball accidentally went over your fence, and if you'll let me get it, I'll try not to do it again. . . . I'm sorry."[10]

What angry man would not respond nicely to this perceptive little boy?

In another study the same researchers tried to link children's skills in listener adaptation (adopting the perspective of another person) and their persuasiveness with others; they found a solid relationship between the

[10]*Ibid.*, p. 336.

two.[11] The persuasive tasks presented to the children (second graders to ninth graders) were the following:

1. asking parents to buy them something they wanted very much
2. trying to get their mothers to allow them to have an overnight birthday party
3. urging a woman they just met to keep a lost puppy

The children's persuasive approaches were scored for their manner of communication and the type of support used in the plea. Level-one support showed awareness that the listener (a mother, for example) had a distinct perspective:

"I know you don't really know this puppy."

Level-two showed a recognition of the counterarguments the other could use: use:

"I know it costs money, and I don't have enough."

Level-three persuasion focused on the advantages of the plea's fulfillment to the listener:

"Gosh Mom, I'd be such a fun person to live with if I had that coat."

These two studies were based on a classic study by Kerby Alvy. Alvy studied 180 white grade-school children from upstate New York, 60 each at three age levels (six, nine, and twelve years).[12] He found a steady development in the children's quantity and quality of listener adaptations in performing what he called a "multisituational" task. One task, for example, involved these instructions:

Situation 1: This girl cries a lot when she hears sad things or bad things. Pretend that this girl's kitten just got into a fight with a mean dog and you have to to go her house and tell her about it. What would you say to her?
Situation 2: This girl is strong and never cries. (same general instructions follow)

Young children were found to make less complex assumptions about their listeners, and their assumptions were based mainly on observable behaviors of the listener. They might say, "Don't cry, but your kitten is in a

---

[11]Ruth Anne Clark and Jesse Delia, "Cognitive Complexity, Social Perspective-Taking, and Functional Persuasive Skills in Second- to Ninth-Grade Children," *Human Communication Research*, 3 (Winter 1977), 128–34.

[12]Kerby T. Alvy, "The Development of Listener Adapted Communications in Grade-School Children From Different Social-Class Backgrounds," *Genetic Psychology Monographs*, 87 (1973), 33–104.

fight." An older child might adapt in a way that is more complex and less tied to behaviors of the listener: "Don't worry, your kitten is okay, but she did get into a little fight."

Children show improvement with age in their persuasive abilities. Their persuasiveness seems linked to their ability to take on the perspective of the other person. Actually, we might say that persuasiveness *is* taking the other's perspective in a practical way. The course of learning listener adaptation is not a fast and easy one: children meet with failures and struggles as they experiment in different situations. Our awareness of the stages children go through in their mastery of listener adaptation can help us as we assist them in their struggle to acquire this skill.

the effect of communication strategies on communication power

A power philosophy of education is concerned with moving a child from a powerless position in society to a position of power.[13] Our particular concern is with "communication power," which can be defined as the ability to select from among communication options the ones best suited for accomplishing a particular objective. The two chapters that follow outline a basic approach to communication power for children. This approach defines the major communication functions that children must acquire (controlling, sharing feelings, informing and understanding, ritualizing, and imagining) and then proposes a competence-acquisition model for learning those functions. The acquisition model begins with the repertoire of strategies, but includes a more complete system for learning those strategies:

1. An adequate *repertoire* of communication strategies is developed for dealing with every-day situations.
2. *Selection criteria* are used to select the most effective and appropriate communication strategies for these situations.
3. Verbal and nonverbal choices are *implemented* in communication situations.
4. The effectiveness of their communication attempts are *evaluated* by the children.

The goal of communication instruction is to provide learning experiences that will help children develop the communication tools they need in their power move. To accomplish this goal, children should be given opportunities to participate in communication situations that allow them to enhance their language-performance skills through a wide variety of activities. These activities should represent the realistic and sometimes difficult situations children face in their struggle to make sense of themselves, the world,

---

[13]Beverly L. Hendricks, "The Move to Power: A Philosophy of Speech Education," *Speech Teacher*, 19 (1970), 151.

and others. A program of communication instruction should strive to increase children's repertoire of communication strategies so that when they are faced with a new and difficult situation they can choose from available options the most strategic route to effective communication.

Effective communication: the coorientational approach. In our discussion of communication strategies thus far it may appear that children's effective communication means that they get their own way. We certainly are not implying that educators should plan units on how children can raise their allowance or how they can avoid household chores. Admittedly, these might be attractive goals for many children, but our approach is not quite so child-centered. Our concern is not only with an individual's *success*, but also with the nature of the *interactive process* by which the goal is accomplished.

Many of us consider effective communication to be the successful accomplishment of our goal in communicating. If a girl's communication goal is to gain sympathy from her friend, and if this goal is consistent with her friend's motives for communicating, few problems arise in considering "success" in accomplishing her goal a measure of effective communication. Problems arise, however, when the persons engaged in communication have different motives and, consequently, inconsistent goals. If the girl seeking sympathy is met by a friend who wishes to give no sympathy, her communication goal is not compatible with that of her friend. When such situations arise, as they often do, the coorientational approach is necessary for judging communication effectiveness.

The coorientational approach to communication effectiveness requires cooperation in the identification of a joint goal. Both participants reveal their initial goals in their expressions of the communication task. If the goals conflict, attention must be paid to this difference. If a child's goal is to obtain permission to go to a friend's house to play and the mother's goal is to have the child help care for a younger sister, we have a clear mismatch of goals. The coorientational view of communication we adopt is that both parties—the mother and the child—must weigh their initial goals in terms of several factors:

1. their degree of *compatibility* (Can they both happen at once, or can they occur one after the other?)
2. their *importance* to the needs of each participant (Is one goal more strongly tied to an individual's needs than the other?)
3. their relationship to the *ground rules* of the family (Have there been prior agreements about the care of siblings?)

All of these factors have to be weighed in resolving the conflicting goals and producing a joint goal of communication. A judgment of communication effectiveness for either participant, the mother or the child, must be expressed in terms of the joint goal, not the conflicting initial goals. Consequently, when we discuss children's communication power we are not talking about their ability to get their own way. Instead, we are talking about children's ability to communicate their needs and desires as they coincide with those of the other person(s) in the situation.

Let's "turn it on"! Children are not completely powerless when they enter school. As we learned from our study of children's communication strategies, very young children are able to use language successfully to deal with the "problems" of their very narrow world. As children grow older, however, the situations they must face represent a wider world, and the problems are in many ways more difficult than those of their preschool days. Children are now expected to function with ease in almost every social situation, yet their training has done little to provide them with communication tools for social situations that are often complex. It is up to the school, then, to activate children's power potential: the school must provide an open environment in which children can test and discover alternative communication strategies that they can use in the everyday situations they encounter. In other words, schools must help to develop children's communicative competence—their ability to perceive and categorize social situations and act accordingly.

Children must feel a sense of confidence in their own abilities as communicators—we call this *felt power.* They must also be able to use language successfully and creatively in their everyday encounters with various persons, settings, topics, and tasks of conversation; to do so gives them *expressive power.* Communication strategies give children opportunities to achieve both kinds of power. The classroom must become an accepting environment in which children are allowed to experiment with communication strategies that could be of critical importance in their everyday communication encounters.

As children grow older they learn how the factors of a situation make certain kinds of talking more appropriate than others. They learn which factors of the communication situation place demands upon *what can be said* and *how it should be said.* To "turn on the power," using the phrase of the children's television program *The Electric Company,* let's take a closer look at the four parameters of the communication situation in terms of communication power.

Participants. In trying to understand children's communication it can be extremely important to ask this question: To whom was the child speaking? Conversely, when looking at how a child responds to another person's speech it is important to inquire about the other person, the person's status in relation to the child, and the control or power the person has in the eyes of the child. These participant-related factors may explain the child's response better than any other parameter of the situation.

Children with communication power know that they must gear their style of language to the person with whom they are talking. They must be able to recall past experiences with that person and draw on personal information that may be relevant to the present encounter. A young boy with communication power knows that his interview with the principal is likely to be about the incident in which he swore at his teacher in class. He also knows that the principal is a man who does not tolerate excuses but is impressed with neat appearances and good manners. Armed with this information and the task of trying to get off the hook, he is better able to plan his communication strategies. Perhaps a simple explanation of why he was so angry and an apology for swearing (which he now knows is wrong) will suffice. Then again, maybe he should just appear in his best clothes and wear a sad face.

Setting. Different settings provide different atmospheres for communication. A setting can refer to a physical locale—such as a schoolroom or a grocery store—or to a time or an occasion—such as when father returns home from work, or during a math exam. It is often said about children's communication that their motives are worthwhile but their timing is horrid. They ask their father for that new football just as he walks into the house after a tough day's work. They wait to obtain permission to go someplace at the very time when they must be at that place. The child with communication power knows how to weigh the factor of communication setting—the time and place of a conversation. The child with a basic understanding of timing and places knows that it's better to ask for that football after Dad relaxes and has eaten dinner. And permission is far easier to receive when the child plans ahead instead of waiting until that last tense minute.

Topic. Children want to be able to discuss matters that touch on their interests in some way. Children rarely need to be taught to become interested in something. All children turn their natural curiosity in some direction. It is often necessary to expose children to a variety of topics, giving them experience in discussing and listening to various approaches that can be taken in a conversation or discussion. Children become more powerful communicators as they develop a greater number of topic options, or subjects that they can talk about. Of greater importance, however, is that children know the "rules" concerning how and when a subject can be discussed. In other words, not only do children with communication power have a wealth of options concerning the topics they can discuss, but more important, they know which options to select in a particular communication situation. If an eight-year-old girl is attempting to discuss with her parents her belief that she is old enough to stay up an hour later at night, it might be wise for her to avoid crying or name calling. It might also be beneficial for her to avoid this subject after complaining that she was too tired to clean up her room or do her homework.

Task. It is often helpful in attempting to understand children to ask this question: What is the child's real objective in communication? Too often, more attention is paid to children's grammar and pronunciation than to what they are trying to communicate. Children should be exposed to the variety of ways in which language can be used to accomplish communicative tasks. Children may benefit from seeing and hearing others in the act of apologizing, asking questions, begging, and persuading. These communication acts are important in children's everyday experiences with others. Yet none of them can be learned from a set of how-to-do-it rules. Instead, there are various methods of accomplishing the same task, and the success of any one method depends on the factors of the communication event: the participants, the setting, and the topic. A six-year-old boy may find that the best way to "talk" his mother out of punishment is to lock himself in a room, bang a few things around, and then remain perfectly silent, refusing to eat. This method may work for this child but may prove to be a very hungry experience for other children. Another young boy may have discovered that the best way to make up with his mother after an argument is simply to apologize with a kiss and say "I love you." The child with communication power has more than one option or method to accomplish the same objective.

The four parameters of the communication situation form the dynamics of the communication event. Children should be given opportunities to discuss and participate in critical communication situations in the classroom setting. By hearing and observing how their peers handle such situations and by listening to ideas offered by the teacher, children can learn about novel approaches to a communication situation and can experiment with new strategies.

In order to see some of the communication strategies that children use, we interviewed Karen, an observant but very typical fifth-grade girl. We asked her to talk about three important persons: her mother, her teacher, and a friend. She described critical communication situations she experienced with each, and we analyzed these situations according to the four communication parameters. What follows is a report of this interview.

Karen's "tough task" with her mother. Karen said that the most difficult job she has in talking with her mother is convincing her that she should be allowed to choose her own clothes to wear to school. It seems that Karen is *the only* person in the fifth-grade class whose mother buys and selects clothes for her daughter "without even asking." As a result, Karen is the "worst-dressed girl in the class." When Karen was asked what she said or did to try to change the situation, she said she told her mother 500 times that all the other girls in the class make fun of her clothes and that they all were allowed to select their clothes. Further, Karen said she always screamed to her mother that she wasn't a baby anymore but was always treated like one. Her mother's usual response was that Karen should stop acting like a baby.

Karen's "tough" situation with her mother can be outlined like this:

Topic: clothes selection (or Karen's maturity)

Task: Being allowed to choose her own clothes

Setting: in Karen's bedroom, before she goes to school

Participants: Karen and her mother

Verbal communication strategies:
repetition (asking again and again—500 times!)

plea ("Others are making fun of me.")

conventions ("Everyone else does!")

reason based on age ("I'm not a baby anymore.")

Nonverbal communication strategies:
"screaming" (raising her voice)

Karen's "tough task" with her teacher. Karen has a lot of trouble convincing her teacher that the reason she does so badly in math is that she isn't good at math, not that she doesn't study enough. The other day, when Karen received a poor grade on her math assignment, she knew she had to talk to the teacher about it. She approached the teacher at an appropriate time and whispered her "excuse." With her "sincere" smile she began to explain her predicament. She said she could spend all day doing math problems and she still wouldn't do well. Therefore, it's silly to spend much time doing math when she loves reading history. The teacher has told Karen's mother that the child would do significantly better on her math assignments if she would only spend more time on them in the evening. Karen thinks her teacher simply doesn't understand her. In fact, this misunderstanding is probably based on the fact that her teacher just doesn't like her—because of her clothes! (Karen snickered when she made this statement, but the interviewer thought she might have been pretty serious.)

Topic: mathematical inadequacies

Task: making excuses for poor performance

Setting: in the classroom, when assignments are returned to students

Participants: Karen and her teacher

Verbal communication strategies:
reason based on ability ("I'm incapable!")

reason based on experience ("More time wouldn't help.")

related information ("I'm better in history.")

plea ("You just don't understand me.")

Nonverbal communication strategies:
  "sincere" smile
  whispered voice

Karen's "tough task" with her friend. Karen has trouble persuading Eric that he should be her boyfriend. Eric doesn't really like girls very much, but even if he did, he probably wouldn't like Karen (her own analysis). Eric even refuses to come over to her house after school. She asks him in a "polite" voice, but it doesn't work. To show Eric that he isn't being nice, Karen calls his house and hangs up when he answers the telephone. (We were told that this was "confidential information," not for release to Karen's mother or Eric's mother.) Karen also has her girlfriends call Eric and hang up. As you might have guessed, Karen blames her lack of success on her terrible clothes (see, she was serious!) and on the fact that Eric is "too dumb" to listen to "reason." Karen asked the interviewer for her opinion as to the best method for capturing Eric as a boyfriend. The interviewer, wise in the ways of fifth-grade boys, suggested that perhaps Karen should find a new boyfriend and, at the least, stop calling Eric.

Topic: someone you'd like as a friend

Task: getting a person to "notice" you and like you

Setting: a variety of places—homes, school, neighborhood; times: during school, after school, at night—any time!

Participants: Karen and Eric; Karen's friends

Verbal communication strategies:
  direction question (the invitation)

Nonverbal communication strategies:
  use of a "polite" voice
  fussing and bothering (all the telephone calls)

In spite of the light tone in our descriptions of Karen's problems, these problems are real situations in which Karen feels *powerless to act*. These are critical communication situations for Karen. She claims to have tried everything she could think of, without much success. Her communication strategies—strategies that she thinks are reasonable—lack something in most cases. Other children may excel in similar situations but have difficulties in others. Maybe Karen could learn something from her classmates if classroom activities were constructed on the basis of the factors in the critical communication situations Karen has described.

SUMMARY

When children's language is viewed from the standpoint of the communication situation the full impact of verbal and nonverbal language choices is understood. One way to understand the communication situation is to cast the event into a dramatic framework in which each participant is an actor with a script and a character to play. The "performance" of both communicators relating to each other takes place in a "scene." Communication can also be viewed in terms of categories of usage. Situations are categorized in terms of the appropriate communication behavior required—for instance, "be forceful" or "be quiet." A third view of the communication situation is based on the four communication parameters: participants, setting, topic, and task. A fourth approach is that communication situations are governed by the mutual goals of the participants and a mutual respect for the norms that guide interactions. The third and fourth approaches are fruitful ones for communication instruction.

Communication strategies are the results of three types of learning:

1. *Random learning:* children happen to discover an effective strategy and incorporate it into their repertoire of strategies
2. *Observational learning:* children observe the behavior of persons with "personal power" around them, note their strategies, and use them
3. *Learning from tutors:* siblings, parents, and teachers directly teach children which approaches are desired and which are not.

Children develop communication strategies by learning to adapt their messages to others. At first their adaptations are undifferentiated, global strategies, such as "Can I play with your truck, pretty please?" A more elaborated, differentiated approach might be a bargain: "If you let me have your truck, I'll give you a marble." In regard to children's development of persuasive techniques, studies have found that children first show an awareness of the other's perspective, then show recognition of counterarguments, and finally are able to state the advantage of their plea.

The purpose of communication instruction is to give children opportunities to increase their repertoire of strategies for critical communication situations, and to develop a set of selection criteria that will help them decide which strategies are best for a particular situation. Children need to develop the tools necessary for functioning effectively in their important relationships. With greater experience with different participants, a variety of communication settings, different topics, and different tasks, children will be able to cope more successfully in communication situations that are significant to them.

REFERENCE

ERVIN-TRIPP, SUSAN, and CLAUDIA MITCHELL-KERNAN, *Child Discourse.* New York: Academic Press, 1977.

12

the communication framework

In order to become socially competent, children must learn certain communication skills in their elementary-school years. The "talents" of the competent six-year-old include the ability to gain the attention of an adult in a socially acceptable way, the expression of affection to peers and adults, competition with peers, and the expression of a desire to grow up.[1] As we discussed in Chapter 1, these communication skills are important for the effective socialization of children.

Chapter 13 discusses communication competencies that children must acquire. This chapter outlines a framework for communication axioms and communication functions:

1. The *axioms of communication* tell us how communication works in our important relationships: we cannot *not* communicate; messages have content and relationship components; we "punctuate" our communication exchanges; communication is both analogic and digital; and we communicate in complementary or symmetrical interchanges.
2. The basic functions of communication are manifested in our daily lives: controlling, sharing feelings, informing and understanding, ritualizing, and imagining.

The axioms of communication provide us with the most realistic *perspective* of the communication process, and the five functions of communication provide the basic *content* of communication development.

---

[1]Burton White, "Critical Influences in the Origins of Competence," *Merrill-Palmer Quarterly*, 21 (1975), 243–66.

A PERSPECTIVE OF COMMUNICATION: FIVE AXIOMS

Three psychologists interested in helping persons and families in trouble have developed an exciting perspective on communication called the *pragmatic approach*.[2] They present five axioms about how communication works, saying that these axioms are supported by our everyday experiences and intuitions about communication in relationships. They can serve as guiding principles of how communication functions for children of all ages, as well as for adults. A knowledge of these axioms is beneficial for anyone, but is especially important for those who work with children in their development of communication competencies.

we cannot *not* communicate.

People usually equate communication with verbal language, and so they say that not talking to someone is not communicating. In actuality we find that people respond to "nonmessages," as they should. Why? All of our behavior is communication; we don't have to talk to communicate. Our bodies, our choice of words, or our tone of voice can say something to another person. Likewise, our not wanting to talk says a lot. Yet we tend to think of communication in terms of strictly verbal dimensions.

Guideline. If we use interesting examples and keep the explanations clear, children are fascinated by a discussion of this axiom. The impossibility of not communicating is an issue to challenge their minds in the classroom or in a family discussion. Bringing this axiom to their attention can only benefit their development of social awareness as well.

messages have content and relationship components.

Our messages are not simply packages of information with words inside them. In addition to its content, our message says something about our relationship with the person we are talking to. Our messages may indicate how we view ourselves at the moment, as well as how we view the person we are talking with. Many adults underestimate the extent to which children understand the nonverbal communication channels. "Talking down" to children is an example of this: how often have we heard a child say, "She talks to me like I'm a baby."? Children offer relationship statements in their messages too. Whether it's an "I'm special" or "I am not sure of myself at all" message, the relationship implications are present and important.

[2]Paul Watzlawick, Janet Beavin, and Don Jackson, *The Pragmatics of Human Communication* (New York: Norton, 1967), pp. 48–71.

Guideline.   When children's relationship messages surprise or please us, we can comment on them to their senders. For example, if we see that a child is proud of an accomplishment, we might comment, "I see you're proud of that sand castle, aren't you, Billy." They might ask, "How did you know?" We can tell them it was their face, their expression, or whatever else gave us the clue. We can also bring negative messages into the open in this way, teaching children that they communicate a lot more than they put into words: "I get the idea that you really don't want to go. Is that right?"

we "punctuate" our communication exchanges.

We tend to think about our communication with others in terms of actions and reactions. Usually, we talk as if our actions are strongly affected by the actions of others, so that we are always reacting. When we say "You make me so mad" or "I feel so good when I'm with you," we are punctuating our interpersonal communication; we are attributing *our* feelings to the behavior of *others*. Instead, theorists suggest, our feelings should be our own; we feel the way we do because of how we feel about ourselves. In punctuating communication sequences we often view a communication problem in terms of cause-effect relations, such as "You made me do it." The classic example offered by the three psychologists is of a husband and wife who aren't getting along well.[3] She seems to continually nag him and he seems always to withdraw. She says that his passive behavior makes her nag, but of course he says her nagging drives him to withdraw. Both see their own behavior as resulting from the other's. A more profitable view of communication is to note that although people do tend to punctuate, we should strive to eliminate such behavior by accepting ourselves as masters of our own actions and feelings.

Guideline.   Most adults have made statements such as "You make me so angry" or "You drive me nuts." At times like these we must stop ourselves and ask, "Why must I let myself become so angry? What can I do to stop this craziness?" Theorists say we drive *ourselves* crazy; no one else does. If we can understand the pitfall of placing blame or cause on others in our communication, then we can bring it to the attention of children when they do the same thing. When they say "He made me talk—he asked a question" or "She made me be late from recess," we can point out to them that it is all a matter of perspective.

[3]*Ibid.*, pp. 56–58.

communication is digital and analogical.

When we communicate with others we usually use a verbal code that we call *digital language*. Children learn their digital code orally before they enter school and throughout their elementary-school years. They learn the written digital code in their early elementary years. The *analogic code* includes the nonverbal channels of our message (body, voice, and space) and the context of communication. Two-year-old children can communicate affection with words, but even babies and toddlers can use analogic means to communicate: a pretty dandelion, a shiny rock, a smile, or a big hug tells us "I love you." The theorists stress that both the digital and analogic means of communication have their strengths and weaknesses. While the digital is clear and precise in the form of a message, it is often unable to express the warmth of relationships. On the other hand, the analogic is good for expressing underlying feelings of affection or hostility, but the interpretation of an analogic message is not always clear and precise. An example is the appearance of the husband (who has been "working late" a lot in the past month) at the front door with a bouquet of flowers for his wife. While the flowers can communicate "I love you and I'm sorry I've been working late," they can also say "I'm late, I feel guilty—you should know what I've been doing—and I want you to take these flowers to relieve me." Children must learn that both the digital and the analogic modes of communication are important, and that both have strengths and weaknesses.

Guideline. Children like to use analogic means of communicating positive messages. They offer gifts, they ask if they can help, and they give you their treasures. We can accept these objects, knowing that they are a special, analogic way of saying "I like you." Elementary-school children know that to say "thank you" they can send a card or a gift, say nice words, or smile. They can learn that some of these are verbal ways of communicating while others are messages without words, but messages nonetheless.

relationships can be symmetrical or complementary

In terms of who is "up" and who is "down" relationships can change every second or remain relatively constant. Patterns of interaction can represent either a complementary (unequal-status) or symmetrical (equal-status) relationship. Probably the most unequal-status relationship that exists is that of the mother and her newborn, whose life is virtually dependent upon her care. Yet studies also tell us that the baby's personality has a powerful effect on the mother's behavior. So, even this most classic complementary relationship has elements of role change: the child can assume the one-up position and dictate the flow of events.

It is important for adults and children to know that neither the symmetrical nor the complementary pattern is "better." Instead, healthy relationships can flow back and forth between different roles and patterns. Moreover, in some of our relationships we are the boss, and in others we play more submissive roles. The most important realization for us is that when a role bothers or pleases us we have the right to say something about that to the other person.

Guideline. We may feel that relationship roles are getting "out of hand": "Jimmy, you seem to be acting like you are in charge here and you're not. What's the problem?" (A parent hates to be ruled by a child, right?) Express your view of a relationship snag when it occurs, so that children will realize that such snags occur naturally but that they can figure out what to do about them. Now consider this situation: "Jill, we seem to be arguing and bickering about this. You say this and I say that. We don't seem to be seeing things the same way, do we?" (Symmetrical bickering is common; neither one gives an inch because neither wants to admit being "the loser.") In these cases our observation of the relationship lays the groundwork for settling the problem in a way that doesn't downgrade either person: (1) the parent can now insist that a rule be followed; (2) the parent can now "agree" that he or she has a view that differs from the child's, but that both could be "right."

We have just considered five communication axioms: (1) we cannot not communicate; (2) messages have content and relationship components; (3) we "punctuate" our communication exchanges; (4) communication is analogical and digital; and (5) relationships can be symmetrical or complementary. With this perspective of communication in mind let's turn to the basic functions of communication—the *content* of the skills necessary for effective communication development.

THE FIVE FUNCTIONS OF COMMUNICATION: COMMUNICATION CONTENT

The basic skills in communication are built upon the dominant functions of language in its social uses. These communication functions serve as the basic content of messages, and in this sense they reflect axiom 2 (all communications have content and relationship components). When we use one of the five communication functions we share content ("I'm going to tell you a secret") and relationship ("I trust you; I like you") messages. Communication functions seem to combine the two elements of our messages, the informational and the relational. The following framework of the content of these functions was drawn from a system proposed by Gordon Wells, which in turn was derived from the study of children's speech.[4] This system categorizes about one hundred speech or communication acts under several functional headings. Here are brief descriptions of the five functions that serve as the content of instruction:

1. The *controlling* function involves attempts to direct or affect the behavior of another person, as well as responses to control. Requesting, suggesting, warning, acknowledging, refusing, and assenting are examples of this function.

2. *Sharing feelings* involves communication acts such as praising, commiserating, ridiculing, approving, apologizing, and rejecting. All are messages we use to express feelings to another.

3. The *informing* function occurs when we provide ideas and information to others, as in naming and giving examples, as well as when we respond to information given by others, as in answering, questioning, and denying.

4. When our messages help sustain our social relationship with someone we may be *ritualizing*. This function involves such acts as greeting, thanking, introducing, and teasing.

5. The *imagining* function involves dealing creatively with reality through language; examples are speculating, fantasizing, storytelling, and dramatizing.

Communication in everyday situations involves a fluid flow of ideas, feelings, and statements, such that no one person is either "the speaker" or "the listener." Instead, persons serve the roles of speaker and listener simultaneously: they speak, observe, and listen at the same time, though in most of their vocalizing they follow rules in taking turns. Functions serve both initiating and responding purposes. For example, a request may initiate a complaint or a response; both communication acts are categorized as controlling. All five communication functions include acts or strategies for initiating and responding.

Another feature of communication is that each communication situation typically includes multiple functions rather than one: a person can be controlling and sharing feelings at the same moment. One of the functions may be primary and the other(s) secondary.

A third feature of communication functions is that all of them are accomplished by nonverbal as well as verbal means. Gestures, facial expressions, postures, and hand and arm movements may help communicate a sense of urgency for a plea (the controlling function), the emotion of sadness (sharing feelings), physical dimensions (informing), a greeting (ritualizing), or a dreamlike state in fantasizing (imagining).

In conclusion, the content of communication instruction involves developing the five communication functions. While even two-year-old children have acquired communication acts in each of the five functional

---

[4]Gordon Wells, "Coding Manual of the Description of Child Speech" (Bristol, England: University of Bristol School of Education, 1973).

categories, further development must occur throughout their preschool and elementary years. Learning takes the form of expanding children's repertoire of communication acts under each of the five categories and developing more finely tuned criteria for selecting from among the range of alternative strategies. All learning takes place in a context in which children also learn to initiate and respond, use multiple communication functions effectively, and employ verbal and nonverbal strategies. Let's look now at developmental information on each of the five functions.

learning to control

Deborah (five years): Here Kathy, be the mother and feed the baby.

Kathy (five years): What should I feed her?

Deborah: Feed her spinach . . . and mostaccioli—yes, I made some yummy mostaccioli for dinner.

Kathy: Yuch.

Deborah: Come on, get going. (bossy tone of voice)

Kathy: I thought you said I was the mother.

Kathy is the victim of Deborah's rather dominant controlling strategies. She uses direct requests (such as "Feed her spinach"), but she also uses more subtle tactics:

1. Deborah makes Kathy think she's "the boss" when she tells her to be the mother, seeming to build up her status.

2. However, she turns around and orders mother to "get going," a strategy hardly respectful of this ascribed status. Kathy does not seem pleased with the situation, so she reminds her buddy of her mother status, but her approach is one of a hurt puppy rather than an assertive person.

This dialogue is typical of a certain kind of conversation that children engage in. The focus is on controlling communication. Children learn to adapt their controlling strategies to characteristics of the particular situation: persons, setting, topic, and task. A strategy that may result in compliance in one situation, such as Deborah's forceful approach to Kathy, may not work in another situation, say with a stronger peer unwilling to give in. Children may find it easy to "boss" their younger sisters or brothers into doing just about everything, but the use of bossy tactics with older buddies may have disastrous results.

Just as adults assume dominant and submissive roles in their communication encounters, children communicate in equal- and unequal-status relationships. Though relationships among children can change from moment to moment, some children often find themselves in one role, as "boss" or as "follower." With experience in peer relationships children acquire flexibility in alternating among roles of dominance, equality, and submissiveness.

Catherine Garvey analyzed children's requests for action.[5] She developed an elaborate classification of the requests into three basic forms (direct, indirect, and inferred) and noted the rules underlying the use of those forms. She concluded that preschoolers know the pragmatic rules underlying requests for action. She found that on the whole preschoolers got their way with about 53 percent of their direct requests (such as "Gimme that truck!"), the most popular form with preschoolers. Indirect requests ("Will you gimme that truck?") were more effective (75 percent compliance) but occurred much less frequently in their conversations than direct forms (a one-to-nine ratio).

Let's consider more closely the more indirect forms of asking for something. Do children understand these request forms:

1. *Affirmative indirect:* "Can you give me the truck?"
2. *Negative indirect:* "Can't you open the door?"
3. *State of affairs:* "Must you hog the game?"

Four researchers attempted to answer this question.[6] They found that even the youngest age group in their study understood the first two types. They performed the required actions when necessary (such as changing a light bulb) or ceased an action (for example, a noisy activity). The negative-indirect form didn't tempt the children into performing the opposite action, a prediction the researchers had considered. However, only the six-year-olds understood the third request form, two types of which were studied:

1. "Must" types: "Must you bite the pen?"
2. "Should" types: "Should you erase the writing?"

These indirect requests suggest an action quite the opposite of the action stated in the predicate. While the four- and five-year-olds understood affirmative and negative indirect requests for initiating and ceasing actions, only the six-year-olds understood the more complex forms, which often required an opposite action or no action at all.

Elizabeth Bates studied children's development of politeness in their

[5]Catherine Garvey, "Requests and Responses in Children's Speech," *Journal of Child Language*, 2 (1975), 41–63.

[6]Lawrence Leonard, M. Jeanne Wilcox, Kathleen Fulmer, and G. Albyn Davis, "Understanding Indirect Requests: An Investigation of Children's Comprehension of Pragmatic Meanings," *Journal of Speech and Hearing Research*, 21 (1978), 528–37.

directives.[7] At least in their conversations with adults, children must learn polite forms to meet with adult expectations. Bates plotted the development from two to five years of age of children's use and understanding of polite forms. Her results show a steady increase in children's repertoire of polite cues. The children begin with the direct forms:

"Gimme that truck, okay?"

They then develop more indirect forms for accomplishing the same purpose:

"Do you think I can have that truck?"
"It's my turn for the truck."

Claudia Mitchell-Kernan and Keith Kernan examined children's use of directives in a role-playing task. They found that older children (seven to twelve) had acquired all of the directive forms and that they were aware of social factors affecting their choices among these forms.[8] For example, children in the role-playing situation used directives more frequently with persons of lower or equal status than with persons of higher status (a five-to-one ratio).

We found that compliance to directives varied greatly among children from three to five years of age.[9] The children occupied either a dominant ("one-up") or nondominant ("one-down") position. Requests and orders (the more forceful versions of requests) were about equally effective for the younger children in the dominant position. In fact, some of the younger children rarely failed in their attempts to control the actions and behavior of their buddies. The index for the three- and four-year-old children in the dominant position was 92 percent, an exceptionally high figure. But the one-down children in the younger age group had very poor compliance levels, in the range of 25 to 33 percent. Results were not as extreme for the older age group, though the pattern was similar: the older one-down children also showed poor compliance levels. Pairs of children who were about equal in their power or dominance in relation to each other showed indices within a range closer to Garvey's figure of 53 percent.

[7]Elizabeth Bates, "Pragmatics and Sociolinguistics in Child Language," in *Normal and Deficient Child Language*, ed. D. Morehead and A. Morehead (Baltimore: University Park Press, 1976), pp. 441–63.

[8]Claudia Mitchell-Kernan and Keith Kernan, "Pragmatics of Directive Choice Among Children," in *Child Discourse*, eds. Susan Ervin-Tripp and Claudia Mitchell-Kernan (New York: Academic Press, 1977), pp. 189–208.

[9]Barbara Wood and Royce Gardner, "How Children 'Get Their Way': Directives in Communication," *Communication Education*, 29 (July 1980), 264–72.

In the same study we examined children's politeness in their directives, expecting to find answers to two questions:

1. Do older children use more politeness cues in their directives than younger children?
2. Do polite directives to peers have higher levels of compliance than directives without politeness cues?

On the basis of the research of Bates, we expected to find a greater number of polite forms in five-year-olds' directives than in three-year-olds' directives. Our results did show this. However, our answer to the second question was not a simple one; results varied greatly with the status relationships of the children in the conversations. For example, one-up children used few politeness cues, yet their directives often met with success. The child using the greatest number of politeness cues was the one-down child. The nondominant child frequently attempted to be polite to get her way, but rarely did anything seem to work. Politeness seemed to be associated with compliance only for older children in equal-status dyads. This suggests a guideline for children's directives to their peers: Be polite, and it may help if the other person is about equal to you in power; otherwise, more assertive and forceful strategies are likely to work best.

A more advanced stage in the development of control through directives is achieved when children use subtle strategies like those in the dialogue between Deborah and Kathy. Two strategies characterize this advanced stage of development: the "pretend" approach, where children manipulate each other with language games, and the "perceptive" approach, where children use hints and a more devious manner to get what they want. Let's discuss each of these approaches.

The pretend approach has been explored by Susan Ervin-Tripp. Look at this example:

A: Pretend this was my car.

B: No!

A: Pretend this was our car.

B: All right.

A: Can I drive our car?

B: Yes, OK. (smiles and moves away)

A: (turns wheel, making driving noises)[10]

The climax of the pretend approach is the use of the permission strategy, "Can I drive our car?" The boy's use of the inclusive pronoun "our" shows

---

[10]Susan Ervin-Tripp, "Wait for Me, Roller Skate!" in *Child Discourse*, ed. Ervin-Tripp and Mitchell-Kernan, p. 177.

extraordinary deftness, says Ervin-Tripp. The status game is also part of the approach because "A" is trying to make "B" think he is not losing something but rather is sharing or gaining.

Later, children acquire even more subtle tactics of control. Uncovering them requires observation over a period of time with careful attention to detail, for the most advanced forms are not explicitly stated and depend on careful use of timing and content. Hints play a major role in the perceptive approach, where children seem to avoid being direct and obvious but at the same time act firmly. Take a look at Ervin-Tripp's key example of this strategy:

Six-year-old in supermarket: Can I have a penny?
Mother (surprised at small request): Why, yes.
Ten minutes later, at another shop, child deposits penny in gum machine.[11]

According to Ervin-Tripp, the child would have been denied the penny in a more "obvious" situation, say when the child was next to the gum machine. Forecasting such behavior from her mother, the child arranges the use of the directive so that negative factors are not brought into the mother's mind when it is communicated. This is a rather brilliant consideration of the communication parameter of setting (timing). Here are some other examples of the subtle approach with directives:

1. *Bargaining:* "I'll clean up my room if you give me a penny."
2. *Gentle reminder:* " 'Member, you gave Billy a penny once—I never got one before."
3. *Nonphysical threat:* "If you don't give me a penny, I might hafta walk real slow."

The trend in children's development of control through directives seems to take this general course:

1. *Direct requests:* "Give me that truck."
2. *Indirect requests:* "Can I have that truck?"
   Polite requests: "Please, can I have the truck?"
   Indirect negative requests: "Can't you give me the truck?"
3. *State-of-affairs requests:* "Must you always play with the truck?"
4. *Pretend directives:* "Pretend you're the garage man, and you tell me where to drive the truck."
5. *Subtle directives:* "Just give me a little turn with the truck and I promise that you can keep it forever and ever, today."

The forms of control move from direct to indirect, from explicit to less explicit, and from simple to complex.

[11] *Ibid.*

learning to share feelings

Burton White's study of the seven key communication talents of the elementary-school-aged child has been noted in this text. Three of the seven talents clearly require the sharing of feelings, the second communication function:

1. expressing affection to peers and adults
2. expressing hostility to peers and adults
3. showing pride in one's accomplishments

These talents are critical to children's effective functioning in all of their close relations with friends and family. While psychologists have devoted a great deal of research to children's emotional development, few studies have focused on the development of children's communication of feelings in important relationships. What if a six-year-old child does not express her affection easily, or what if a seven-year-old rarely expresses pride in his accomplishments? Studies are needed to examine the development of these key talents in children. The approach to communication competency in Chapter 13 plays close attention to children's feelings.

One research project examined the sharing-feelings function in an interesting context—third and fourth graders' arguments.[12] A sense of what children learn in their struggle to share their feelings can be found in the content and tactics of these disputes. Let's examine the feelings statements children used with their opponents:

1. *Threats:* "I'll kill you if you don't give it to me."
   "If you don't help me, I won't be your friend."
2. *Bribes:* "I'll give you some of my bubble gum if you let me play with it."
3. *Insults:* "You're a dummy, and I think you stink."
4. *Praise:* "You sure have big muscles."[13]

These feelings statements are important communication strategies that children learn to use in arguments with their peers. Other strategies listed by the authors used the controlling function (as in a command) and the informing function (as in a simple assertion). Third- and fourth-grade children rely on the sharing of feelings to handle themselves in disputes with their peers. Threats, bribes, insults, and praise are important means of doing this.

The more interesting phase of this study was the researchers' analysis

---

[12]Donald Brenneis and Laura Lein, " 'You Fruithead': A Sociolinguistic Approach to Children's Dispute Settlement," in *Child Discourse*, eds. Ervin-Tripp and Mitchell-Kernan, pp. 49–65.
[13]*Ibid.*, pp. 51–52.

of patterns or tactics children use in their disputes. Three basic patterns of argument characterize children's disputes: repetition, escalation, and inversion.

Repetition.   Children rely on repetition of feelings or self-beliefs in struggling for the top position:

Brad: I'm the strongest kid in class.
Tom: No, I'm the strongest.
Brad: I am.
Tom: I am.

This verbal dispute could continue for several turns, each boy continuing to boast about his strength.

Escalation.   In an escalation dispute each statement is more imaginative, more striking, more powerful, or more "something" than the one before it:

Dave: I'll bust your brains out.
Jim: I'll tear yours out first.
Dave: I'll knock your teeth down your throat.
Jim: I'll punch your head off.[14]

Note the build-up of imagery and associated feelings.

Inversion.   This pattern is rather like the use of opposites: successive statements are based on a category (dumb-dumb) and its inverse (non-dumb-dumb):

Dave: . . . you dumb-dumb.
Larry: I'm not no dumb-dumb, dodo.
Dave: Yes, you are.
Larry: No, I'm not.
Dave: Yes, you are.
Larry: No, I'm not.[15]

Of course, the more advanced communicator familiar with these sequences may anticipate the opponent's behavior and trick him into admitting he is dumb while they are battling about who is smarter:

---

[14]*Ibid.*, pp. 56–57.
[15]*Ibid.*

Ann: I am.
John: I am.
Ann: I am.
John: I am.
Ann: You are dumb.
John: I am.[16]

Children develop rather sophisticated feelings and controlling strategies in order to perform effectively in their disputes with peers. This study of disputes illustrates well the principle that important communication exchanges often involve multiple functions.

children's development of informing and understanding

This function is similar to what many communication theorists call the referential function. It entails people's use of information-related strategies, such as statements, responses, questions, and answers. Our discussion focuses on key studies in each of two areas: describing (and responding) and questioning (and answering).

Describing.   A landmark study in children's communication development was conducted by Robert Krauss and Sam Glucksberg.[17] They devised for pairs of kindergarten, first-grade, third-grade, and fifth-grade children a communication game requiring them to describe a graphic figure adequately enough for their counterpart to "find it" in a similar display. They found that the kindergarteners never seemed to adjust to the task: they were unable to use referential statements that were specific and adapted enough for their listener to understand. Error rates for the children in the higher grades gradually decreased, and the fifth graders were fairly successful in the task. That children gradually develop communication skills for referring specifically to objects probably depends to some extent on their use of verbal feedback from their listener. Children learn gradually to respond appropriately to feedback given by their listeners, and obviously this is a key ability in the task of referring to specific objects or events.[18]

When do children become competent from an adult point of view in making specific, clear statements about an object or event? Krauss and Glucksberg reported in their 1969 article that on the basis of some unpub-

    [16]*Ibid.*, p. 57.
    [17]Robert Krauss and Sam Glucksberg, "The Development of Communication Competence as a Function of Age," *Child Development*, 40 (1969), 255–66.
    [18]Sam Glucksberg and Robert Krauss, "What Do People Say After They Have Learned How to Talk?: Studies of the Development of Referential Communication," *Merrill-Palmer Quarterly*, 13 (1967), 309–16.

lished data they gathered, ninth graders' performance is not yet up to adult standards. Referential communication skills appear to continue emerging even in the teens. A study of the factors that assist children in performing referential tasks found that children imitate the communicative style of an adult or model almost without regard to whether it does them any good in the task. The author argues that children "do not learn to be good communicators by listening and reacting to the poor communication of others. Instead, they adopt the style of communication to which they are exposed, be it informative or incomplete."[19]

How then do children learn to respond appropriately and correctly to descriptions and explanations? Most studies of this aspect of communication agree that "listener proficiency" develops earlier, so that children develop skills in responding before they are able to initiate referential communication effectively. The learning process spans a fairly long period, and children are still developing informing skills in their junior-high and high-school years.

Questioning.   In our chapter on children's syntactic development we examined children's acquisition of yes/no questions and wh-questions. Developmental norms tell us that the first questions to be used by preschoolers are the yes/no variety; the question is marked by intonation only:

"You are going home?"

In a later stage of syntactic development children invert the subject and linking verb to produce a more sophisticated yes/no question:

"Are you going home?"

The wh-questions develop later, but with a similar pattern of emergence. First, the wh-element is attached to the question:

"Where you are going?"
"Why you are doing that?"

Again, by paying attention to word order children gradually produce questions with adultlike grammatical features:

"Where are you going?"
"Why are you doing that?"

---

[19]Grover Whitehurst, "The Development of Communication: Changes with Age and Modeling," *Child Development*, 47 (1976), 473–82.

However, it is not uncommon to hear even first-grade children using wh-questions with the uninverted word order. The order of learning of wh-questions types was investigated by Dorothy Tyack and David Ingram.[20] They found evidence to support the following developmental pattern:

1. *What:* "What this is?" "What you doing?"
2. *Where:* "Where you going?" "Where my bear-bear?"
3. *Why:* "Why the clock stopped?" "Why are you crying?"
4. *How:* "How do you do this?" "How can I fix this?"
5. *When:* "When is dinner?" "When are we going to Grandma's?"

In the same study the researchers tested children from three to five and a half years of age and found that the number of correct responses to wh-type questions increased with age. Children make response mistakes in a predictable fashion, using certain question-answering strategies:

Strategy 1: If you know the question type (such as the easy "what" questions), then give an appropriate "subject" answer.

Strategy 2: If you have not acquired the question word, respond on the basis of the semantic feature of the *verb.*

Each of the verbs the researchers tested had its own pattern of reaction. They used six verbs, three transitive (touch, help, ride) and three intransitive (sit, smile, sleep). Certain features of these verbs led children to respond in certain ways, which happened to be incorrect. Let's examine the rather interesting response patterns for the transitive verbs the children were not familiar with.

When children heard the verb "touch" they tended to focus on *what* was touched and *where* the touch occurred. So, if a child heard the question "Who is the boy touching?" she might have responded "The ladder" or "His head" instead of saying "The man with the book." These responses, which refer to objects or places, are called *nominal responses.* "Touch" was considered a "very transitive" verb because children tended to respond with the place or object of touching whether this was appropriate or not.

When children heard the verb "help" they focused first on *cause* (why) and then on manner (how) and location (where). This would explain why children hearing the question "Where is the girl helping?" (a man in trouble) might answer "Because he's in trouble" rather than "Right here, at the doorway."

"Ride" elicited responses that focused on *location* (where) and then on

[20]Dorothy Tyack and David Ingram, "Children's Production and Comprehension of Questions," *Journal of Child Language,* 4 (June 1977), 211–24.

cause (why); time was a critical factor. This would explain why the question "What is the girl riding?" elicited "She's right here" or "She likes to ride" rather than the correct response, "The bicycle."

What do children have to learn when they are acquiring the subtle, technical rules of interpreting questions? First, it seems that when children have not acquired the more difficult wh-question forms, they use a processing strategy based mainly on the verb in the question. Certain verbs elicit certain patterns of response that dictate the child's behavior and her ultimate interpretation. Since questions are one of the major strategies children use in finding out about their world, they have to understand the rules of their use before they can employ them properly. Further, to communicate with the adults in their lives who tend to ask questions repeatedly, they must develop competence in answering.

David Townsend and Melinda Erb examined how children develop strategies for interpreting complex comparative questions.[21] Children between three and six years of age were given questions such as these:

"Which box is taller than it is fat?"
"Which box is fatter than it is tall?"
"Which box is shorter than it is fat?"
"Which box is thinner than it is tall?"

Children tended to select the largest box, regardless of the adjectives in the question. The older children were a bit more discriminating in that they tended to focus on the first adjective in the question. For example, if they were given the question "which box is fatter than it is tall?" they would select the fattest box, without regard to its height. After the experimenters provided the kindergarten children with feedback on the procedure their errors of picking the biggest box all the time tended to decrease. But they still tended to select the box that fit the first adjective. Though five-year-old children know the meanings of the adjectives and the questions, the processing of comparatives at this stage of their development is difficult if not impossible. This study shows the problems that children must handle in becoming competent users of the informing function.

learning to ritualize

Probably one of the first functions to develop in the infant due to conscious teaching by the parents is the ritualizing function. When they are babies children are taught to say "Hi" and "Good-by" and to play little

---

[21]David Townsend and Melinda Erb, "Children's Strategies for Interpreting Complex Comparative Questions," *Journal of Child Language*, 2 (November 1975), 271–77.

social games like peekaboo and pat-a-cake. Greetings, farewells, and social games highlight the social relationship between infants and others. The words, motions, and rules are easy in these rituals, and the rewards are immediate: those involved feel closer together.

Children learn a host of culturally based rituals necessary for effective functioning in their peer groups and families. The following is only a small sampling of rituals or social graces that develop from the more basic skills in the use of ritualizing communication:

1. Developing culturally sensitive ways to greet and say farewell to your friends
2. Practicing effective turn-taking skills in conversation so that a balance of communication is established
3. Using effective techniques (such as teasing, praising, or gossiping) to emphasize qualities of our relationships
4. Introducing oneself and others in an effective and friendly manner.

The list could include any behavior that communicates the importance of maintaining social ties between the persons involved.

Gossiping is a form of ritualizing among children that provides an interesting window to the child's social sense. Psychologists studying children's gossiping are often surprised that even three-year-olds begin to talk about the qualities and actions of other children who are not present in the conversation. While early gossip contains little evaluative content, the gossip of four- and five-year-olds is adult-like in many ways. Nevertheless, Gary Fine found that elementary-school children's gossip has four components that distinguish it from adult gossip.[22]

First, children's gossip is ritual communication primarily because it is used in a socializing manner. Children transfer information for the purpose of solidifying a relationship rather than relating or receiving specific facts or opinions. For older children sexual and aggressive behaviors were frequently the topics of gossip—who kissed who, who beat up someone, and who chickened out of a fight. The primary purpose of gossip, however, is a relational one: keeping close to your buddies.

Second, gossip in children's communication is usually evaluative, and carries the norms of children's peer groups. The emphasis on conformity among children is highlighted when gossip occurs, and gossip is likely to occur when norms are broken by someone in the group. Children who are the targets of gossip, especially those from eight to eighteen years of age, seem much more affected than adults. Their peers' evaluations are taken very seriously.

[22]Gary Alan Fine, "Social Components of Children's Gossip," *Journal of Communication*, 27 (Winter 1977), 181–95.

Unlike the adult rule that you never gossip about someone in their presence, children frequently gossip about someone right in front of them. Teasing is a public form of gossip that frequently occurs, though the child target is expected to "remain cool" and offer some form of defense to the charges. Children do not consider gossiping something that will be evaluated negatively by their peers. They admit to doing it and find it important; only some realize it can be cruel.

Third, like adults, children are interested in maintaining their reputations in certain areas. Because gossip is something that can be used against someone's reputation, the person who gossips has a profound effect on the social order among his or her peers. Higher-status children are not as likely to be the targets of gossip: Fine found that a Little League baseball player who made a poor play and broke into tears would be comforted by his buddies if he were considered good by his teammates. But if our little ballplayer is a lower-status child, watch out: the gossip about his babyish behavior on the ball field will spread quickly in the schoolyard and the neighborhood. In contrast, targets of adult gossip are more often high-status persons.

Fourth, ability and competence are key elements in the effective use of gossip. Studies of children's gossiping in front of targets show that performance skills are important for both the sender and the receiver. Children must learn to develop poise in responding to gossip, when they are teased for childish behavior, and to insults. Probably most important, children have to develop storytelling skills in communicating interesting gossip that their peers will want to listen to.

"Talent" in gossiping leads nicely into the last communication function important in children's communication development—that of imagining. In this final area of concern, children must engage effectively in the more imaginative uses of language.

developing the imagining function

We could read volumes on children's development of imagining functions. Much has been written about the development of pretending, role-playing, and storytelling, three of the key manifestations of imagining. Our purpose in this section is to highlight some of the key imagining skills children develop, skills that have bearing on their development of communication competence. Remember that Dr. White stressed one of the most important imagining functions that emerges in the talented child: the role-playing of adults, which expresses the desire to grow up. Children's interest and skill in pretending is probably one of the most important areas in their development, and has been receiving careful attention from researchers in the past few years. The area we are about to explore is called pretending by some, make-believe by others, and pretend-play by still another group. Though we could draw some rather specific contrasts among these three activities, we will consider all forms of pretending in terms of the imagining skills children learn. When they engage in pretend-play children tie together aspects of their communication in very creative ways:

1. Children use the speech and language of the person or being that they are playing, whether it is a mother, father, teen-age brother, or younger sister.
2. Children vary the delivery of their pretend-play messages so that their body language, voice, and proxemic cues fit the identity of the person.
3. The content of pretend-play talk includes topics and messages the person typically uses.[23]

Pretend-play gives us a picture of how children view their sisters, brothers, parents, and teachers. It also allows us to see how children enact such familiar roles as the police officer, the bank teller, and the gangster. Children's make-believe gives them opportunities to experiment with roles they value in some way or roles they wish to learn about. The imagining function has its origins in pretending, and then expands into these more complex acts:

1. *Commentary:* Children learn to provide language that explains ongoing actions. ("My heavens, look at that guy punch him—he's falling. . . .")
2. *Expressive speech:* Children learn that a vivid way to express themselves is to use imaginative images for how they feel. ("Everything went perfect in the ball game—I feel like a superstar right now!")
3. *Heuristic speech:* Children learn to provide creative models for events or characterize things according to schemes. ("I have to be careful and get up early enough; otherwise, I can't make it in time for the bell.")

Pretend-play, or role-playing, requires the use of all the communication functions in the sense that pretending involves total role enactment. For this reason the imagining function is probably the most complex, difficult, and manifold function. The imagining function is the basic method of communication development outlined in the final chapter of this text.

SUMMARY

Communication competencies are developed in an atmosphere that is sensitive to the five axioms of communication: (1) we cannot not communicate; (2) messages have content and relationship components;

---

[23]Catherine Garvey, "Play with Language and Speech," in *Child Discourse*, eds. Ervin-Tripp and Mitchell-Kernan, pp. 27–47; see also Catherine Garvey, "Some Properties of Social Play," *Merrill-Palmer Quarterly*, 20 (1974), 163–80.

(3) we "punctuate" our communication exchanges; (4) communication is both digital and analogic; and (5) communication can be symmetrical or complementary. These axioms provide the perspective for all thinking about communication, and suggest guidelines for communication development for children.

The five functions of communication constitute the content of communication development. They are based on the social uses of language. The controlling function includes directives that are used in children's conversations with their peers. Children using the sharing-feelings function learn to express affection, hostility, pride in accomplishments, and emotion-packed statements in their disputes with peers. The key strategies of the informing function include making and responding to statements and asking and answering questions. The ritualizing function focuses on behaviors such as greeting, teasing, and gossiping. In the development of the imagining function children's pretending gives way to their perceptions of social roles and language appropriate to those roles.

SUGGESTED READINGS

WATZLAWICK, PAUL, JANET BEAVIN, AND DON JACKSON, *The Pragmatics of Human Communication*, Chaps. 2–3. New York: Norton, 1967.

WHITE, BURTON, "Critical Influences in the Origins of Competence," *Merrill-Palmer Quarterly*, 21 (1975), 243–66.

WOOD, BARBARA, ed., *The Development of Functional Communication Competencies: Pre-K Through Grade Six*. Urbana, Ill.: ERIC Clearinghouse on Reading and Communication Skills, 1977.

13

communication
competencies

When children are given an opportunity to say what they think about something, almost anything can happen. *Life* magazine gave children the opportunity to say what they thought about their own communication, their parents, weekly allowances, their school, and a number of other very important topics. Children were encouraged to complete a questionnaire and mail it to the editors of *Life*.[1] The polling firm of Don Bowdren Associates tabulated the responses of over 250,000 children and presented the results to the editors. A follow-up article was based on the children's responses.[2] Over 5,000 children attached letters to their questionnaires that explained their opinions and feelings in greater detail. Most of the children's responses indicated a strong awareness of a lack of effective communication between children and adults.

Children took advantage of such a rare invitation to communicate their opinions and ideas. Comments made by children illustrated their desire to be heard and to play a more powerful role in everyday communication situations:

"Just because we're short doesn't mean that we can't say something worth listening to."

"My family has what they call a family meeting. Every time I make a suggestion I am told to be quiet."

[1]"For Children Only," *Life*, October 17, 1972, p. 66.
[2]Tom Flaherty, "250,000 Children Have Their Say: 'We Don't Want to Rebel, Just Be Heard,'" *Life*, December 29, 1972, pp. 87–88D.

"My parents really don't listen to me. [They] think of me as a little child, and why should they listen to a child's opinion, right?"

"My parents only listen when they're mad at me."

"Did you know that parents and teachers can scream at you, but you cannot scream at them? We have feelings too."

In fact, one child suggested that the situation was serious enough to deserve serious action:

"I think there should be a Children's Lib."

These children seem to be asking for help in dealing with critical communication situations. They seek personal powers so that they can say something that will be heard, make suggestions in a discussion, express anger if they feel it, and in general, communicate effectively.

This chapter explains the *target* of communication instruction and guidance—what children should aim for in becoming competent communicators. With a background on the communication situation (Chapter 11) and the perspective and content of communication learning (Chapter 12), we move to the objectives of learning, the communication competencies necessary for functioning effectively in everyday life. The communication competencies are presented in terms of a *developmental framework* and the *minimal competencies* that must be mastered by children in their elementary-school years. The framework for developing communication competencies includes, (1) a repertoire of communication strategies, (2) selection criteria for choosing from among these strategies, (3) experience in implementing choices, and (4) practice in evaluating communication experiences. In the second section of the chapter minimal communication competencies are suggested for each of the five communication functions: controlling, sharing, informing, ritualizing, and imagining.

Our conclusion is a commentary on an original theme in the book: communication, the child's power play. We end where we began, but with a new view, a new framework, and what we hope are new ideas about what children do when they learn to communicate.

THE COMPETENCY FRAMEWORK

A complex behavior such as communication is learned most effectively in a special framework. Such a framework has been proposed by Kevin Connolly and Jerome Bruner. It consists of four basic steps necessary in developing communication competencies:

1. developing a repertoire of communication strategies
2. learning selection criteria
3. implementing choices
4. evaluating communication[3]

Let's consider each component in terms of its relevance to children's communication development.

developing a repertoire of communication strategies

At the core of any child's communication competencies is a repertoire of strategies for dealing with critical communication situations. Some theorists call these strategies "communication acts" and others call them "speech acts," but whatever their name they are the basis of the child's power. We could formulate hundreds of communication strategies if we defined them specifically enough. But for an idea of the core strategies children must acquire, see the following list.[4]

control function

1. *Wanting:* "I want my bike back."
2. *Offer:* "I'll help you fix it."
3. *Command:* "Get my coat for me."
4. *Suggestion:* "Let's play ball."
5. *Formulation:* "You're 'sposed to put away the basketball before you go."
6. *Permission:* "You can use my radio."
7. *Intention:* "I'm going to the store."
8. *Query want:* "You wanna play cards?"
9. *Query permission:* "May I drive your car?"
10. *Query intention:* "Are you playing or not?"
11. *Promise:* "I'll always defend you."
12. *Threat:* "I'm gonna tell your dad."
13. *Warning:* "You're gonna fall."
14. *Prohibition:* "Don't touch me."
15. *Condition:* "If you help me (I'll play ball too)."
16. *Contract:* "I'll give you some gum if you let me have a turn on your cycle."
17. *Command regarding verbalization:* "Tell her about it." *or* "Stop talking right now."

---

[3]Kevin J. Connolly and Jerome S. Bruner, *The Growth of Competence* (New York: Academic Press, 1974), pp. 3–7.
[4]Barbara Wood, ed., *Development of Functional Communication Competencies: Pre-K–Grade 6* (Urbana, Ill.: ERIC Clearinghouse on Reading and Communication Skills, 1977), appendix.

18. *Assent:* "Sure, OK."
19. *Refuse:* "No, I won't."
20. *Rejection:* "I don't want to go."
21. *Evasion:* "We'll see." *or* "I don't know."
22. *Query justification:* "Why did you do it?"
23. *Justification:* "Because my dad told me to." *or* "It's not right to do." *or* "We aren't allowed to do that."

feeling function

1. *Exclamation:* "Wow!" *or* "Nuts!"
2. *Expression of state/attitude:* "I feel just terrible today." *or* "I really don't like that program."
3. *Query state/attitude:* "How do you feel now?" *or* "What do you think about our math teacher?"
4. *Taunt:* "You're a real sissy."
5. *Challenge:* "I bet I can throw farther than you."
6. *Approval:* "You had a nice idea."
7. *Disapproval:* "You did a dumb thing."
8. *Cajole:* "You know how—come on."
9. *Congratulation:* "Good for you!"
10. *Commiseration:* "I'm sorry you were hurt."
11. *Endearment:* "I'm your best friend."
12. *Tale-telling:* "And then he hit me with the truck and . . ."
13. *Blaming:* "John broke the glass, not me."
14. *Query blame:* "Who wrote on the wall?"
15. *Command to apologize:* "Say you're sorry."
16. *Apology:* "I'm sorry I broke your picture."
17. *Agreement:* "I hate him too."
18. *Disagreement:* "I think you're wrong—he's nice."
19. *Rejection:* (same as control function)
20. *Evasion:* (same as control function)
21. *Condition:* "I'd like her if she was nice to me."
22. *Query justification:* (same as control function)
23. *Justification:* (same as control function)

informing function

1. *Ostension:* "That's [pointing] the car I like."
2. *Statement:* "I never hit other people."
3. *Question—positive/negative:* "Is that your car?"

4. *Content question:* "Who runs fastest in your neighborhood?"
5. *Why question:* "Why does he always win?"
6. *Query name:* "What's that thing called?"
7. *Response:* "Bill runs the fastest."
8. *Affirmation:* "You're right."
9. *Denial:* "No, you're mistaken."
10. *Rejection:* "No, it's not terrible."
11. *Evasion:* (same as control)
12. *Condition:* (same as control)
13. *Justification:* (same as control, but wider in scope—includes all supporting material)

ritualizing function

1. *Greetings:* "Hi, how ya doin?"
2. *Farewells:* "See you tomorrow."
3. *Turn-taking:* "And what do you think?" *or* all nonverbal cues signalling the back and forth flow in conversation.
4. *Call:* "Nancy . . ."
5. *Availability response:* "Yeah? You called me?"
6. *Request to repeat:* "Say that again."
7. *Repetition:* "I said 'Give it to me.'"
(other rituals include *introducing* someone, *welcoming* a person, *acknowledging* another's new status, and so on.)

imagining function

1. *Commentary:* "And then the old man put his cane down . . ."
2. *Expressive language:* "Wow, you sure are a pretty doll!"
3. *Heuristic language:* "When the sun goes out, then it gets dark and then the moon appears."

Our discussion of the five functions of communication in Chapter 12 included information on communication strategies for each function. For example, in the discussion of controlling we plotted children's development of directives from age two to about age eight. The process started with simple, explicitly stated directives such as "Gimme truck" and progressed to more complex and subtle strategies such as "I'll give you a turn on my bike if I can play with your truck for a minute." Studies all seem to indicate that children increase their repertoire of communication strategies during their elementary-school years. Bur this rather natural process of development should not discourage us from giving further attention and assistance to children's development of this repertoire.

learning selection criteria

Children need guidelines they can follow in selecting the most effective and appropriate strategies for any communication situation. Probably the most practical criteria are the four parameters of the communication situation:

1. *The participants:* Who are you communicating with? What attributes about this person are important to you and to him or her? Is the person a close friend or a stranger? Is the person a peer or a high-status person? All important characteristics of the other participant should be weighed in selecting the communication approach.

2. The *setting* of communication: What physical and psychological factors of the communication situation are relevant to your communication right now? Is the conversation in school, on the playground, or in your own home? Does it take place in the evening, after breakfast, or during recess?

3. The *topic* of the conversation: What is the content of the communication? Is it small talk or is the topic one of serious import?

4. The *task(s)* of those involved: What does each person hope to accomplish by the communication event? What basic functions are paramount for each person? Motives, concerns, and objectives play a role.

These four parameters must be considered as we adapt our communication to the situation and to the person we consider to be our listener. In Chapter 2 we noted that even two-year-olds can "revise" their communication when they perceive that others are not understanding them.[5] Carole Menig-Peterson attempted to determine if slightly older children would naturally adapt their communication to the situation and listener in some more specific ways.[6] In one situation, the listener had participated in an experience with the child; in the other, the listener was ignorant of the experience. That both the three- and four-year-olds in the study were able to use some types of selection criteria is evident from these findings:

1. Children seemed to talk more and need less prompting when they were talking to the naive listener. They used many more *references* (which were defined as specifically named objects or events from the experience). Pronouns and general references were not used as frequently as in the condition with the knowledgeable listener.

2. Children talking to the knowledgeable listener were much more general in their manner of talking and methods of referencing.

[5]Tanya M. Gallagher, "Revision Behaviors in the Speech of Normal Children Developing Language," *Journal of Speech and Hearing Research*, 20 (1977), 303–18.

[6]Carole Menig-Peterson, "The Modification of Communication Behavior in Preschool-Aged Children as a Function of the Listener's Perspective," *Child Development*, 46 (1975), 1015–18.

The four-year-olds seemed to be better at using the specific references than the three-year-olds. The sensitivity of children to their listener is clearly developing in the preschool years.

The studies on the development of communication strategies cited in Chapter 11, specifically the Delia and Clark studies, offer additional evidence on the development of children's ability to use selection criteria. The developmental process shows that in their elementary years children begin adapting to their listeners in very general ways. At first they are able to show their awareness that the listener has a distinct perspective; for example, they might say, "I know you'll probably say 'no,' but can I get a candy bar?" Next their adaptation shows a recognition of counterarguments that the other person could use: "You'll probably say I'll get cavities from it, but can I spend my money on candy?" The richest use of selection criteria shows adaptation and persuasiveness: "Mom, I know candy has sugar and it's bad for my teeth, but if I brush right away, can I get a Hershey bar?" Now that shows use of selection criteria, doesn't it?

implementation: children's practice

Successful implementation of our communication choices is not something that comes easily to most of us. We may experiment with a new approach or idea, but this does not ensure its effectiveness. Our fear of failure or our lack of confidence may hold us back from even trying new communication approaches. It is extremely important that we continue to offer children comfortable communication environments in the home and in the classroom so that they can develop their communication competencies. Communication apprehension—the fear and general avoidance of communication—strikes many of our children. Of even greater significance, however, is that communication apprehension seems to increase for both boys and girls as they progress from first grade to their high school years.[7] Unless special attention is given to these trends, and especially if teachers are unaware of the role of environment in "feeding" communication apprehension, the situation becomes even worse, for teachers seem to form negative expectations of children who are high communication apprehensives.[8] The vicious circle continues because these negative expectations only help to dampen the spirit of the child who finds it difficult to communicate "in public."

We have discussed how useful role-playing and pretend-play can be in

[7]John Garrison and Karen Garrison, "Measurement of Oral Communication Apprehension Among Children: A Factor in the Development of Basic Speech Skills," *Communication Education*, 28 (May 1979), 119–28.

[8]James McCroskey and John Daly, "Teachers' Expectations of the Communication Apprehensive Child in the Elementary School," *Human Communication Research*, 3 (Fall 1976), 67–72.

the development of children's communication. Make-believe can be encouraged for younger children, while role-playing can serve as the instructional tool for older children. Role-playing gives children opportunities to try out the communication strategies and roles that are important in their development. Studies in role-playing often reveal that when children pretend to be someone else they use a more varied repertoire of communication strategies than whey they "play themselves." In a study where children were asked first to say something and then to suggest what another person would say back, children offered a more diverse and creative repertoire of strategies for *the other* than for *the self.*[9] When children are communicating as themselves they are perhaps more cautious. The risks are less in playing other persons because the failures may seem to be less their own. Because of this tendency in children's behavior we must capitalize on the effectiveness of role-playing in advancing children's communication.

An in-depth analysis of a child's communication when he was playing alone, with a friend, and with his mother revealed that his playing-alone communication was very special.[10] It included dramatic dialogues in which he played a variety of roles, from policemen to magicians. He seemed to communicate effectively with his invented people, using creatively orchestrated communication exchanges: "The invented characters had appropriately modulated tones of voice and stylistic differences attributed to them."[11] Children's natural creativity in communication is something we must take advantage of in instructional practices.

evaluating communication

The final step in developing communication competencies in children is to see that they have opportunities to learn how to evaluate their communication behavior and assistance in doing so. In the classroom the evaluation process must be built into the activities themselves. In more general social settings we can encourage discussion or evaluation and attempt to answer the two most basic evaluation questions:

1. How effective was I in achieving the goals I had for this communication situation?
2. How effective was this communication exchange in maintaining our relationship?

The focus of discussion can be the issue at the heart of all persons in the process of communication:

---

[9]R. R. Allen and Kenneth Brown, eds., *Developing Communication Competence in Children* (Skokie, Ill.: National Textbook Co., 1976), p. 205.

[10]Margaret Martlew, Kevin Connolly, and Christine McCleod, "Language Use, Role and Context in a Five-Year-Old," *Journal of Child Language*, 5 (1978), 81–99.

[11]*Ibid.*, 85–86.

3. How sensitive was this person to my needs, background, interests, and goals?

Materials are available that offer specific suggestions to teachers on how to manage an instructional approach that develops the five basic functions of communication in role-playing exercises and question-and-follow-up activities that focus specifically on the four basic components of communication competence: repertoire, selection criteria, implementation, and evaluation.[12]

BASIC COMMUNICATION COMPETENCIES

Just what are the basic communication competencies we should expect of children in their elementary-school years? How would we go about defining them? Using resources that we can count on for their sound approach and general acceptance, we attempt in this section to outline a set of basic communication competencies. Two major sources were used to compile these guidelines: Burton White's study of young children and their basic social/communication talents and the Speech Communication Association *Guidelines for Minimal Competencies in Speaking and Listening for High School Graduates.* The rationale for using the first source is clear: this text has cited Dr. White's work frequently and supports the guidelines it suggests. The second source may seem puzzling because the target is high-school graduates, not elementary-school graduates. It contains a carefully derived set of objectives in each of three critical areas of life: occupation (work setting), citizenship, and "maintenance" (daily life). An explanation of the Speech Communication Association's method of compiling competencies will help justify our scaling them down for the elementary-school child.[13] In fact, this adaptation of the competencies was natural.

A task force of communication experts conducted a search to identify speaking and listening skills that school districts, state education agencies, and communication experts listed as essential for any person graduating from high school. The search included an exhaustive review of literature with the assistance of a computer and a more personalized investigation of states' policies, curriculum guides, and administrative stances. Only those speaking and listening skills that met the following criteria were included: the skill had to be functional, educational (appropriate for classroom instruction), and

---

[12]Barbara Wood, ed., *Development of Functional Communication Competencies: Pre-K Through Grade Six* (Urbana, Ill.: ERIC Clearinghouse on Reading and Communication Skills, 1977).

[13]See Ronald Bassett, Nilwon Whittington, and Ann Stanton-Spicer, "The Basics in Speaking and Listening for High School Graduates: What Should Be Assessed?" *Communication Education*, 27 (1978), 293–303.

general (related to children and youth from all over the country). What emerged was a set of minimal competencies in several categories. Since the communication thrust of this text has been the five communication functions, I have regrouped these competencies to fit this approach. The final section of this chapter, then, simply presents the results of the extensive search and the translation for elementary-school children.

I have tried to state the basic competencies in terms of what we could expect of children midway through their elementary-school years.

One word of explanation seems necessary before we proceed to the lists of competencies. You will notice that some categories are quite short (such as the imagining competencies) while the informing category is rather lengthy. Two major factors probably account for this discrepancy: (1) educators are more trained in informing skills, and so would include them in any lists for study and rate them as important, and (2) informing skills are more clear-cut and less intricate psychologically.

basic competencies in controlling

1. Assumes control in peer-related activities. (W)[14] The child is able to take charge in a game of tag, setting the rules and boundaries.

2. Follows the lead of peers. (W) The child accepts the suggestions of others on how to spend their time during recess.

3. Competes with peers; exhibits interpersonal competition. (W) The child is able to participate in a dispute with a peer about who is the fastest runner.

4a. Expresses and defends dissatisfaction with a toy or product purchased. (S) If a Big Mac doesn't taste right or if a toy breaks upon use, the child tells the clerk about it and asks for a new one.

4b. Expresses and defends a basic belief about how to behave. (S) A child can persuasively explain to others why it is dangerous to pet strange dogs.

5. Identifies clearly what are commercials on television. (S) The child is able to identify even the testimonial TV commercials as commercials.

6a. Understands weather bulletins broadcast on TV or radio. (S) After hearing a weather report or bulletin the child is able to decide what to wear and whether or not to carry rain gear, for example.

6b. Understands a doctor's directions to take medication. (S) The child knows how to take a pill three times a day, for example, and helps monitor the process.

6c. Understands basic household rules. (S) Knowing that it is important to follow procedures involving the house keys, the child is able to hold onto a key and keep doors locked.

---

[14]W (B. White); or S (SCA) indicates the source of the competency.

7a. Describes viewpoint of a store clerk to whom merchandise is being returned. (S) If a squirt gun doesn't work properly or a game has missing pieces, the child is able to explain the problem to a clerk in the store but at the same time realize that returning things adds work to the clerk's responsibilities.

7b. Describes the viewpoint of a family member or peer in a disagreement. (S) The child is able to say what the view of a friend or family member is in an argument over how they should spend time together.

basic competencies in sharing feelings

1a. Expresses affection to peers. (W) The child is able to tell friends "I really like you" when he feels good about their friendship.

1b. Expresses hostility to peers. (W) The child is able to express hostility to friends when she is displeased with how a certain communication event is proceeding.

2. Expresses affection to adults. (W) Feeling affectionate toward a parent, the child is able to express the affection in verbal and nonverbal ways.

2b. Expresses hostility to adult. (W) When the child becomes terribly angry in the home, she is able to express anger effectively.

3. Shows pride in accomplishments. (W) If he builds a fine airplane model, the child shows, verbally and/or nonverbally, that he is pleased with his work.

4a. Expresses dissatisfaction to a store clerk. (S) If a child is unhappy with a product she purchased at the store, she is able to express her feelings to the clerk.

4b. Expresses approval to siblings for their accomplishments. (S) If a younger sibling has just learned how to ride a bicycle, the child is able to express appropriate approval for the accomplishment.

4c. Expresses feelings of regret to a friend who has met with misfortune. (S) If a peer has had a prize possession stolen, the child expresses regret and empathic feelings to the person.

5a. Describes differences of opinion with family member about what to watch on TV. (S) When there is a disagreement about what to watch on TV, the child is able to present the feelings of both self and other siblings, for example.

5b. Describes differences of opinion with regard to household expectations. (S) The child is able to express her feelings about a household task, say doing the dishes, and also present the wishes of the parent.

6. Uses nonverbal signs in the expression of sympathetic messages to peers. (S) If a friend has experienced misfortune in the family, the child is able to convey sympathy with his body and his voice.

7. Expresses and defends feelings in a family discussion. (S) When

family members are discussing a serious disagreement, the child is capable of expressing his feelings to other family members.

8a. Distinguishes facts from opinions in advertisements. (S) The child can tell the difference between scientific evidence and personal testimony in a TV commercial on a new breakfast cereal.

8b. Distinguishes facts from opinions with regard to nutrition. (S) The child knows the difference between foods that taste good, such as corn chips, and those that are "good for you," such as fruit, as they are presented in advertisements.

basic competencies in informing

1. Uses others as resources when a task is too difficult. (W) If a child is having trouble finding something in a library, she is able to ask for help from the librarian; if she does not understand a teacher's instruction, she asks for clarification.

2a. Teaches peers how to play a game. (S) The child is able to present the basic rules of a new game in teaching it to his friends.

2b. Teaches a younger sibling how to do something. (S) The child is able to show and describe to a younger sister or brother how to draw something on paper.

3a. Recognizes when a parent doesn't understand what is necessary in a situation. (S) If a child needs to bring something special to school and asks for help from a parent, he is able to see when the parent doesn't understand what he is asking for.

3b. Recognizes when a friend does not understand a direction. (S) In a game of hopscotch a child realizes when her friend does not understand a particular rule she is explaining.

4a. Summarizes a public-service message on safety. (S) The child is able to effectively give the point of a message on street safety to others.

4b. Summarizes for family members a telephone conversation. (S) After a conversation with a peer about a party coming up, the child gives a basic description of what events are to occur.

5a. Answers a doctor's questions about illness. (S) When a doctor asks the child to tell about "where it hurts," the child is able to explain the pain and its location.

5b. Answers a parent's question to explain behavior. (S) When asked to answer questions about where or why she did something, the child is able to explain.

6a. Explains a malfunction of a toy to a parent. (S) The child is able to explain why a toy is not working properly by locating the source of the problem.

6b. Explains a task to a family member. (S) The child is able to tell others, with adequate illustration, what must occur for a job to be done, such as collecting objects or money for a purpose.

6c. Explains values to peers. (S) The child is able to explain the ground rules or values important in his family: curfew, secrecy, and promise keeping.

7a. Obtains information about the rules and procedures of a group. (S) When a child belongs to a group or club, she knows how to ask questions and acquire information on what is expected of her in terms of rules and procedures.

7b. Obtains information about product use. (S) A child knows how to ask for information regarding how a toy or product works, such as whether or not it includes a battery or whether extensive work is required to put it together.

8a. Describes an ailment to parents. (S) So that they will understand why she doesn't feel well, the child is able to explain an ailment to her parents.

8b. Uses language effectively in reporting a problem situation to school officials. (S) If the child reports details of a problem situation (such as a fight or property destruction) to school officials, his report explains adequately the events of the situation.

9a. Uses gestures to enhance a friend's understanding of how to play a game. (S) In explaining to a friend how to play the ball game called "ledge," the child uses arm and hand movements to show the procedures.

9b. Uses gestures effectively in showing others how to operate something mechanical. (S) The child is able to use gestures to clearly show the movements necessary for operating a mechanical toy.

10a. Obtains main idea in TV news stories. (S) The child is able to tell what the main idea is in a news story about her community.

10b. Identifies the main idea in a weather-warning broadcast on TV or radio. (S) The child is able to tell what weather condition might occur.

basic competencies in ritualizing

1. Gains and maintains the attention of adults in socially acceptable ways. (W) The child is careful not to interrupt a conversation rudely in getting someone's attention.

2. Makes small talk in conversations. (S) The child learns to talk about subjects like homework or the weather in keeping social conversations going with peers.

3. Introduces peers to each other. (S) The child is able to introduce one of her friends to another.

4. Introduces self to other children. (S) The child is able to introduce himself to other children he does not know but wishes to know.

5. Speaks with an appropriate rate, volume, and clarity in conversa-

tions with peers. (S) The child talks so that others can keep up with her, hear her well, and understand what she is saying.

basic competencies in imagining

1. Is able to role-play adults and generally expresses the desire to grow up. (W) The child knows how to make believe he is a parent, a child, an authority figure, or almost any other person by adapting characteristics of that role.　　*Speech Comm. Assoc*

While the focus of the SCA document did not include basic competencies in the imagining function, the thrust of the entire document suggests that effective instruction in *all* of the competencies listed would include the ability to effectively role-play the situations in those competencies. Thus, if we were to list the imagining skills necessary for the growing child, we could list the basic competencies under all of the other functions, stressing that children should be able to implement their "pretend choices" in each situation. In this sense the imagining function is probably the most important communication function of all, because if children lack skills in that function, their communication development suffers greatly.

COMMUNICATION: THE CHILD'S POWER PLAY

Communication power does not mean that children should always get their way in their families, nor does it mean that they should be in charge of their classrooms, deciding what they'd like to learn. Instead, communication power is personal; it is a sense of well-being that says "If I want to enter into a dispute with my friend about who is the fastest runner, I can do it with a degree of effectiveness." The powerful communicator is able to get the attention of her peer when she has something to tell her. It is not that some children have no choices for accomplishing these two tasks while other children have many; instead, we suggest, we need to consider expanding the repertoires for all children.

Let's examine two examples of what we mean by communication power. The first one concerns the ability just mentioned—to get the attention of a peer in an activity. We observed a group of children playing in a nursery-school playroom; because we had videotaped their interactions, we were able to analyze their strategies to gain the attention of their peers.[15] In one situation Bree tried several strategies for obtaining the attention of Rebecca, her buddy. She asked her questions, suggested things to do, and

[15]Barbara Wood and Royce Gardner, "How Children 'Get Their Way': "Directives in Communication," *Communication Education*, 29 (July, 1980), 264–72.

tapped her on the shoulder, but Rebecca was too busy playing with a toy cash register. So she tried this approach:

Bree: Rebecca, you know what? I wear size-two underpants.

Rebecca: (continues to play; seems to disregard Bree)

Bree: Isn't that something, Rebecca? Size two!

Rebecca: (does not answer; continues playing)

Bree: Isn't that something?

Rebecca: Here, hold this for me.

Bree's strategies were varied and her last attempt was rather innovative, yet no matter what she did Rebecca didn't pay any attention to her. In this example the variety of strategies *may* not have been vast enough or the use of selection criteria not appropriate. Many who have analyzed our video-tapes of this interaction have suggested that Bree should have given Rebecca a yank on the arm and said, "Hey, I'm talking to you—listen!"

The second situation illustrates the complexity of what we mean by personal power in communication. In this situation Deborah and Kathy (both five-year-olds) are role-playing a family. Let's follow a portion of their dialogue:

Deborah: You can be the mother, okay?

Kathy: Okay, I'll make dinner. You want some carrots and celery, honey?

Deborah: Gimme some food, Mom.

Kathy: Just hold your horses, baby.

Deborah: I'm not a baby; I'm Deborah.

Deborah enjoyed assigning high-status roles to her friends when they engaged in pretend-play; here she allows Kathy to be the mother. But notice how Deborah turns around and bosses her mother. Kathy noticed this but was never quite able to cope with Deborah's tactics. How did we analyze this encounter? Which strategies were used? It is difficult to connect the principles one might draw from this dialogue with any of the communication competencies just presented, though it is clear that each child was controlling the other through the imaginative function. The complexity of this communication does not allow an easy, straightforward analysis of what was done and what could be done to improve the relationship. Some teachers who have watched our tapes of the two children have suggested that if they had the opportunity to talk to children who play with Deborah, they would tell them to watch out for Deborah because she will let them think they're the boss but then try to boss them instead. Our studies with children's reactions to controlling messages from their peers suggest that children as young as four and five can identify when their peers are "bossing" rather than "asking." That they are able to differentiate the two communications is evidence that we can focus on this skill in our instructional practices.

Designing communication instruction is not an easy task. More and more books, booklets, and guidelines are being published to assist parents and teachers in their creation of effective models for the development of communication in children. This chapter has offered a starting point for what must be learned—a developmental framework and a minimal set of communication competencies. In this last section we warn that the notion of communication as the child's power play does not mean simply the learning of several communication strategies. Notice how little this did for our friend Bree. Nor is communication the ability to use complex strategies in playing out various social roles. We must also introduce notions about what it means to relate to one another in a caring fashion.

The aim of this text was to provide those who care about children and who work with children an understanding of communication development. The factors influencing development were explored, and implications for development were noted. Verbal and nonverbal communication was examined in a stage-by-stage fashion so that we could understand how it normally unfolds in children. Our final concern was the development of children's communication competencies, and for this a framework for the communication situation was proposed and discussed. Our objective is the development of communication as the children's power play so that children can make sense of themselves, others, and the world around them.

SUMMARY

To develop communication competencies in children in their elementary-school years, we must include the four basic components of communication competence in our guidance and instruction:

1. Children must develop *a repertoire of communication strategies* for dealing with everyday communication situations.
2. Children need to acquire *selection criteria* that they can use to select from among the repertoire of strategies the most appropriate ones for any situation.
3. Children need *practice in implementing their communication choices* so that they can improve their effective delivery of them.
4. Children need experience in the *effective evaluation* of how well their communication met their goals and maintained their relationship with the other person.

Finally, we proposed what might be the basic communication competencies of children who are midway through their elementary-school years. These competencies represent all five of the communication functions. These competencies are practical for everyday situations, they are educational and can be developed in the home and in school, and they are general in that they apply to children from across the country.

SUGGESTED READINGS

ALLEN, R. R., AND KENNETH BROWN, *Developing Communication Competencies in Children.* Skokie, Ill.: National Textbook Co., 1976.

BASSETT, RONALD, NILWON WHITTINGTON, AND ANN STANTON–SPICER, "The Basics in Speaking and Listening for High School Graduates: What Should Be Assessed?" *Communication Education*, 27 (1978), 293–303.

HOPPER, ROBERT, AND NANCY WRATHER, "Teaching Functional Communication Skills in the Elementary Classroom," *Communication Education*, 27 (1978), 316–21.

WOOD, BARBARA, ed., *Development of Functional Communication Competencies: Pre-K Through Grade Six.* Urbana, Ill.: ERIC Clearinghouse on Reading and Communication Skills, 1977.

index

CHILDREN AND COMMUNICATION,
Second Edition, is an up-to-date
revision of a successful "landmark"
survey of the child as a communicator.

Presenting a comprehensive view of
the development of communication
skills in children, the book considers
the development of verbal language,
nonverbal language and communication competence. Unique examples
and illustrations reflect the child's
perspective on the journey toward
functioning autonomously in his/her
environment.

PART I explores the forces—
intrapersonal, such as the biological
and genetic, as well as interpersonal, particularly the family—that
affect a child's communication
development.

PART II takes full advantage of
recent research and theory in the
field as it views the emergence
of vocabulary, syntax, and semantics
in children.

PART III, also updated with the latest
theory and research, considers
children's development of communication through their body language,
voice, and proxemics.